A THEORY OF FOREIGN POLICY

A THEORY OF FOREIGN POLICY

Glenn Palmer and T. Clifton Morgan

PRINCETON UNIVERSITY PRESS

PRINCETON AND OXFORD

Published by Princeton University Press, 41 William Street, Princeton, New Jersey 08540

In the United Kingdom: Princeton University Press, 3 Market Place, Woodstock, Oxfordshire OX20 1SY

Library of Congress Cataloging-in-Publication Data

Palmer, Glenn, 1954–
   A theory of foreign policy / by Glenn Palmer and T. Clifton Morgan.
     p.   cm.
   Includes bibliographical references and index.
   ISBN-13: 978-0-691-12359-2 (13-digit hardcover : alk. paper)
   ISBN-10: 0-691-12359-4 (10-digit hardcover : alk. paper)
   1. International relations.   I. Morgan, T. Clifton, 1956–   II. Title.
   JZ1305.P35 2006
   327.1'01—dc22   2005016522

British Library Cataloging-in-Publication Data is available

This book has been composed in Minion

Printed on acid-free paper. ∞

pup.princeton.edu

Printed in the United States of America

10 9 8 7 6 5 4 3 2 1

To our children
Einav and Ethan,
and
Tom and Emily

Contents

List of Figures

List of Tables

A Theory of Foreign Policy

As often happens in research, this project began as an investigation into one phenomenon and ended as an investigation into something somewhat different. We were always focused on the implications of considering foreign policy to be directed at achieving two goals, but we set out to explore how this would influence our understanding of the role of domestic politics in the making of foreign policy. We soon came to realize that understanding how domestic politics influences policy requires that we first have a base, ideal-type model of what foreign policy would be without the pushing and pulling of domestic actors. This book presents our efforts to develop such a model.

We are primarily motivated by a belief that traditional ways of evaluating foreign policy are fundamentally flawed. The most significant shortcoming is that analysts typically treat foreign policy as though it is aimed at achieving only one goal—maintaining the security of the state. Many have noted that "security" is an ambiguous concept and that almost anything can be said to enhance it. Our complaint is not that "security" is too abstract; rather, it is that we cannot understand foreign policy decisions if we assume they are aimed at producing only a single good. Accepting that foreign policy decisions often involve trade-offs is essential to understanding those decisions; this requires that we recognize that policy is aimed at achieving multiple goals.

There are an almost infinite number of interests states can pursue through their policies. It would not aid our understanding to enumerate them all, even if that were possible. To understand things, abstraction is necessary. Since we believe assuming that states have but one goal is unproductive because it stops us from seeing the trade-offs that decision makers confront and assuming that states have many goals is unproductive because it inhibits our ability to generalize, we take the simplest possible remedying step by assuming that states pursue two goods through their foreign policies. We call these *change*, which constitutes efforts to alter the status quo, and *maintenance*, which constitutes efforts to prevent changes in the status quo. This is clearly an abstraction, but it allows us to consider trade-offs and it is the simplest model that can do so.

We believe that the theory built upon this assumption is far superior to the alternatives. It provides a solid basis from which to explain specific decisions and it can serve as a foundation upon which to build a general understanding of the patterns in a particular state's policies over time. Most important, it leads to a large number of testable hypotheses. Many of these are surprising;

many are unique to this particular theory and enjoy a great deal of empirical support. Our efforts in this book are aimed at convincing our readers of these points.

Our theory is mathematical, and the hypotheses are formally derived. We subject many of the hypotheses to statistical tests. We have tried to make this book accessible to a broad readership, however, so the first half is presented in a non-technical fashion. The formal version of the theory is presented in chapter 5, but we first present an intuitive version in chapter 2. Chapters 3 and 4 are devoted to showing that the theory can provide a useful conceptual basis from which to describe and understand actual foreign policy events. We provide an account of U.S. foreign policy since World War II, an explanation of New Zealand's decisions that effectively ended the defense agreement among Australia, New Zealand and the United States (ANZUS), an explanation of the Bolshevik decisions leading up to the Treaty of Brest-Litovsk, and an account of changes in the pattern of Chinese foreign policy. In chapters 6 and 7, we present the results of a number of statistical tests of the theory's hypotheses. We hope that this provides a convincing case that our theory is exceptionally rich and useful.

In the end, we hope to have accomplished several things. First, we hope to have developed a useful, fruitful, and general theory of comparative foreign policy. We seriously considered titling this book "A Theory of Comparative Foreign Policy," but we have a strong sense that our sales would be hurt because most international relations scholars consider that to be a dead field. It should not be. Much can be learned by looking for general patterns in the foreign policies of various types of states and for looking for the factors that determine why states behave differently. Our theory is intended to apply universally. It does not account for just one state's behavior, nor does it apply only to a brief historical era, nor does it explain only one type of behavior. It allows us to see commonalities across all these dimensions, and it provides an explanation for variations in behavior. We believe our theory provides a framework from which we can understand the specific decisions and general patterns of behavior adopted by all states at all times.

We also hope to have provided a theory that can serve as the basis for a great deal of additional research. We present the results of a large number of statistical analyses in this volume, but these test only a few of the hypotheses generated by the theory in only a few empirical contexts. The theory is amazingly rich in terms of the hypotheses that follow from it, particularly with respect to the phenomenon of foreign policy substitutability. Testing other hypotheses can serve to increase our confidence that this is a useful way of looking at the world—or convince us that we are on the wrong track. Moreover, we do not consider the job of developing this theory complete. In particular, the present version does not allow us to consider the effects of strategic interaction (that is, given that decision makers can anticipate how their actions will influence the actions of others, they should account for those anticipations in their decisions), nor does it allow us to consider the effects of domestic politics on foreign policy choices. These considerations would certainly complicate matters, but we believe they can be accommodated by generalizing, not completely changing, the theory.

Further, we hope to have developed a theory that can inform policy debates. To a great extent, we believe that what we have to offer on this score comes from a superior conceptualization of what foreign policy should accomplish. Accepting that some of foreign policy is directed at changing the world and that this is not necessarily "bad" could only improve policy debates. The belief that foreign policy should provide only "security" and that "security" means protecting what we already have leads to patently nonsensical arguments. As this is being written, the United States is engaged in a war to replace the Hussein regime in Iraq. The administration has argued that this war is being fought to protect Americans and to enhance their security. These arguments are clearly absurd. From the perspective of our theory, this war was meant to change the status quo more to the liking of the United States. Were the administration able (because of an accepted conceptualization of foreign policy that granted legitimacy to change-seeking actions) to acknowledge that, the debate over the policy would be much more fruitful and make much more sense. We could argue sensibly over whether overthrowing the Iraqi regime was, in fact, a change that should be preferred and over whether the resources used to procure that change could have been better spent somewhere else.

Consider a more specific example. In his second inaugural address, President George Bush outlined the direction of U.S. foreign policy in his second term: "[I]t is the policy of the United States to seek and support the growth of democratic movements and institutions in every nation and culture, with the ultimate goal of ending tyranny in our world. . . . The difficulty of the task is no excuse for avoiding it. America's influence is not unlimited, but fortunately for the oppressed, America's influence is considerable, and we will use it confidently in freedom's cause."

This is a statement calling the United States to bring about a tremendous change in the world: the elimination of tyranny. As a statement of policy preference, it serves as the basis for useful discussion and analysis. Debate over this policy could fruitfully be focused on three sets of issues. First, is the elimination of tyranny an end that the United States desires? Is this something Americans want? Second, resources would be required if the United States were to strive to reach this goal. Are the resources necessary to achieve this goal available? If there is a limit to the resources available, or a limit to the resources we are willing to allocate to reach this end, what is the probability of achieving this goal within those limits? Third, what opportunity costs are associated with pursuit of this goal? In other words, would the resources required to achieve this goal be better used toward the realization of some other desired end? If we pursue the end of tyranny, what other desired changes will we have to forego?

President Bush's speech did not address these points. Instead, the reason America should pursue this goal, according to the president's address, was to enhance the security of the United States: "[A]s long as whole regions of the world simmer in resentment and tyranny—prone to ideologies that feed hatred and excuse murder—violence will gather, and multiply in destructive power, and cross the most defended borders, and raise a mortal threat. . . . The survival of liberty in our land increasingly depends on the success of liberty in other lands."

It is standard for political leaders to justify foreign policy proposals as enhancing security: it is consistent with the accepted paradigm that says foreign policy is exclusively about security. For example, those who supported expansion of the American presence in Vietnam and those who supported its immediate withdrawal each defended their recommendations as adding to American security. Support for and opposition to arms control agreements with the Soviet Union similarly were each justified by their positive effect on U.S. security. One might argue that President Bush's goal of eliminating tyranny worldwide would diminish rather than enhance U.S. security, by, for instance, replacing those tyrannical systems (which are opposed to groups threatening their ability to rule) with weak, unstable regimes that would be incapable of controlling terrorist groups based within their borders. Our point here is not to suggest an opinion as to whether the elimination of tyranny would enhance or weaken U.S. security. Rather, we want to point out that it would be far more useful to center the policy debate on the more precise questions we have outlined rather than focusing on whether the proposed action enhances American security.

There is an important implication to accepting that trade-offs must be made over valued goods and resources, as suggested by this theory. Understanding that foreign policy must accomplish more than enhancing "security" requires us to consider the opportunity costs associated with policy actions. This requires a change in the way we evaluate policy. Typically, we focus our judgments on specific actions; for example, U.S. sanctions on Cuba have "failed" to bring about a change in Cuba's behavior. From the perspective of our theory, we must continue to make such judgments, but that is not sufficient. We must also evaluate foreign policy as a portfolio. That is, we must consider whether the full range of policies adopted provide for the optimal mix of the goods being produced. This could lead us to be more accepting of some seemingly bad policies (if they are part of an overall strategy that produces a good mix of foreign policy outcomes) or to be more critical of some seemingly good policies (even if every action "works" in the sense of accomplishing the stated goals, the overall outcome could be worse than is possible given the resources available).

The extent to which we have accomplished our goals is, of course, a judgment that our readers must make. As with any body of research, we view this as a work in progress, and we sincerely hope that others will find what we offer to be worthy of criticism. We believe we are on to something, and we look forward to seeing it improved. Obviously, we could not have made it to this point without the help of many who have so selflessly provided support, advice, and criticism. We owe a debt of gratitude to all those we are about to thank and, as is customary, we absolve them of all but a tiny bit of responsibility for any remaining blunders.

First, we have received substantial financial support from a number of sources. Much of our research was supported by the National Science Foundation, through grants SBR9511289 and SBR9507909. Some of the work appearing in chapter 4 was supported by the Baker Institute of Public Policy at Rice University. Much of that chapter was written at the International Peace Research Institute, Oslo (PRIO), and we thank Scott Gates and Nils Petter Gleditsch for making Glenn Palmer's visit there fruitful. The School of Social Sciences and the Department of Political Science at Rice University provided funds to host a conference on an earlier version of this book. Our thanks go to Bob Stein and Rick Wilson for making this possible. Our home departments at Binghamton University, Texas A&M, Penn State University, and Rice University have also been generous and supportive of our work, especially in providing office space to whichever of us was visiting the other.

Second, a number of current and former students have assisted us in much of the research and have provided many useful suggestions. We are indebted particularly to Archana Bhandari, Sean Bolks, Sky David, Dennis Foster, Faten Ghosn, Xiaoling Ji, Heather Pace Marshall, Michaela Mattes, Anne Miers, Dawn Miller, Peter Partell, Matt Rupert, Luke Shi, and Scott Wohlander. Each contributed significantly to the development of our arguments. This a better book because of their efforts.

Third, many colleagues have given us helpful comments, criticisms, advice, and support over the years it has taken to complete this book. Many offered general suggestions and encouragement along the way and many offered pointed criticisms. All were extremely helpful and served to focus our thinking. Stuart Bremer, Bruce Bueno de Mesquita, Paul Hensel, Walter Isard, Jacek Kugler, Doug Lemke, Zeev Maoz, Sara Mitchell, Will Moore, Jim Morrow, Randy Siverson, Dale Smith, Harvey Starr, and John Vasquez deserve special thanks in this regard.

Finally, there are a number of people who have made a substantial impact on our work by offering directed suggestions after having endured reading all, or at least large portions of, various versions of the manuscript. Michael Bernhard, Bob Harkavy, Mark Jones, Steve Quackenbush, Jeff Ritter, and Paul Senese have each led us to make specific changes for which we are grateful. Words cannot convey our gratitude to Ashley Leeds, Tamar London, Mike

McGinnis, Bill Reed, Dani Reiter, Ric Stoll, and Rick Wilson. The efforts they made to help us with every aspect of this book are truly humbling. We consider ourselves blessed to have such friends and colleagues.

We, of course, have the nagging sense that we have forgotten to acknowledge the contributions of some. If that is the case, we apologize. It is due to our fading memories and not our lack of appreciation.

We would also like to thank our families for their love and support. Our wives, Tamar and Kay, have been supportive, helpful, understanding, and, most important, tolerant. Our children, Einav and Ethan, Tom and Emily, have brought us great joy and inspiration. We have dedicated this book to them and we hope that our work, in at least some small way, makes their world a better place in which to live.

Finally, we would like to acknowledge with extreme admiration the work of Jim Henson, whose creative talents certainly contributed to the betterment of humankind.

A THEORY OF FOREIGN POLICY

1

Introduction

WHY DO COUNTRIES do what they do in their dealings with other states? That question is at the heart of much of the discourse and analysis that has been focused on international relations, and it is the question we seek to answer in this book. Answers to that question can be fruitful, and we see these answers as having four applications. The first regards individual policies that states choose and is typically the focus of much of the work on international behavior. Valuable work has been done, for instance, on why states choose to start wars, wars that may kill millions of people. Why do states impose sanctions that may inflict suffering on the innocent citizens of another state? Why do states make alliances? These types of questions address the issues that most directly affect all of our lives and pique the interests of scholars and policymakers. As a research community, we have spent centuries investigating questions like these, and while we now know a great deal about the causes of such behaviors, much more remains to be learned.

The second application is about the relationship between a state's policies in a specific situation or at a specific time. Policies are tools that states use to get what they want. Why do states choose particular policies? For instance, why might a state choose to impose sanctions on another state instead of attacking it? Why might a state increase its foreign aid allocation and simultaneously decrease its military spending? Why might a state break an alliance with another country and decrease its trade barriers with it? All foreign policy actions are a matter of the choices made by the leaders of states (or nonstate organizations). These leaders often have several options for dealing with any particular issue, and we would like to know what influences the particular choices they make.

The third application is relevant to choices leaders make between similar sets of policies in different situations. The United States, to take an example, is friendly with Denmark and Israel, states with about the same population and with similar levels of wealth.[1] The United States, however, has a formal military alliance with Denmark but not with Israel, and gives Denmark no foreign aid while Israel receives approximately $3 billion from the United States annually. Why do these differences in policies exist? In many instances the answer to this question might appear obvious. That does not relieve us of the necessity of

---

[1] According to the CIA's *World Factbook 2002*, Denmark has a population of about 5.4 million with a GDP per capita of $28,000. Israel has about 6 million people and its GDP per capita is about $20,000 http://www.cia.gov/cia/publications.

developing systematic and generalizable explanations for such observations. An explanation based only on size, wealth, and amity would not be able to explain the differences in U.S. policy toward Denmark and Israel.

The final application is to provide an understanding about the relationships among policies. For instance, should a leader decide to use sanctions as an instrument of her state's foreign policy, does that imply that the frequency of conflict will subsequently diminish? Does joining an alliance lead to an increase or a decrease in defense spending? To understand the relationship between and among policies requires that we understand why states pursue their policies, which in turn should help us understand foreign policy substitutability. In this book we will offer an approach to the study of foreign policy that provides answers relating to all four applications.

We try to answer the first question posed in this chapter above by doing three things in our analysis that are uncommon in approaches to the study of international relations. First, we view states' actions as components of portfolios, which consist of all their foreign policy behaviors. We do not focus exclusively on conflict behavior, or trade policy, or foreign aid allocations as discrete policies that can be discussed and analyzed without reference to other policies, though our theory has things to say about those separate policies. Instead, we see a state constructing bundles of policies—what we will call portfolios—that, in combination, are designed to achieve things—outcomes—that the state wants. Second, we adopt a general perspective of foreign policy that is designed to apply to all states at all times. Our focus is on a few independent variables and their general effects. While the main focus of the theory is not on explaining, for instance, German foreign policy in the interwar years or American foreign policy during the cold war, we will demonstrate that our theory can be applied to the policies of specific countries. Third, contrary to much theorizing about international relations, we assume that states pursue two general goals through their foreign policies. Typically, international relations theorists argue that states can be analyzed as if they want one thing only—greater security. We will assume that states want to protect things that they value and that they will try to alter things in the international systems they do not like. Since the ability of any state, no matter how powerful, to accomplish what it wants is limited, leaders have to make choices. Leaders have to decide whether they want to protect something they like or attempt to bring about a change in some situation to conform more to their preferences. And it is this choice that we seek to understand and explain in this volume.

The theory presented here is based on a relatively simple formal model. Since many readers might be put off by the technical presentation of the model, we delay that until chapter 5. We introduce the reader to the concepts and general argument of the theory in the next chapter, in which we present a nonmathematical version of the two-good theory more fully. There, we will ask the reader to think about international relations differently from other approaches. So that we may start that presentation cleanly, we use this chapter, first, to introduce the idea of the foreign policy portfolio, that set of policies a state adopts to meet its foreign policy objectives. Changes in a state's foreign policy portfolio represent the key factor that is to be explained by our theory. Second, of course, we want to outline the particulars of the two-good theory and present the main assumptions we make. Our third task in this chapter is to highlight the elements of our approach that distinguish it from other, more traditional theories of international relations.

Foreign Policy Portfolios

One of the central axioms of the two-good theory that separates it from other ways of thinking about international relations is the belief that a state's foreign policy behaviors, the individual policies a state adopts in pursuit of its interests, should be viewed as a bundle of policies. States, in other words, create their foreign policy portfolios to achieve the things that they want, given existing constraints.

Consider some of the actions the United States has taken within the last ten years or so in its dealings with other states:

- During much of the 1990s the United States supported expanding the North Atlantic Treaty Organization (NATO) by admitting states that had previously been members of the Warsaw Pact. This support was essential to the success of the negotiations that resulted in Poland, the Czech Republic, and Hungary joining NATO on March 12, 1999.
- On April 2, 1996, Secretary of Defense William Perry reported that Libya was constructing an underground chemical weapons facility and warned that the United States would use force, if necessary, to halt construction rather than allow the plant to operate. Libya halted work on the facility immediately, and after diplomatic intercession by Hosni Mubarak of Egypt, Libya agreed not to resume construction.
- On April 30, 2001, the United States announced a major arms deal with Taiwan. The United States agreed to sell Taiwan four Kidd class destroyers, twelve P3 Orion anti-submarine planes, and eight diesel submarines.
- In the spring of 2001, the United States reversed its long-held opposition to allowing the People's Republic of China to join the World Trade Organization (WTO). On November 10, 2001, the WTO welcomed China as a member.
- On January 5, 2002, the United States announced that it would not bail Argentina out of its financial crisis; the United States said it wanted to avoid being a "financial firefighter." Argentine President Eduardo Duhalde placed blame for Argentina's situation on the American economic model, pushed by Washington, which stressed deregulation and decentralization. On January 15, President Bush

warned Argentina not to use its difficulties as an excuse to back down from its free-market reforms. On January 31, the United States cut foreign aid to Argentina because, in the words of Treasury Secretary Paul O'Neill, "it just didn't reform."

- On January 14, 2002, the United States and the Philippines prepared for joint military operations against Abu Sayyaf, an extremist Muslim group with links to Al Qaeda. A plan was agreed to by the two countries whereby 650 U.S. military personnel were to be sent to the Philippines within weeks.
- On April 11, 2003, the U.S. government announced that it had reached a settlement with the New York Yankees, in which the baseball team would pay a penalty of $75,000 for violating U.S. economic sanctions against Cuba by negotiating a contract with a Cuban baseball player.

We chose these actions not because they are exceptional but because they are ordinary and constitute good examples of the elements that make up a foreign policy portfolio. Represented among these actions are issues of alliance politics, decisions about foreign aid, matters of trade policy, and steps to enforce a longstanding embargo. Some of the actions are relatively routine or undertaken by officials not at the top of the bureaucratic hierarchy, while others represent decisions made by U.S. leaders. The targets of the actions include states friendly to the United States as well as adversaries. In other words, they reflect the range of actions that a major state can be expected to take in pursuit of its interests during any particular period.

These actions are elements of the American foreign policy portfolio. The United States chose the policies (and others not included here) from among all actions available to it in order to create the most desirable set of international arrangements under the circumstances. Several things are implied by that. First, this means that the United States wanted to change some things in the world that it does not like, such as the regime in Cuba. Other actions, such as the arms deal with Taiwan, were meant to reinforce an existing outcome. The United States, we assume, has preferences and it attempts to realize those preferences through its actions.

A second implication is that these actions all used resources: some required time to reach a decision or to carry out that decision; some needed money; some the extension of U.S. security guarantees; and some the dispersion of military personnel into dangerous places. But none of the acts is free and without cost. If the United States, or any actor, is rational, before undertaking an action it must decide that spending limited resources on a particular policy is a good idea. This means that the actor must determine that two things are true. For the United States—or any actor—to do something, it must decide, first, that the expected benefits of undertaking the action surpass the direct expected costs of the action: the expected value must be greater than the transaction costs. If the costs are greater than the benefits, the actor is better off not adopting the policy and presumably the action would not be selected. The United States prepared to send the 650 troops to the Philippines because it expected a benefit from doing so, and that benefit was greater than the costs in money and threat to lives that sending the troops to the Philippines would entail. A second necessary condition is that the expected benefits of the action be greater than the opportunity costs. That is, the United States—or any actor—places its limited resources into one particular policy, P, rather than putting them into any other policy or policies because its expected return is greatest for policy P. The policy chosen is the most efficient one available at the time for achieving the actor's goals. The United States decided to send its 650 troops to the Philippines, not to Cuba.

The third implication is that we see states as selecting from the menu of available policies the bundle of policies that best suits their needs and goals at a particular time, given their preferences and constraints. Much as an individual consumes a bundle of goods designed to satisfy a range of wants—subject to the limits of the individual's wealth—states adopt policy portfolios to maximize the utility they derive from the world political environment, subject to the constraints imposed by their limited resources and the international system.

Throughout much of this work we will be analyzing foreign policy behavior as a portfolio of policies. In approaching matters this way, we can represent a state's foreign policy as an identifiable point in a two-dimensional space. (Those two dimensions will be defined as we progress.) This allows us to generalize about foreign policy behavior across states and across time. This is critical to our work; we want to look at the effects of changes in environmental factors—an increase in state capability, for example—on various aspects of state behavior so that we can analyze a large number of states simultaneously. More important, we want to say things about how changes in resources given over to one policy are likely to affect the resources given over to another policy. We also want to address the issue of how portfolios might be expected to change if the goals of the state change.

This view of policies making up a portfolio admittedly is an abstraction, but it is an abstraction with which most of us are familiar. It is common for states' foreign policies to be described and analyzed as if they had one purpose motivating them, such that the elements of the policy were tied together, reinforcing and interdependent—that is, as if they were portfolios. During the cold war, the underlying purpose of American foreign policy was held to be the containment of Soviet influence. Elements of that policy included the formation of NATO, allocation of foreign aid to the militaries of friendly states, participation in the Korean War, the development the hydrogen bomb, the establishment of the Marshall Plan, the formation of defense pacts with Taiwan and Japan, and the centralization of military planning. Surely some of these policies were uniquely affected by local, parochial, bureaucratic, or historical circumstances, but those of us who study American foreign policy see them as tied together and designed to accomplish a common end. That they were seen as interdependent by decision makers is demonstrated by the Eisenhower administration's belief that a reliance on nuclear deterrence through the doctrine of massive retaliation would allow the United States to decrease its military spending. Against such a background of generalization, our notion of portfolio does not seem out of place or extraordinary.

The use of foreign policy portfolios allows us to make generalizations and comparisons that are vital to the development of theory. The level of generality achieved permits comparisons of the policies of a state at different points in time or of the different portfolios of different states. We want to be able to say such things as, "As a state becomes more powerful it will attempt more to change the status quo, other things being equal." Such statements have meaning at a very general level, but they are also useful empirically, and using our concept of portfolios does not preclude more focused statements and expectations. Once we are able to identify what elements of a portfolio are designed to accomplish, we will be able to translate general statements into more precise expectations. For instance (without looking too far ahead), if we were to say that, in general, conflict initiation and the granting of foreign aid are good policies for changing the behavior of others, then our general statement is equivalent to saying that states that become more powerful are more likely to initiate conflict and to allocate greater resources to foreign aid, other things being equal. In other words, while the use of portfolios allows us to generalize, we can also disaggregate them into their component parts to analyze specific aspects of states' foreign policies.

Finally, we do not assume that a state's foreign policy portfolio is fixed or constant. Indeed, much of our discussion in the following chapters is directed toward determining when states alter their portfolios, and we discuss environmental factors that we believe lead states to make significant changes in their general orientation. We also present our ideas about *how* states go about instituting the changes they desire. If, for instance, a state wants to alter the existing political situation in a region or between it and some other state, what does it do? What policies, in other words, are good for bringing about changes and what policies are more associated with stabilizing or solidifying the status quo? In doing that, we draw conclusions from our theory that are general and—when we impute general goals to specific policies—can be quite specific.

The components of the state's foreign policy portfolio serve as our dependent variables, those things that we are attempting to explain. We will also be analyzing the relationship among the components of those portfolios, as the two-good theory has some direct implications for foreign policy substitutability. Now, having introduced what we want to explain, we present a short summary of our approach—the two-good theory of foreign policy.

The Two-Good Theory: A Summary

The two-good theory, of course, assumes that states pursue two things—we will call them change and maintenance—through their international behavior and component foreign policies and that they allocate foreign policy resources as efficiently as possible to maximize their utility. That simple statement contains the central components of the theory; but, as we will show, it leads to a large number of implications. Here we introduce some of the basic elements of the theory.

The political universe, we assume, can be viewed as consisting of issues that at least one state cares about. The world, in other words, can be modeled as a multidimensional issue space. The status quo at a particular time is the existing outcome of all those issues. It is evident that states will be happy with some of the outcomes and unhappy with others. All states, we assume, want to protect aspects of the world (the outcomes in the issue space) they like. One of those outcomes is, of course, the fact that they exist. Beyond that, there are such things as desired internal political arrangements, trade patterns, existing alliances, and a host of other components of the status quo that states would like to see unaltered. Simultaneously, all states would like to see some changes in the existing set of outcomes. Not everything is as any one state would like it to be. No state is able to determine the international and domestic policies of all other states, so all states are able to imagine a better world.

We assume that states have goals and that they pursue them through their foreign policies. These goals can be classified in as disparate and precise a fashion as one cares—states can be seen as attempting to ensure nuclear nonproliferation, to increase international respect for human rights, to protect the environment, to bolster democratic forces, to improve the life expectancy of newborns, to weaken the economies of enemy countries, and so on. Focusing separately on the vast array of specific goals and policies that states can adopt makes building general statements and theorizing impossible. Instead, we generalize about the goals states have as much as is fruitfully possible. Rather than saying that states have many, many goals (as many goals as there are issues) or that states have but one goal (either increasing their power or their security, for instance), we think it simplest and most useful to generalize to the point where we say states pursue *two* goals.[2] Specifically, we generalize to say that states use their foreign policies to protect the components of the status quo they like and to change those they do not like. We consider actions designed

---

[2] As we argue throughout, a central consideration for explaining *any* choices that involve the expenditure of resources (which certainly characterizes foreign policy decisions) is an understanding of the trade-offs decision makers must make over things they value. Any such consideration requires us to assume there are a minimum of two things of value. Ours is thus the simplest theory that can allow an investigation of such trade-offs.

to protect existing outcomes as seeking the goal of *maintenance* and those designed to alter aspects of the status quo as seeking the goal of *change*. Foreign policy actions, our theory says, are directed at either maintaining or changing specific components of the international status quo.

Any analysis of foreign policy behavior implicitly or explicitly imputes goals to its actors. Since we wish to develop a fruitful and simple general theory, we have assumed that states have two goals, maintenance and change. The preferences leaders have for each of the two goals are affected by many factors, but the actual ability of the state to realize the desired change or the desired maintenance must be a prominent consideration in deciding what policies to adopt. Among the most important environmental factors that affect the effectiveness of a state's pursuit of its goals are the national capabilities of the state. We assume that the effectiveness of a state's pursuit of change or maintenance varies with its relative capabilities. States with more resources, not surprisingly, are better able to achieve *both* change and maintenance than are the less capable. Nonetheless, we expect to see a difference between more and less capable states in the relative emphasis placed on change versus maintenance, for a simple reason. Specifically, we argue that it is easier to maintain the status quo than it is to change it. That means that more capable states are *comparatively* better able to realize desired changes in the status quo than are weaker states, which have a comparative advantage in maintaining the status quo. This simple assumption—reasonable and defensible, in our view—implies a variety of things. For one, we expect to see that more capable states should be more active in altering the international status quo than weaker states, which, in turn, are expected to place a greater proportion of their resources into policies better suited to maintaining the status quo. In addition, states gaining in relative capabilities are likely to place a greater proportion of their new resources than previously into changing things and will place greater emphasis on policies better suited to bringing about change.

In the next chapter we will explain and justify the assumptions of the theory more fully. We present the logic that moves us from these few and simple assumptions to the theory's conclusions. We will spend considerable effort deriving the empirical implications of the theory so that we might subject them to test. Having summarized the components of the two-good theory, we move now to a short description of some of its characteristics and peculiarities.

Two-Good Theory Characteristics

Our task in this section is to highlight some of the more basic or implicit characteristics of the two-good theory. Our emphasis in this book is on the theory and what it tells us about the way international relations works; we are not prone to engage in extended epistemological discussion. Nonetheless, because the two-good theory may offer a view of international relations that is different from those with which many readers are familiar, we want briefly to outline the two-good theory's positions on some sundry matters.

First, the two-good theory is abstract and general. It is not motivated by a desire to explain and understand only one state's foreign policy or only one type of behavior. Instead, the theory's goal is to understand the factors that affect the foreign policy portfolios of all states at all times. This has the advantage of making the two-good theory widely applicable, and its range is quite large. We can—and in succeeding chapters we will—analyze broad trends in a state's international behavior, such as the general directions of American foreign policy since World War II and of Chinese foreign policy since 1949. The theory can also help us analyze specific foreign policy decisions that are hard to understand using the usual theoretical tools we have for analyzing international relations. We can also have relatively precise expectations about particular policies, such as conflict initiation and alliance formation, and the theory can tell us about how changes in one policy can be expected to affect other policies.

The two-good theory makes no direct statement about the nature of the international system. We do assume, however, that there is no overarching authority capable of enforcing agreements or norms. States may be able to reach mutually satisfying arrangements between and among themselves (such as the formation of alliances and the founding of international organizations), and they may have reasons to abide (or not to abide) by those agreements. But the incidence of cooperation and coordination can and must be explained as functions of the self-interest of the actors, not the operation of supranational entity.

Realism shares this emphasis on the units that make up the system, of course. Neorealism similarly sees the system as fundamentally anarchic, but it also holds that the structure (for example, bipolar versus multipolar) and the distribution of power within the system impose constraints on the behavior of the states (see Waltz 1979). The two-good theory does not provide for system-level variables to affect the behavior of the units. The emphasis of the theory is on the behavior of the actors, the states; its focus is on the units. The theory takes as axiomatic that observed political outcomes are the result of the consequences—intended and unintended—of actors taking actions in pursuit of their self-interest. This focus on the units means that some characteristics, such as their level of national capability and the change in that capability, of those units are central to the theory. Other characteristics are either assumed not to play a significant role in determining the behavior of the states or are such that we are not currently able to make general statements about them.[3]

---

[3] For example, in earlier work we distinguished among presidential, parliamentary, and autocratic political systems in applying the two-good theory (Morgan and Palmer 1996). We anticipate returning to that attention and applying it to domestic political structures, but the current work has assumed that domestic political arrangements have very little effect on foreign policy.

The theory is general, but it is also falsifiable. This is a critical attribute of any good theory. The two-good theory hypothesizes, to take an example, that states increasing in their power are the most likely to pursue change-seeking policies, compared to states that are declining in power or those not changing in power. We have identified the initiation of conflict as a change-seeking policy. If we were to find that states increasing in power do *not* have the highest incidence of conflict initiation, we would conclude that the two-good theory is wrong. We have, in fact, reported instances in this volume where hypotheses generated by the two-good theory are not supported. We do not conclude that the theory is without merit, however, in part because of the number of—often nonintuitive—hypotheses that are supported by the evidence. Indeed, we argue that it represents an advance over prominent and widely used theories of international behavior in part precisely because it is, on occasion, wrong in its predictions. Accepting where one's theory is wrong rather than manipulating it to account for any observed phenomenon is essential for the development of knowledge. Addressing the problems thus revealed is, of course, the subject of further work.

Last, the two-good theory can produce novel expectations about foreign policy substitutability. In other words, it can do more than explain how the environment affects one policy at a time. As the theory assumes that some policies are better at bringing about change while others are better at maintaining some parts of the status quo, and (in keeping with standard definitions of rationality) it assumes that states choose the most efficient policies to accomplish their set of goals, it speaks to the relationship between and among policies. Recall that the traditional understanding of substitutability says that as resources given over to one policy increase, resources given to all other policies decrease. The two-good version of substitutability says that we must know two things about a policy before we can predict the effect of increased allocations to it. First, we must know why more was given over to the policy: is it more efficient at accomplishing its end than previously? Does the state now value the good that policy produces more than previously? Or have the overall resources the state can dedicate to foreign policy increased? Second, we need to know what good this policy is better suited to acquiring. The predictions the two-good theory makes regarding the effects on other policies depend on whether those other policies produce the same or a different good. In viewing states as constructing portfolios—mixtures of particular policies—the theory can explain how substitutability can be expected to operate.

Plan of the Book

We proceed as follows. The next chapter lays out the two-good theory in some detail. We address a number of conceptual issues, we specify our key assumptions, and we spell out the reasoning behind those assumptions. We also state some of the implications from the theory and present some of the many empirical hypotheses that can be drawn. Our goal in chapter 2 is to make the two-good theory accessible and attractive. To that end, we spend some time making the point that the two-good theory really is quite simple and that the assumptions it makes about the relationships between concepts (such as power and the ability to pursue change) are as simple as any theory that has actors pursuing multiple goals can be. We also argue that the primary value of the two-good theory is the breadth of behaviors it can explain.

Chapter 3 begins the application of the implications of the two-good theory. We apply the theory to the general patterns of one country's foreign policy over an extended time—specifically, to U.S. foreign policy since World War II. This case contains a wealth of historical material that will be familiar to many readers. Our purpose is not to provide new historical data but to show how the broad patterns of American foreign policy are interpreted and understood by the two-good theory. We will discuss, for instance, how the theory sees the United States not as a status quo oriented power but as the most change-seeking country in the world after 1945. We will show how the postwar foreign policy consensus resulted less from a widely shared belief about the need to contain Soviet expansion than from the power of the United States, which provided the ability for American policy to meet the desired goals of large numbers of domestic constituents. People who wanted to maintain American supremacy and keep the Soviet Union at bay could be satisfied, as could those who wanted to establish fertile grounds for American business, particularly in Europe. As the relative power of the United States declined, the foreign policy consensus predictably unraveled. Particularly after the Vietnam experience, Americans were caught in a debate about whether the United States should retain the focus on opposing the USSR or reorient its policies toward achieving greater international economic and social coordination. That debate reflected the fact that the United States could no longer simultaneously satisfy the demands of those who wanted American policy to bring about change in the international system and of those who wanted the United States to protect the beneficial aspects of the international status quo. The reinterpretation of postwar U.S. foreign policy will, we hope, show the distinguishing features of the two-good theory as well as provide a better, more scientifically based view of that period in history.

In chapter 4 we apply the two-good theory to different situations to see how it explains seemingly odd events in international relations and how it is useful for analyzing quantitatively the patterns of one state's foreign policy. We do this to show the range of analyses and uses to which the two-good theory can be put. Specifically, we apply the theory to a situation where a large country—Russia—accepted extremely harsh terms in negotiations to end its participation in World War I. The Treaty of Brest-Litovsk is interesting because Soviet

Russia was willing to end its war with Germany even at the cost of a large percentage of its land and about 25 percent of its population. It is also interesting and useful for us because we know a fair amount about the discussions among the Bolshevik leadership leading up to the Brest-Litovsk agreement. The disagreements among the three factions in the leadership—led by Lenin, Trotsky, and Bukharin—can be understood and analyzed easily through the two-good theory.

The second case we discuss involves a small country that took actions knowing that the result would be the end of its alliance with a much larger country. The end of the alliance between New Zealand and the United States in 1985 followed the election of a new government in New Zealand that placed significantly greater value on its independence from the United States on particular policy matters than did its predecessor. This alliance is instructive because some approaches to understanding international politics have a difficult time explaining either why (using Morrow's [1991] language) such "asymmetrical" alliances exist on the one hand, or why there aren't many more of them on the other. The two-good theory does a nice job of explaining both why these alliances exist and why a small country might decide that membership in such an alliance is no longer valued. Last, chapter 4 looks at Chinese foreign policy since 1949 using a variety of statistical analyses. The point of our exercise there is to make some predictions about the general directions of China's policy based on several environmental factors identified by the two-good theory. Chapter 4, we hope, shows how disparate and valuable the uses of the two-good theory are.

After devoting two chapters to the applications and illustrations of the theory, we present the formal, mathematical version of the two-good theory in chapter 5. The chapter provides more rigorous direction and reasoning for the statistical analyses of the two subsequent chapters, and it makes our assumptions more precise and the logic used to derive the hypotheses more explicit. The chapter may be taxing for some, but we think it worth a little effort because one salient conclusion we think readers will come away with is that the theory is remarkably simple in its components and logic. We will argue this point repeatedly throughout this volume, but nowhere is the case made more apparent than in chapter 5.

Chapter 6 presents statistical analyses of some of the hypotheses derived from the theory. For example, we look at the effects of one prominent environmental factor—national capabilities—on the rate at which states initiate and reciprocate international conflict. We find some surprising things that are nonetheless predicted by the theory. For instance, consistent with our expectations we find that less powerful states are more likely to reciprocate conflict than are more powerful states. We also investigate empirically some of the theory's implications for foreign policy substitutability. We look at how foreign aid allocations are affected by such policies as alliance membership, general military expenditures, and international conflict involvement. We will show both that substitutability is more complicated than is often believed and that the implications of the two-good theory's version of substitutability are borne out.

Chapter 7 investigates foreign policy substitutability in greater detail and does so in two ways. First, there is a set of statistical analyses regarding the effects of joining alliances on other aspects of states' foreign policy portfolios. One of the basic points of that analysis is to show the strong support for the theory's two fundamental conclusions regarding substitutability: first, substitutability patterns are affected by the relative efficiency with which specific policies produce change or maintenance; second, the effects on one policy, A, of putting greater resources into some other policy, B, are based on the motivations for increasing the resource allocated B in the first place. Chapter 7 also presents a case study of the Suez Canal Crisis of 1956. It is useful for us to spend some time on this crisis because one of our theory's conclusions is that rather than constraining behavior, alliance membership serves to allow states to pursue their foreign policy goals more actively. The end of the Suez Canal Crisis is frequently portrayed as following the American insistence that its allies, Britain and France, withdraw from Egypt. Perhaps so, but our examination of the case shows that without their alliance with the United States, the United Kingdom, and France (and Israel) would have been militarily and politically incapable of launching their invasion of the Suez Canal in the first place. In terms of our theory, the alliance with the powerful United States provided Britain and France with resources and maintenance, allowing them the opportunity and desire to increase their change. The war against Egypt could not have occurred without the alliance with the United States.

In the final chapter we argue that the two-good theory is an advance in the analysis of international relations. We think the primary cost of the theory—the loss in parsimony—is much less real than appears at first blush. Part of this, we argue, is because realism and neorealism are underspecified; they are not as complete as they need to be. The two-good theory, we demonstrate, is fully specified and as simple a theory as possible, given the assumption that states pursue multiple goals in their international behavior. We argue that the logical completeness and the gain in empirical explanatory power more than justify the two-good theory. We hope, by the end, the reader will agree.

We turn now to a description of the two-good theory.

2

The Two-Good Theory Presented

As NOTED in the last chapter, our goal in this book is to present a general theory of foreign policy that can be used to explain a wide range of foreign policy behaviors as well as a wide range of empirical relationships. Later in the book, we develop a formal version of the theory; our aim here is to provide a more intuitive description of our reasoning. In this chapter we discuss our basic conceptualization of the problem, we present our major assumptions, and we introduce many of the hypotheses to which the theory leads. We also make some effort to contrast our theory with existing models of the foreign policy process.

What Is to Be Explained?

One of the major appeals of the neorealist perspective is that it provides a basis for explaining foreign policy on at least three levels. First, it provides a means for understanding specific foreign policy actions. As analysts, we want to be able to explain such things as why the United States launched a cruise missile attack on targets in Afghanistan and the Sudan in August 1998; why in the mid-1980s New Zealand took actions leading to the dissolution of the ANZUS pact; why Japan spent $37.7 billion on defense and $9.4 billion on foreign aid in 1996 (a ratio of about $4 to the military for every $1 to foreign aid), while the United States spent $266 billion on defense and $12.2 billion on foreign aid,[1] a ratio of about 20:1; and so forth. We can take any such observed action and come to understand it through the realist framework—all that is required is the construction of an argument demonstrating how that action contributed to the security of the state.

Second, neorealism provides a means for understanding the overarching themes in state foreign policies. For example, U.S. foreign policy in the 1950s and 1960s is usually characterized by the term "containment." The general,

---

[1] According to 2002 SIPRI Military Expenditures Database and the Ministry of Foreign Affairs of Japan's Office of Development Assistance 1997 Annual Report, respectively. The latter is available at http://www.mofa.go.jp/policy/oda/summary/1997/02.html. The data for U.S. foreign aid in 1996 was taken from the U.S. Department of State Web site, specifically, http://usinfo.state.gov/journals/ites/0896/ijee/ej3faf2.htm.

stated goal of U.S. policy was to forestall the expansion of Soviet influence, and most specific policy decisions were evaluated in terms of how well they contributed to this goal. Similarly, British policy toward Germany in the late 1930s is characterized as one of "appeasement" and specific actions are interpreted in terms of how they fit into this pattern. Neorealism provides a basis from which to evaluate such themes.[2] It assumes that the goal of a state is to maximize its security and that this goal is sought through the application of power politics. A realist can explain the American policy of containment and the British policy of appeasement by noting that both governments were concerned with security (Truman felt most threatened by unbridled Soviet aggression, Chamberlain by the effects of war) and that both adopted overall strategies regarding how best to apply their power resources. Furthermore, neorealism offers a basis for judging how well states did—the policy of containment was a success, the policy of appeasement a failure.

Finally, neorealism offers a basis for explaining the general relationships in international affairs that occur through the aggregation of foreign policy actions taken by several states. Neorealism can lead us to hypothesize, for example, that we should observe, in general, a positive correlation between changes in defense spending in one state and changes in defense spending in rival states. Similarly, we can draw upon the realist framework to argue that wars should be more frequent, but less serious, in a multipolar international system than in a bipolar system.

Much of the appeal of neorealism rests with its ability to integrate explanations of each of these different sorts of things. We want explanations for all and it seems fairly obvious that they should be related; a single perspective that accounts for each is clearly desirable. One reason that most of the assaults on neorealism have failed to gain wide acceptance may be that they typically can offer explanations for only one thing. For instance, one of the most recent attacks has come from those offering theory and supporting evidence showing that domestic political factors have a significant effect on foreign policy

---

[2] To be sure, we are generalizing about a vast literature, and we run the danger of minimizing the range of thought that is based on the realist and neorealist tradition. Fundamental realist texts would include Morgenthau (1951, 1952, 1965a), Kennan (1954, 1957), and Kissinger (1957). See also Krasner (1978), Gilpin (1981), Mearsheimer (1983, 1990), and Wayman and Diehl (1994) for applications of realism or neorealism to different research questions. A recent debate regarding the fruitfulness of realism includes Vasquez (1993, 1997), Christensen and Snyder (1997), Waltz (1997), and Walt (1997). Additionally, we are treating realism and neorealism similarly for purposes of our discussion while acknowledging that there are significant differences between them. See Waltz (1979), Keohane (1984, 1986a, 1986b), and Walt (1987) for discussions. Some recent discussion about the utility of realism and neorealism include James (1995), Lamborn (1997), Schweller and Priess (1997), Osiander (1998), Denemark (1999), Inoguchi (1999), and Russett, Oneal, and Cox (2000).

choices—a finding that is in direct contradiction of neorealism.[3] This work has shown that explanations other than neorealism better account for general empirical relationships (and we have long known that the general hypotheses derived from neorealism do not hold up well in large-N studies), but thus far, nothing has developed from this work that does a very good job of accounting for specific foreign policy actions or the overarching themes in individual state foreign policies.

Thus, as we develop our general theory of foreign policy, our challenge is to demonstrate that it can offer explanations for a number of different things. In this chapter, we develop our argument at an intuitive, conceptual level. In doing so, we hope to demonstrate that our model can be used to guide explanations of general patterns of state foreign policies as well as explanations for specific foreign policy actions. In explaining the former, we surpass neorealism by showing how our model identifies the conditions under which states alter the general pattern of their foreign policies, enabling us to predict when such changes will occur. We also show that our theory can lead to explanations for specific foreign policy actions. These specific events constitute the observable traces of foreign policy (for example, alliance formation, military action, foreign aid allocation) and are generally what we are concerned with explaining; that is, we want to know why states do the things they do, when, and in what amounts. We will offer some examples showing that our theory provides a basis from which to understand very specific actions. In doing so, we will again show that our theory betters neorealism in that it provides a basis from which we can understand domestic political battles over foreign policy decisions. In a subsequent chapter we formalize our theory. This permits the derivation of general hypotheses that we test through large-N statistical analyses. This will demonstrate that our theory accounts for general relationships better than does neorealism.

Basic Assumptions

A fundamental tenet of our theory is the assumption that foreign policy actions are goal directed. At a general level, this assumption is shared with neorealism,

---

[3] We are referring largely but not exclusively here to the work on the democratic peace. Representative of that large body of research are Small and Singer (1976), Chang (1984), Weede (1984), Doyle (1986), Maoz and Abdolali (1989), Morgan and Campbell (1991), Bueno de Mesquita and Lalman (1992), Maoz and Russett (1993), Dixon (1993, 1994), Ray (1995), Rousseau, Gelpi, Reiter, and Huth (1996), Gleditsch and Hegre (1997), Gartzke (1998), Bueno de Mesquita, Morrow, Siverson, and Smith (1999), and Mousseau (2000). For criticisms of the democratic peace, see Farber and Gowa (1995, 1997), Gates Knutsen, and Moses (1996), Elman (1997), Gowa (1999), and Henderson (2002).

as well as a host of other perspectives on foreign policy and international relations.[4] The difference rests with exactly how we specify those goals.

A fundamental tenet of neorealism is that foreign policy is directed at maintaining and enhancing the *security* of the state. Security is viewed primarily in military terms. That is, the major foreign policy concern is to protect the territorial integrity of the state against encroachment from other, potentially aggressive states. The scope of "security" is often broadened, however, to include the safety of one's citizens abroad, the protection of economic interests, and even the protection or advancement of one's ideology.

Many realists hold that security is paramount and that nothing else in international relations can be sought until security is assured. Others believe that security is the only foreign policy goal. In fact, the implications of either view are nearly identical. Accepting that other goals can be sought once security is ensured does not imply a belief that absolute security can ever be achieved. One can little imagine a state being more secure from military threat than was the United States immediately after World War II. Yet, the American realists of the time still saw a world fraught with danger. If, in practice, no state can achieve sufficient security to turn its attention to other goals, then all foreign policy must be seen as directed toward increasing security.

Part of the problem with the realist conception is that it cannot readily explain the source of states' assumed motivation: if all states are solely concerned with protecting what they have, from where do the threats to a state's security come? One possible answer is that all states at all times do not behave in accordance with the tenets of neorealism. Basically, states expect that on occasion and without significant warning, a madman (such as Hitler) will emerge as a state leader and will set out on a course of conquest. This, according to many realist prescriptions, is exactly what is of concern to states. Since we cannot anticipate when such situations will arise, we must always be prepared to defend ourselves when they do. The problem with such an explanation is that it completely undermines the ability of neorealism to serve as an explanatory or predictive theory. We are basically left with the idea that neorealism works, except when it doesn't.

A somewhat more refined version of this argument can be found in the work of those who separate states into two types—the status quo oriented and the revisionist (Carr 1946; Schuman 1948; Morgenthau 1965; Gilpin 1981; Stein 1990; Schweller 1998). Here, the status quo oriented are entirely defensive,

---

[4] A point we wish to stress throughout is that being critical of neorealism does not require that we throw out every aspect of it. We find some of its assumptions to be quite useful and others to require only modification. Further, some of the insights derived from neorealism are valid, interesting, and useful. Our theory is quite different from neorealism (and other perspectives) in many respects, but it also shares much in common. We hope to retain much of the insight produced by neorealism while overcoming many of the limitations.

but the revisionist states believe that the existing international order undermines their ability to receive their due prestige and security. Revisionist states
threaten the existing order and, if they are strong enough militarily, will attempt to overturn it. The problem facing such an argument is that it quickly
becomes tautological. Revisionist states are seen as destabilizing and "bad" and
we generally label as revisionist either those that lost the last war or those that
are our current enemies.

The more common notion of the source of threats to states can be found in
the concept of the security dilemma (Herz 1951; Wolfers 1962; Jervis 1978;
Snyder 1984). The idea is that even in a world populated totally by peace-
loving and defensive states, fear and suspicion can lead to threat, conflict, and
war. This follows from the fact that the anarchic nature of the international
system means that each state is ultimately responsible for its own protection.
Actions taken by one state to increase its security (for example, increasing
arms, forming alliances, territorial expansion) unavoidably pose threats to
other states. Each state may act to increase its security in a way that is individually rational, but the result is that all states end up being less secure. Since states
can observe only each other's abilities and not each other's intentions, it is only
prudent for each to mistrust the others. Conflict spirals are possible in such an
environment and are motivated solely by defensive concerns. A major problem
with this explanation is that one is left wondering why any two states would
ever cooperate on anything. Why are we not constantly involved in a war of all
against all?

The root of the problem actually rests with the realist notion that security is
the only goal states seek. Any explanation for the source of threat in a world
populated by defensive-oriented states is bound to be unsatisfying. It must be
inherently contradictory to the basic notion and/or take on the feel of adding
epicycles to save the theory. More important, it requires that we adopt a notion
of "security" that is so broad as to render the concept meaningless (Buzan
1983). Territorial expansion is security enhancing because it affords a buffer
zone for forward defense. Or territorial retraction is security enhancing because
it shortens lines of communication and leads to more defensible borders. Giving foreign aid increases security because it stabilizes other regions and produces goodwill. Denying foreign aid, however, improves security by conserving
valuable resources for the military and by denying those resources to potential
enemies. Forming alliances adds to security by ensuring assistance if attacked.
Forming alliances decreases security by forcing the state to fight battles that are
not its own.

Basically, we must presume that any observed action was taken to enhance
the state's security and the method for explaining that action is to devise a
story, however tortured, showing how the observed action could be interpreted
as being security enhancing. Any foreign policy action that is observed can be
made consistent with realist theory simply by constructing an argument that it

contributed to the state's security. In fact, any foreign policy action that has not yet occurred can be justified in similar terms. Thus, we have interesting policy debates in which each side argues that its preferred alternative is really the one that will maximize security. During the Vietnam War, for example, proponents of American policy argued that U.S. national security required that the war be fought to prevent the fall of another domino and to maintain the credibility of American commitments. Opponents, on the other hand, argued that getting out of Vietnam would enhance American security by preserving valuable resources and maintaining the country's moral standing.

The bottom line is that the realist tenet that all foreign policy is directed toward the goal of security, broadly defined, makes neorealism conceptually vacuous, theoretically tautological, and empirically non-falsifiable. While maintaining the notion that foreign policy is purposive, we must do better in terms of conceptualizing that purpose. In particular, we must recognize that states pursue more than one goal. Even individual political actors value several things, and one of the key features of political life is that these actors often must make trade-offs across the things they value. This is particularly true of "actors" that, like states, are amalgamations of individuals.

The Assumptions of the Two-Good Model

In developing our model, we begin with the notion that politics, whether international or domestic, occurs over issues. An issue is anything meeting the following conditions: it can take on more than one value; political actors have some influence over which value obtains; at least two actors have different preferences over the range of values; and the actors are aware of these things. In the international realm, common issues can range from the question of who rules a particular territory to the determination of precise tariff levels to the decision regarding whether the citizen of one country can enter another country. The essence of politics is the struggle among political actors to achieve favorable outcomes on issues.

We assume that every political actor has an idea of what bliss would be like and that every actor can tell whether any change in outcome on an issue moves closer or farther from that ideal. That is, for every salient issue, an actor can rank the possible outcomes in terms of its preferences. It can identify which outcome would be the most desirable and it can compare any two possible outcomes and determine whether it is indifferent between them or one is preferred to the other. It is common to represent this notion spatially, and an example is provided in figure 2.1.

In this figure, we depict a world in which there are two actors, i and j, and two salient issues: the level of military expenditures by actor i and the tariff level imposed by j. We leave the units unspecified but presume that as we move

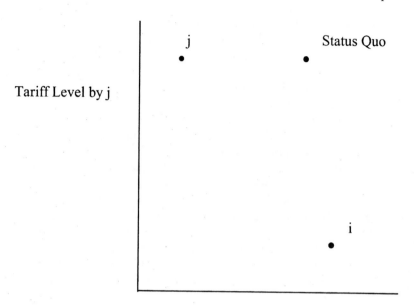

Figure 2.1. Issue Dimensions in Foreign Policy

from left to right in the figure the level of military expenditure increases and that as we move from bottom to top the tariff level increases. Each actor is located in the space by a point that corresponds to its most preferred outcome on each issue (actor j prefers higher tariff levels and lower military expenditures than does actor i), and we associate distance with preferences. That is, the farther away an outcome is from an actor's ideal point (its most preferred outcome) the less preferred it is.[5] We have also associated a point with the status quo, which represents the current levels of military expenditures and tariffs. Notice that actor i is relatively happy with its level of military expenditures, though it would like an increase and would prefer to see j reduce its tariff levels. On the other hand, j would like to see a substantial reduction in i's military expenditures and has its tariffs set at its most preferred level.

We presume that international politics is characterized, for all practical

---

[5] In fully developed spatial models the exact relationship between distance and preference is specified. These relationships can take on fairly complex forms and can allow the actors to place different salience weightings on the issues and to have its preferences on one issue tied to the expected or actual outcomes on the other(s). See, for instance, Hinich, Ledyard, and Ordeshook (1973); Enelow and Hinich (1981, 1984); Morgan (1984, 1994); and Morrow (1986).

purposes, by an infinite number of issues.[6] Every issue may not be particularly salient for every actor, and some issues that are salient may not be in contention at every moment in time. While we may be able to identify and focus on specific considerations of specific issues, we are unlikely to be able to enumerate all issues. Even though our theory is founded on the notion that politics occurs over a multitude of issues, developing the theory in a manner that requires the identification of each specific issue is unlikely to meet with much success. Though the realist position that only one foreign policy issue is salient for any state—its own security—creates the problems noted above, it does at least provide a starting point for analysis. Holding fast to the notion that an infinite number of issues are of concern to states, and thereby to foreign policy analysts, cannot produce a tractable theory. Understanding political behavior is not possible if we cannot analyze and generalize about the trade-offs political actors make over things they value, but comprehension requires that we abstract from the infinite list of goods that states could pursue.

We begin to address this problem by asserting that every political actor is relatively unhappy with the status quo on some issues and relatively content with the status quo on other issues. That is, we assume that neither heaven nor hell exists on earth—every political actor can always find more to want—and yet, as long as an actor exists, things could be worse. From this we are led to the notion that for any political actor, some of its behaviors will be devoted to changing the things it does not like and some will be devoted to maintaining the elements of the status quo it does like. In figure 2.1, for example, it is clear that actor j would devote its policy energies toward reducing i's military expenditures and maintaining its own tariff levels while actor i would work to reduce j's tariff levels. With respect to the issue of i's military expenditures, however, i might make an effort to increase them or i's policy might have to focus on preventing them from decreasing.

Following from the notion that some of any state's foreign policy behaviors will be devoted to changing aspects of the status quo it does not like and that some of its behaviors will be devoted to maintaining the elements of the status quo it does like, we find it useful to characterize states as seeking to produce two composite goods through their foreign policies. This produces the simplest model possible that still forces us to consider trade-offs across goods. We identify the first foreign policy value that states try to produce as *change* and the second as *maintenance.* All efforts and resources devoted toward altering aspects of the status quo are considered to be directed toward the production of *change*, while all efforts and resources devoted to preserving aspects of the

---

[6] For discussions of the role of issues on international behavior, see Mansbach and Vasquez (1981), Diehl (1992), Senese (1996), Hensel (1996, 2001), Mitchell and Prins (1999), Leeds, Long, and Mitchell (2000), and Gibler (1997).

status quo are considered to be directed toward the production of *mainte-nance.*

The major advantage in conceptualizing two (rather than one) composite goods is that we make it possible to consider trade-offs that actors must make in their political decisions. This makes it far easier to explain actions that seem perplexing from the one-good, realist perspective.[7] Consider Iraq's invasion of Kuwait in 1990, for example. If we assume that states seek only to maximize their security, our explanation for the event must be quite tortured, or we must fall back on asserting that Hussein was a madman (with the implication that such events cannot be explained, let alone anticipated or predicted). The two-good model provides a more reasonable explanation by allowing for the possi-bility of an actor who is willing to sacrifice *maintenance* for *change*; that is, one that is willing to risk losing outcomes it likes on some issues for the prospect of gaining outcomes it desires on others.

A related advantage is that the two-good model offers a straightforward ex-planation for why two states would come into conflict. If one seeks to change the status quo on a particular issue while the other attempts to maintain the current outcome, their interests and policies would collide. As simple as this statement is, it is surely more reasonable than the notion that conflicts arise from the security dilemma produced by two purely security-seeking states.

A key question regarding foreign policy that emerges from this involves ex-plaining the particular balance of *change-* and *maintenance-*seeking policies adopted by states. Before developing that aspect of the theory, however, we dis-cuss the two-good conceptualization more fully and offer some examples. We recognize that we are asking the reader to accept an unfamiliar conceptualiza-tion of foreign policy and that the burden of clarification rests with us. We also acknowledge at the outset that some degree of ambiguity will remain in that it may not always be obvious whether a specific action is meant to alter or pre-serve a particular aspect of the status quo. We will attempt to diminish that ambiguity.

The first aspect of the two-good conceptualization that must be emphasized is that it is an abstraction. Maintenance and change are not tangible goods. We use these concepts to represent two foreign policy goals that do involve tangi-ble issues (for example, territory). Some abstraction is necessary simply to make analysis manageable, and we find this abstraction far more useful than the common one of viewing "security" as the only goal of foreign policy.

A second point that must be emphasized is that we assume that all states, at all times, seek both *change* and *maintenance.* We do not assert that some states

---

[7] Compare also to any other perspective that assumes foreign policy is directed at only one good, of which David Lake's (1999) treatment of American foreign policy is an excellent example. He explicitly views foreign policy as intended to produce a good, which he calls security. His con-ceptualization is similar to ours in that regard, but the restriction to a single good prohibits any consideration of decisions regarding trade-offs between things of value.

seek only to change the status quo and that other states seek only to maintain it. In our view, the status quo is multidimensional and every state is relatively pleased with some aspects and relatively displeased with other aspects. Each state thus pursues a mixture of *change-* and *maintenance-*seeking policies. To be sure, some states will emphasize one over the other—in fact, that is what we think is important to explain—but we do not expect one to be sought to the exclusion of the other. We do note that the theory is sufficiently general to allow for the possibility that a state could seek only one of the goods, but we expect this to occur so rarely (if ever) that it should be an extreme case within the theory, not the only case that can occur.

We also note that we make no general moral judgments about state desires to preserve or change various aspects of the status quo. We presume simply that these desires are rooted in state preferences regarding the underlying issues. We do accept that some preferences can be immoral and that it is appropriate for scholars and citizens to make such judgments. Our point is that the morality of a preference is not rooted solely in whether it is to change the status quo or to maintain it. The preference to preserve the institution of slavery was immoral, as is the preference to change the status quo by eliminating a particular ethnic group. The important point is that our explanation for state behavior is not dependent on whether any state's preferences are moral or not.

Finally, we must emphasize that our notion of the status quo is not static. We accept that the status quo is constantly changing, more on some dimensions (issues) than others. Accepting the notion of a dynamic status quo is a necessary consequence of viewing politics as occurring over a multitude of issues.[8] Thus, maintenance-seeking behavior is not aimed at preserving all aspects of the status quo; rather, it is aimed at preserving some aspects over which the state has some control through its foreign policy.

This also requires that we address how, exactly, we can identify whether a particular behavior is change or maintenance seeking. While this determination is usually obvious, there are many cases in which the status quo is harder to pin down, especially since we allow for a dynamic status quo. For example, when the United States and its allies went to war against Iraq in 1991, was the goal to maintain the status quo of an independent Kuwait or was it to change the status quo of an Iraqi-dominated Kuwait? We address this by considering the status quo on an issue to refer to a trend[9] that is generally (not necessarily universally) accepted to identify actors' anticipations on that issue for the fore-

---

[8] To push this point to an extreme, in a very real sense, every birth, every death, every crop that is grown or that rots in the field, and every product that is created or destroyed changes, at the margin, the distribution of resources across states. By viewing the status quo in terms of all possible issues (even those that may be of very low salience for foreign policy decision makers), we are forced to accept that it cannot be static in all dimensions.

[9] Keep in mind that a trend can be flat, that is, unchanging. So, for example, the trend regarding the territory contained within the United States has been unchanged for years and the expectation is that it will continue to be unchanged in the foreseeable future.

seeable future. A generally accepted anticipation is not changed by fluctuations in the outcome that occur while the issue is being contested. That is, a change only becomes the new status quo when it becomes generally accepted as such. We offer a few examples to illustrate.

First, Iraq's invasion of Kuwait in 1990 is a clear example of change-seeking behavior. Because the change in the issue—from an independent Kuwait to a Kuwait controlled by Iraq—was not generally accepted as a new status quo, the actions of the United States and its allies to liberate Kuwait were maintenance seeking. As the accepted and established status quo included an Iraq led by Hussein, had the United States continued the war in an effort to overthrow him, that would have been change-seeking behavior. Second, the current anticipation is that China will, at least in the near future, continue to develop economically. Efforts by another state to keep China at its current level of economic development would thus constitute change seeking because these efforts would be directed at altering the anticipated trend. Third, in the early 1950s, the efforts to gain Vietnam's independence from France were change seeking, while the efforts to retain Vietnam as a French colony were maintenance seeking. The agreement that led to the French withdrawal from Indochina established a new anticipation (status quo) of a single, independent Vietnam that, after the agreed upon elections, would probably be under Ho Chi Minh's rule.[10] The actions of some countries, notably the United States, to alter this anticipation by creating two Vietnams were change-seeking behaviors. The fact that South Vietnam was sustained until 1975 is not sufficient to characterize U.S. behavior as maintenance seeking. Indeed, the very imagery of the "domino theory" presented a United States working to counter an anticipation. This is a case in which the challenge to the accepted anticipation took many years to resolve, but the notion of two Vietnams never became generally accepted.

Finally, we note that while some policies are directed at producing "potential" change or maintenance, as opposed to producing realized change or maintenance, we do not make this distinction. For example, many states devote resources to the military in order to protect their territories from invasion. We consider this an example of maintenance-seeking behavior, even if no attack occurs and the military is never used. This example seems intuitive, but the point becomes more difficult when we consider change-seeking behavior. Many states adopt policies that are designed to gain influence over the actions of other states. This is considered change-seeking behavior, even if the influence is not exercised overtly. "Finlandization" during the cold war is an obvious example. The Soviet Union rarely, if ever, overtly interfered in Finnish politics. It was widely believed, however, that if the Finns had, say, elected a prime minister

[10] The work on this point is extensive, and examples include Gelb with Betts (1979); Karnow (1983); Herring (1979); and Gardner (1988).

who was not to the Soviets' liking, such interference would be forthcoming. Thus, the Soviet policy toward Finland was change seeking. Another such example can be found in the 1847 alliance between Austria and Modena and the 1848 alliance agreement between Austria and Parma. In these treaties, Austria agreed to come to the defense of these Italian states in the event of a foreign invasion and they, in turn, "granted extensive rights of intervention and occupation" (Schroeder 1994, 778). Austria at the time was greatly concerned about what it saw as the threat to political stability represented by "the revolution," and the treaties allowed it to intervene to put down such threats and to bolster the Italian leaders. The terms of these treaties provide good examples in which Modena and Parma gained *maintenance* and Austria gained *change*.[11]

We offer one more clarification. Suppose a state undertakes a new policy or alters some situation in the world—produces change—with an eye toward protecting some existing outcome in the status quo. As an example, imagine that the United States acquires a naval base in the Philippines, whose primary purpose for the United States is to protect sea-lanes in the western Pacific. Is that a change-seeking action? How does the two-good theory distinguish between an action and the strategic or political purposes motivating that action? The two-good theory sees the status quo as multidimensional, with the each dimension capturing the outcome on an issue of contention between states.[12] One dimension, in this example, pertains to the absence or presence of an American base in the Philippines, while another describes the relative security of sea-lanes in the western Pacific. American acquisition of the naval base alters the status quo, and to accomplish this the United States adopts change-seeking policies; it might rent the land from the Philippines, offer an alliance or trade concessions in exchange, physically occupy the territory without Philippine consent, grant generous foreign aid terms, or adopt any other policy designed to alter the situation. Once that base has been acquired, the status quo on that specific dimension has been altered; the United States would now be described as acting to maintain two aspects of the status quo that it likes: the presence of an American naval base in the Philippines and open sea-lanes in the western Pacific.[13]

Before turning to the remaining assumptions contained in our theory, it is useful to compare our conceptualization with other common perspectives. We have already noted many of the comparisons between our theory and neorealism. We believe the primary advantage of our theory rests with the assumption that states pursue two goods, maintenance and change, through their foreign

---

[11] We thank Ashley Leeds and Jeff Ritter for providing us with this example.

[12] The word "contention" is important here. If all states agree on some issue—that the Gulf of Mexico should not be drained to aid in oil exploration, for example—then a situation of harmony is observed, and no political interaction will occur.

[13] Robert Harkavy raised this specific example with us, and we are grateful for his having done so.

policies. Clearly, thinking of all policies as designed to produce one of these abstract goods is more complicated than viewing all policies as designed to enhance one abstract good (security). The two-good approach is more useful, however, because it allows for the consideration of trade-offs that states must make, and, as we shall show, it provides for better, less tortured explanations of observed events.

Other theories, notably power transition theory and hegemonic stability theory, emphasize that a state's satisfaction with the status quo is an important determinant of its behavior (Organski 1968; Organski and Kugler 1980; Kugler and Lemke 1996; Tammen et al. 2000; and Gilpin 1981). These theories posit that an extremely powerful state, or hegemon, typically dominates the international system. This state uses its power to structure the rules of the system (for example, by establishing a mercantilist or capitalist economic system) in a manner that serves its own interests. Over time, the dominance of this state decreases and it is challenged by another state seeking to establish itself as the hegemon. A key feature of each of these theories distinguishes states as being either status quo or revisionist powers (or, similarly, as satisfied or dissatisfied powers) on the basis of whether the rules of the system benefit or harm their interests. Major challenges to the hegemon come from the revisionist (or dissatisfied) states and major wars occur when a revisionist state is overtaking the hegemon in terms of power.[14]

It must be stressed that the conceptualization of the status quo in these theories is *very* different from that which we adopt. In the first place, the concept of the status quo in these theories is unidimensional, and a state's preference for the status quo is dichotomous—that is, it either favors the system established by the most powerful state or it does not. Our notion of the status quo is multidimensional and we assume all states like some aspects of it and dislike other aspects. Second, the concept of the status quo in these theories is static. It only changes when the identity of the hegemon changes, and changes in the status quo are cataclysmic events. In our view, the status quo is constantly changing and most changes are incremental in nature.

Finally, there is a tendency in these theories to associate support of the status quo with promoting peace and stability and to associate dissatisfaction with the promotion of war and instability. Thus, revisionist states have typically been portrayed as threatening, bent on world domination, and, in a moral sense, bad. Consider that the recent major revisionist powers are identified as Napoleonic France, Nazi Germany, and the cold war Soviet Union. This leads to some curious interpretations of events. For example, U.S. behavior in

---

[14] We recognize that this brief characterization of power transition theory and hegemonic stability theory does not capture the full flavor of either. It also serves to conflate the two theories that do have notable differences. Our point focuses on the conceptualization of the status quo and states' orientation toward it, which is very similar in both theories.

Vietnam is interpreted as stabilizing and meant to maintain the status quo while the Soviet invasion of Afghanistan is interpreted as destabilizing and meant to expand Soviet influence.

Again, we make no sweeping value judgments regarding change and maintenance. We assume all states engage in both, and we presume that for both change and maintenance seeking, some policies are morally good while others are bad. Some states may make great efforts and take great risks to seek great change. We would judge some such efforts to be bad (for example, Nazi Germany's attempt to dominate Europe and eliminate Jews) and other such efforts to be good (for example, the post–World War II efforts by the United States to reconstruct Europe, end colonialism, and promote stable, free trade). Similarly, some efforts to maintain the status quo can be good (for example, the efforts to resist Hitler) while others can be bad (for example, the French efforts to maintain colonial control over Vietnam and Algeria). The important point for our theory is only whether an action is change or maintenance seeking; moral judgments, while important, are another matter. Thus, we can consider both the U.S. action in Vietnam and the Soviet action in Afghanistan to be change seeking while allowing the moral judgment of each to depend on whether one thinks advancing or hindering the spread of communist rule is a good thing.

Furthermore, as we shall see, many of the states identified in hegemonic stability theory or power transition theory as being status quo, or satisfied, powers are viewed by our theory as being among the most change-seeking states in history. Britain in the eighteenth and nineteenth centuries and the United States in the latter half of the twentieth century are the clearest examples. They may have favored and worked to maintain rules of the system that served their interests (for example, free trade), but they also engaged in many activities designed to alter the (multidimensional) status quo. It is hard to view the British acquisition of colonies as preserving the status quo, for example. Similarly, no state today is as active in attempting to alter the international status quo as the United States: the American efforts to change Iraqi domestic and international policies, and the negotiations aimed at changing North Korean security policy are but two obvious examples. The important point to remember is that when we refer to a state as seeking to maintain or change the status quo, we are referring to its actions intended to affect the outcome on a particular issue. This should not be confused with other concepts of the status quo that refer to a unidimensional notion of system control.

Thus far we have developed our key assumption that states seek to produce two goods, change and maintenance, through their foreign policies and we assume that all states at all times seek to produce some of each good. We further assume the production of foreign policy goods, like the production of any good, requires resources. These resources can be anything that is used in foreign policy—cash, material goods, political influence, or the time and energy of diplomats. We assume that these resources are largely fungible across goods but that any unit of resources devoted to the production of one good cannot also be used to produce the other. The foreign policy actions that we typically try to explain (for example, dispute initiations, alliance formation, foreign aid grants, diplomatic protests) are the observable manifestations of the expenditure of these resources in the pursuit of change and maintenance. We explain variations in these observed foreign policies by specifying which good a behavior (for example, dispute initiation) is intended to produce (an issue to which we turn below) and identifying the factors that account for the amount of change and maintenance sought by a given state.

We assume that two general types of factors account for the amount of change and maintenance sought by a state. The first are the environmental constraints that determine the limits on the amount of change and maintenance that can be sought. The second are the preferences of the state that capture the willingness to make trade-offs across the two goods. Here, we discuss each in more detail.[15]

As noted above, we assume that foreign policy actions require resources. These may be physical resources such as minerals, agricultural produce, or human capital, economic resources such as cash or industrial produce, diplomatic resources such as the time and attention of ambassadors, or anything else that can be used to pursue foreign policy objectives. Environmental constraints determine the amount of resources a state has available for foreign policy and the efficiency with which these resources can be used to produce change and maintenance.

In general, we assume that the single most important environmental factor is a state's resource endowment. Not surprisingly, we assume that a state's ability to produce change and maintenance is directly related to the amount of resources that it has, relative to other states. States with relatively more resources are able to produce more foreign policy goods than can states with fewer resources, ceteris paribus. We recognize that there are many demands on a state's resources. Some must be devoted to domestic political issues, some to consumption, and some must be invested. Thus, we expect that a number of factors could affect the proportion of a state's resources devoted to foreign policy. For example, as the level of threat emanating from the international system increases, we expect that the proportion of resources devoted to foreign policy would increase. We have every reason to believe that the relationship between

---

[15] Our discussion of these issues in this chapter is primarily conceptual. Some ambiguity will remain until chapter 5, when the formal version of this theory is developed. As will be seen, the formalization is based on precise functional forms of these assumptions and produces specific equilibria.

resource endowment and resources devoted to foreign policy is monotonic, however. That is, as resource endowment increases, those given over to foreign policy also increase.

The basic assumption that states with relatively more resources will engage in more foreign policy activities than will states with fewer resources is quite intuitive. A key feature of our theory is that we make this assumption much more precise by asserting that the efficiency with which resources can be used to produce change and maintenance follows two distinct patterns with respect to the overall level of a state's resources.[16] In particular, we assume that as a state increases in resources, its ability to produce maintenance increases at a decreasing rate while its ability to produce change increases at an increasing rate. That is, an additional unit of resources will produce less additional maintenance for a strong state than for a weak state while an additional unit of resources will produce more change for a strong state than for a weak state.

Notice that one implication of the pattern for production of change would be that any state, no matter how powerful, that increased its resources would continue to increase its ability to produce change at an increasing rate. We suppose that, at some point, this relationship has to flatten out. That is, once a state has so many resources that it can do whatever it wants, additional resources will not continue to increase its ability to produce change. We do not believe that any state has ever reached this point, however, nor do we believe that any state is likely to attain such status in the future.[17] It is hard to imagine a state more dominant than the United States in the early post–World War II period; yet even the United States at that time faced severe limitations on its ability to alter the world to its liking. Thus, we are comfortable assuming that the ability to produce change grows at an increasing rate as a state's resource endowment increases—at least over the range of capabilities that we have observed in the international system.

We offer three justifications for this "distinct pattern" assumption. First, it is intended to capture the notion that it is easier to defend the status quo than to change it. Scholars working in a number of research traditions have noted that the status quo is "sticky." It is typically far easier for the opponents of change to succeed in legislative bodies than it is for the proponents of change. Proponents must pass several hurdles—committees, amendment procedures, floor votes, perhaps two houses, and so on. Opponents need only win at one of these stages. Furthermore, in voting, the status quo is usually the reversion point; that is, it remains the outcome if no alternative can gain a majority, even in those cases in which a majority would not vote to retain it. Similar arguments

---

[16] At this time, we discuss the general flavor of this assumption. It will be made much more precise when we present the formal version of the theory in chapter 5.

[17] Furthermore, if any state did become this powerful, it is likely that we would no longer need theories of international politics and foreign policy.

can be found in the international relations literature. For example, there is a conventional wisdom in security studies suggesting that in order for an attack to be successful, the attacker must have a significant superiority over the defender.[18] International norms, particularly those respecting sovereignty, are typically conservative in nature, designed to preserve actors and their "rights." The greater burden is on actors wishing to effect change. Our assumption captures this notion in that it allows even weak states some ability to defend elements of the status quo they care about, even if they have little ability to bring about changes they desire. It is only after a state has amassed a fairly large endowment of resources that it sees its ability to pursue change increase substantially. On the other hand, a state that is high in capabilities can protect most of what it values. Additional capabilities can do relatively little to enhance this ability.

Second, this assumption is partially motivated by the recognition that, in the international system, there are many states with few capabilities, a few states with modest capabilities, and very few states with great capabilities. Thus, a weak state that enhances its capabilities would be able to defend its interests against a larger number of potential challengers than would a strong state that enhances its capabilities by a similar amount. This weak state would not necessarily be able to challenge others, however, given the preceding argument. Since there are relatively few states that the strong can surpass by obtaining additional capabilities, growth does relatively little to increase the number of potential challengers against whom they can defend.[19] Since they do have sufficient capabilities to challenge others, however, additional resources can be used to increase the number of issues over which they seek change and/or to increase the amount of change they seek on issues already in contention.

Finally, this assumption is meant to capture some of the traditional realist idea that states must assure their security before they can turn their attention to other matters. There are important differences between our argument and neorealism. Notably, keep in mind that our argument holds that all states, at all times, seek some amount of both change and maintenance. The realist presumption does contain some important insight, however. Most states do seem to devote more attention and resources to protecting what they have than to pursuing change. While we do not go so far as to suggest that states must assure their ability to provide maintenance before they will seek change, our assumption does capture the realists' insight in this regard.

---

[18] For instance, in battle, the attacking side needs something like a 3:1 advantage to prevail, assuming soldiers of equal abilities and materiel (Levy 1984, 1987; Quester 1977; Walt 1989; as well as Mearsheimer 1989; Epstein 1989; and Dupuy 1989).

[19] Consider the following: If Uruguay were suddenly to increase its capabilities, it could greatly enhance its ability to defend its interests against Argentina and Brazil without necessarily gaining the ability to challenge their interests and certainly without gaining the ability to challenge the interests of Thailand.

We can draw from economics for an analogy to make this point. Essentially, our model treats maintenance as though it is a necessity and change as though it is a luxury good. Necessities, such as food, are seen as "inferior" goods. As income rises, one's consumption of food will increase (perhaps in quality if not quantity), but at a decreasing rate. This is because once one's needs are met, additional increases in consumption increase marginal utility at a decreasing rate. On the other hand, as income rises, one's consumption of luxuries, such as vacations or jewelry, will increase at an increasing rate. This is because once one's needs are met, the marginal utility for the consumption of luxuries increases with increases in income. Note that even the very poor typically devote some of their resources to luxury goods. A high proportion of any additional income will be devoted to necessities, however, whereas for the wealthy, a high proportion of any additional income will go toward luxuries.

We believe that our specific assumption captures the realist insight that states defend aspects of the status quo they like before they attempt to change the aspects they dislike. We capture this insight without the realist shortcoming that prohibits considering trade-offs across things of value. As we shall show below, this assumption also drives many of our conclusions. Once we associate specific foreign policy behaviors with change and maintenance, this assumption will allow us to derive precise and explicit hypotheses relating changes in relative capabilities to the occurrence of these behaviors.

In addition to environmental constraints, the second factor determining the balance of change and maintenance pursued by a state is preferences over the two goods. For much of this book, we assume that states are unitary actors and will speak of preferences as being characteristic of "the state." Our theory does not require this assumption, however, and we will make some note of how the preferences of substate actors come into play. In general, we consider domestic politics to be the process by which individual and group stakeholders aggregate their preferences into single policies for a state. Most of our analyses can be carried out under the presumption that this process has already occurred and has resulted in a set of social preferences on which the state will act.

Again, we assume that every state is happy with many aspects of the status quo and is dissatisfied with many others. We expect that every state will, at all times, seek some maintenance and some change. However, since resources are limited and since resources devoted to the pursuit of one good cannot be devoted to the pursuit of the other, each state must decide what proportion of its foreign policy resources can be devoted to each good. This is determined partly by preferences over the two goods. That is, states that value change over maintenance will devote more resources to the pursuit of change, and vice versa. To a great extent, we believe that these preferences are given; that is, some people simply value change (Hitler, perhaps) and others simply value maintenance (Chamberlain). We do believe that preferences are generally affected by two factors, however.

First, the distance (weighted by the importance of the issues for the state) between the status quo and the state's ideal point (its most preferred outcome on every issue) directly affects its relative preferences over change and maintenance. The closer the status quo is to the state's ideal point, the more the state will prefer maintenance and the farther the status quo from the state's ideal point, the more it will prefer change, ceteris paribus.[20] This seems a straightforward assumption to make. In the hypothetical extreme, a state that is able to establish a global situation that perfectly matches its ideal point on all dimensions would prefer only to maintain the existing structure. At the other extreme, a state for which the status quo is far from its ideal point on many issues would prefer to change the world dramatically.

Second, we assume that the level of threat coming from other states affects state preferences regarding change and maintenance. We assume that as the level of threat increases, ceteris paribus, the relative preference for maintenance over change also increases. That is, state preferences are partially determined by the actions, occurring and expected, of other states. A state that faces no challenges to its interests will prefer to pursue more change than will a state that is threatened with adverse alterations on many issues, all else being equal. This assumption also seems reasonable. If no other is trying to bring about adverse changes on any issues about which a state cares, it has no reason to pursue any maintenance. On the other hand, as state that faces many challenges on many issues will want to pursue a great deal of maintenance.

It is also useful to specify an assumption that we do not make. We make no assumption associating state preferences in foreign policy to state power. That is, we presume that it is entirely possible for a weak state to be relatively change seeking (perhaps Libya under Khaddafi) or maintenance seeking (present-day Burma may be an example), and it is possible for a strong state to be relatively maintenance seeking (perhaps the United States prior to World War II) or change seeking (Nazi Germany comes to mind). This is worth noting because many arguments in the international relations literature would suggest that state power is associated with state preferences. It is common, for example, to presume that the weak must be dissatisfied with the status quo and that the strong must be satisfied—or at least that the probabilities tend in this direction. We avoid this assumption primarily to avoid conflating the effects of capabilities and preferences, which would lead to non-falsifiable statements. Capabilities and preferences each have a prominent role in the theory and we will be able to derive hypotheses associating each with foreign policy behaviors. We

---

[20] If a state valued all issues in the multidimensional space equally, the distance between the status quo and the state's ideal point would be measured in simple Euclidean (straight line) distance. States are allowed to care more about some issues than others, however, so the distance between the status quo and the ideal point should be thought of as weighted by the salience the state places on the various issue dimensions. See Enelow and Hinich (1981) or Morgan (1994) for a more technical discussion.

shall show that we expect the strong to behave differently from the weak, but we will not be forced into asserting that these differences arise simply because they have different preferences.

Furthermore, to anticipate our conclusions somewhat, this aspect of our theory produces conclusions that are at variance with much of what is commonly believed in the international relations literature; but we shall show that these conclusions offer a better understanding of observed empirical patterns. Specifically, many theories suggest that the weak would prefer to change the status quo precisely because they are weak but that they are unable to because of a lack of capabilities. Strong states, on the other hand, are seen as typically wanting to maintain the status quo simply because they are strong. Our theory also leads to the conclusion that the weak will seek little change. In many cases this might correspond with the preferences of the weak, and when it does not, their lack of capabilities will serve as a severe constraint. Our theory suggests that the strong will be quite change seeking, however. We shall argue that this conclusion conforms quite well to the evidence and that it offers a far better explanation of, for example, U.S. behavior in the post–World War II world than do previous explanations. Assuming that the strongest state in the system must prefer to maintain the status quo forces us to overlook the fact that a great deal of American behavior (and British behavior during its hegemonic period, Roman behavior in the days of the empire, and so on) was directed at bringing about international changes that it desired. Disassociating capabilities from preferences makes for a far better theory and leads to a far better understanding of how capabilities and preferences interact to affect behavior.

The assumptions presented thus far constitute the core of our theory. Additional assumptions will be added to produce many of our hypotheses, but those discussed above will remain unchanged in the model. Before developing our hypotheses, it is useful to present a pictorial representation of the basic model that has been developed to this point. This is depicted in figure 2.2.

Our basic assumption that foreign policy can be seen as the pursuit of two goods, maintenance and change, suggests that a state's foreign policy can be depicted in a two-dimensional space, as is seen in the figure. The vertical axis depicts the amount of maintenance sought by the state and the horizontal axis depicts the amount of change. The state's foreign policy portfolio will reflect the overall amounts of maintenance and change sought by all its policies in aggregate and can be associated with a point in the space. The northwest to southeast curve represents the production possibility frontier, or the maximum amount of maintenance and change that can be provided given the capabilities of the state (relative to other states) that are devoted to foreign policy. The state cannot possibly adopt a portfolio of policies that would produce a mix of maintenance and change above this curve, and if it adopts a portfolio that places it below the curve it could produce more change and/or maintenance. The state will maximize its foreign policy benefits if it adopts a set of

Maintenance

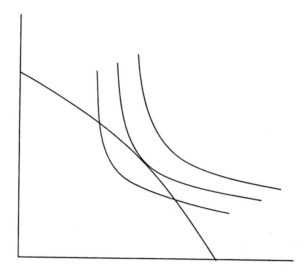

Change

Figure 2.2. Maintenance and Change: The Goals of Foreign Policy

policies that places it on this curve. At that point, it can increase change or
maintenance only at the expense of the other.

The other curves in the figure represent the state's indifference contours. It
is indifferent between any two policy portfolios that fall on a single curve and
it prefers any portfolio that places it on a curve farther to the northeast over a
portfolio on a curve closer to the origin. The state depicted in the figure values
change and maintenance about equally. A predominantly change-seeking state
would have indifference contours that are more vertical while a state that is
predominantly maintenance seeking would have contours that are more horizontal. We would expect the state to adopt a portfolio of foreign policies plac-
ing it at the point where its indifference contour is just tangent to the production possibility frontier. This point provides it with the most preferred foreign
policy that it can have.

The elements of this figure capture the essential features of our theory outlined thus far. The mixture of the two composite goods sought by the state is
reflected in the spatial representation and we can see the trade-offs over these
two goods that the state must make. The assumption that environmental
factors—in particular relative capabilities—affect foreign policy is reflected in
the production possibility frontier—as capabilities increase this frontier moves
outward. Finally, preferences are reflected through the shape of the indifference contours. Much of our analyses involves determining how we expect foreign policy to change with respect to changes in these curves.

Hypotheses

The conceptualization and assumptions we have set forth so far are sufficient
to produce our simplest hypotheses, those focusing on the effects of environmental changes on individual policies considered singly and separately from
each other. We begin this section by specifying those hypotheses, and then expand and complicate the theory by adding other assumptions and present the
additional hypotheses to which these extensions lead. The additional hypotheses pertain to foreign policy substitutability.

Single-Policy Hypotheses

The first conclusion to be drawn from the two-good model is that states with
more resources will engage in more foreign policy behaviors, of all types, than
will states with fewer resources. This is completely intuitive and, if left at this
level, tautological. It is important to note, however, that this hypothesis speaks
to general patterns and not necessarily to specific cases. That is, it is possible
for there to be a particular weak state that devotes more resources to change
(or maintenance) than does a particular stronger state. This could occur if the
weak state's preferences were such that it devoted a large proportion of its foreign policy resources to change while the stronger state's preferences led it to
devote a small proportion of its resources to change. The hypothesis suggests
that, holding preferences constant, a state will engage in more change seeking
and more maintenance seeking as its relative capabilities increase. Since we do
not assume that there is any association between relative capabilities and preferences, we can conclude that more capable states will engage, on average, in
more of all types of behavior than will less capable states.

Our second conclusion is that increases in change- and maintenance-
seeking behaviors will follow different specific patterns as capabilities increase.
Maintenance-seeking behaviors will increase at a decreasing rate while change-
seeking behaviors will increase at an increasing rate. Again, this is by assumption and thus, if left at this level, tautological. It is testable, however, and can
provide a very good indication as to whether the theory is on the right track.
To render these hypotheses less tautological, we make a number of assumptions associating specific types of foreign policy behavior with the pursuit of
each of the two goods. This leads us to expect particular relationships between
capability levels and the frequency with which these behaviors occur.

At a very general level, we recognize that virtually every type of foreign policy
activity can be used in the pursuit of either change or maintenance, depending
on the intentions of the actor. Military force can be used to change the status
quo, as when one country attempts to overthrow the government of another,
or to maintain the status quo, as when force is used to keep sea-lanes open. An
alliance can be formed with the intention of protecting the signatories against

the challenges of another, or with the intention of joining forces to attack another. Foreign aid can be given in an effort to influence the recipient's behavior or in an effort to help the recipient defend its interests against some threat. We believe, however, that various types of foreign policy action can be classified as being either change seeking or maintenance seeking, in general.

We assume that the initiation of militarized disputes is change-seeking behavior. States that initiate military conflict are usually (though not always) attempting to bring about some alteration of the status quo. Conflict reciprocation, on the other hand, is viewed as maintenance-seeking behavior. States that respond to another's use of force in kind are generally attempting to prevent a change in the status quo from occurring. Similarly, we see an emphasis on covert operations, or the support of "terrorism," to be an example of change-seeking behavior, in general. These activities are almost always intended to alter the status quo in some fashion. Efforts at counterterrorism or to combat other countries' covert operations are seen as maintenance-seeking behaviors.

With respect to defense spending, we view a state's overall level of expenditures as indicative of the degree of maintenance-seeking behavior in its foreign policy. This assumes that defense spending is typically designed to offer protection of the state's interests rather than to bring about changes in the international system. We recognize that the military is often used to seek change and therefore further assume that the degree of change-seeking behavior in a state's policy is indicated by the particulars of the state's force posture. That is, militaries that are organized around force projection capabilities are indicative of a change-seeking state. Large navies, particularly those with force projection capabilities (aircraft carriers, troop transports), long-range aircraft, and other expensive hardware, all indicate a force projection capability. Thus, we assume that the capital intensiveness of a state's military indicates the level of change seeking in a state's foreign policy portfolio.

In the case of foreign aid, we assume that this is intended to produce change. Foreign aid that is given with the expectation of some quid pro quo (which much is) is clearly change-seeking behavior. Similarly, aid that is given from a higher motive—to help those in need—is also clearly change seeking. A problem regarding the intent or goal of foreign aid arises because some aid is provided to bolster weak regimes against their internal or external enemies. Much of this aid may actually be change seeking, however. First, some has strings attached; that is, the recipient is obliged to behave in a manner favorable to the donor. Further, supporting a regime that would be expected to fall because of internal trends fits with our definition of change. Aid is an example of maintenance only when it is provided to defend a regime against an external threat and when that is the primary motivation for the donor. We therefore feel comfortable with the assumption that foreign aid is indicative of change-seeking behavior.

Finally, we view some forms of alliance behavior as change seeking and others as maintenance seeking. This determination is based on the capabilities of the alliance partners. Following Morrow (1991), we consider a state that has aligned with a stronger power to be gaining maintenance from the alliance, while a state that has aligned with a weaker power gains change from the alliance. Partly, this reflects the realities of international politics. Weak states can add only marginally to strong states' defensive capabilities, so the strong must typically get something else from the alliance. This is frequently reflected in actual alliance treaties. Often, treaty obligations require a strong state to come to the defense of its weaker ally while the weaker is required to allow the stronger trade concessions or some control over the weaker's policies.

With these additional assumptions associating types of foreign policy behavior with either change or maintenance, we can present our first, simple hypotheses:

H1: As state capabilities increase, defense spending will increase at a decreasing rate.

H2: As state capabilities increase, the extent to which force postures are geared toward power projection will increase at an increasing rate.

H3: As state capabilities increase, the rate at which militarized conflicts are initiated will increase at an increasing rate.

H4: As state capabilities increase, the rate at which militarized conflicts are reciprocated will increase at a decreasing rate.

H5: As state capabilities increase, the extent to which covert operations and/or international terrorism are used will increase at an increasing rate.

H6: As state capabilities increase, the extent to which measures are taken to combat terrorism will increase at a decreasing rate.

H7: As state capabilities increase, foreign aid donations will increase at an increasing rate.

H8: As state capabilities increase, alliances with strong powers will increase at a decreasing rate.

H9: As state capabilities increase, alliances with weak powers will increase at an increasing rate.

Hypotheses on Substitutability

Each of these hypotheses involves a single type of foreign policy behavior. While we expect all of the relationships to hold, empirically, we should also expect the relationships to be relatively weak. In general, this is because of one particular gap in the argument. The model associates capabilities with change-and maintenance-seeking behavior—but it says nothing about which specific components of the foreign policy portfolio will be used in the pursuit of the foreign policy goods. Consider a hypothetical example: suppose a state experiences a sudden increase in its resources available for foreign policy. It would devote some proportion of these resources to produce change, but how? It could initiate a dispute, it could provide foreign aid, or it could upgrade its force projection capabilities. The theory leads us to expect an increase in the overall production of change, but it does not tell us precisely which behaviors will be used. Thus, when the theory indicates that we should expect an increase in change seeking, sometimes we will see an increase in dispute initiation and sometimes we will not because the state chose to increase the production of change through some other means. While we can hypothesize a positive relationship between expected increases in change seeking and dispute initiation, we should anticipate that the relationship would be weak.

This problem is essentially the one Most and Starr (1984) have identified as the phenomenon of foreign policy substitutability. Their argument, in a nutshell, is that our statistical studies of international relations typically have found weak relationships because states have numerous, "substitutable" policy tools available for dealing with any particular problem. In the terms of their argument, for example, a state wishing to enhance its security can do so either by increasing its own armaments or by joining an alliance; thus, arms and alliances are viewed as substitutes. We devote parts of chapter 6 and all of chapter 7 to the application of our theory to an investigation of foreign policy substitutability, but it is useful to offer a brief, non-formal preview at this time. (We give the formal argument in chapter 5.) Among the most interesting hypotheses following from our theory are those that specify associations among foreign policy actions. Previous studies that have explored the substitutability phenomenon have presumed that there should be an inverse relationship between any two behaviors that are substitutable. Our theory produces much more refined expectations. We show that this inverse relationship can hold, but only under certain circumstances. Under other conditions, substitutable policies should vary directly.

Several studies have sought to uncover empirical evidence that substitutability occurs. Since Most and Starr did not develop their argument as a complete theory in and of itself (the idea was that substitutability should be considered in any theory), this previous work essentially appended substitutability to neorealism. The basic assumption was that foreign policy behavior is directed at enhancing state security and that specific policies, such as arms expenditures and alliance formation, are directed at that goal. The hypothesis guiding these studies was that since arms expenditures and alliances are substitutable policies for the provision of security, we should expect an inverse relationship between them. The empirical work conducted on this question has shown that, contrary to the hypothesis, arms expenditures and alliances tend to vary directly.[21] This could suggest a fatal flaw in the substitutability argument, point out a serious shortcoming in neorealism, or indicate that the theoretical expectations following from the substitutability argument have been misspecified. We suggest that the argument has been misspecified, and in chapter 5 we demonstrate that the properly specified theory leads to an understanding of substitutability that is at variance with the expectations of neorealism.

Our argument regarding substitutability requires that we adopt one additional assumption. The assumption is an intuitively reasonable one, but it leads to some interesting and surprising conclusions. We assume that when states are deciding which foreign policy tool to use in the pursuit of either change or maintenance, they select the tool that is most efficient. That is, they will engage in the behavior that produces the most change or maintenance for a given amount of resources consumed. For example, if conditions suggest that a state will seek additional change, it will engage in the change-producing behavior or combination of behaviors (such as dispute initiation, foreign aid provision, or the imposition of economic sanctions) that will provide the most change given the available resources. This captures the essential idea of substitutability.

We are not led to expect that substitutable policies will necessarily vary inversely, however. Previous studies have presumed that if more resources are devoted to one policy (for example, alliances), resources must be taken away from another policy (for example, armaments). Our expectation is a bit different. If one focuses on a particular policy, say arms expenditures, and notices an increase, the expectation of how this will affect other policies depends on *why* the increase occurred. In the context of our theory, there are three reasons for a state to devote additional resources to a particular type of foreign policy behavior and each has different implications for what we should observe regarding other policies.

First, if the overall amount of resources available for foreign policy increases (or decreases), we must see the resources devoted to at least one policy increase (or decrease). Generally, we would expect an increase in change-seeking behavior as well as an increase in maintenance-seeking behavior, and it is likely that more resources would be devoted to all types of foreign policy activities. We certainly have no reason to expect that the resources devoted to any policy would decrease. Thus, when an observed change in policy is the product of a change in the resources available, we can expect either no change or a change in the same direction in all other policies, including those that are substitutable for the observed policy. This expectation is directly contrary to that guiding previous research, and if many policy changes were driven by changes in resources, this would explain the previous findings that substitutable policies tend to vary directly.

---

[21] See, for instance, Diehl (1994), Palmer and Souchet (1994), and Morgan and Palmer (1995).

Second, the resources devoted to particular policies can be reallocated when the state's relative preferences over change and maintenance are altered. That is, when something causes a state to increase or decrease its valuation for change relative to maintenance it will adjust the components of its foreign policy portfolio accordingly. Such a shift in preferences could occur as a result of demographic evolution, a turnover in leadership, or as a response to the behavior of other international actors. In this case, we would again expect to observe behaviors that are substitutable to vary directly. That is, if the state shifts resources away from maintenance seeking and toward change seeking, all maintenance-seeking behaviors would either stay the same or decrease while all change-seeking behaviors would either stay the same or increase. Interestingly, we would expect an inverse relationship between behaviors that are not substitutable—that is, those that produce different foreign policy goods.

Finally, the resource allocation across policies can shift when something causes a change in the relative efficiency with which the policies produce the foreign policy goods. For example, a technological breakthrough could increase the efficiency with which military expenditures can provide maintenance; or if a state that was previously unwilling to form an alliance became interested in doing so, that potential alliance could become more attractive. When this occurs, we expect to observe the inverse relationship between substitutable policies. If arms become more efficient at producing maintenance, we expect the state to shift resources from other maintenance-producing policies and devote these resources to armaments.

This leads to three general hypotheses that can be tested in a variety of ways:

H10: In general, the use of policies that produce the same foreign policy good should vary directly.

H11: If we control for changes in capabilities and state preferences, the use of policies that produce the same foreign policy good should vary inversely.

H12: If we control for changes in capabilities and in the efficiency of foreign policy behaviors, the use of policies that produce different foreign policy goods should vary inversely.

These arguments provide an explanation for the relationship between any pair of foreign policy behaviors. We would, for example, expect armaments and maintenance-seeking alliances (that is, those with stronger powers) to vary directly, unless we control for changes in resources and preferences. These hypotheses can be tested in a variety of ways simply by examining the relationship between any pair of foreign policy behaviors.[22]

While our theory leads us to expect numerous interesting relationships

---

[22] We do not wish to imply that conducting these tests is necessarily easy or straightforward. As will be seen when we turn to this task in chapters 6 and 7, designing a test that incorporates appropriate controls and captures the specified relationship is quite difficult.

between the uses of various foreign policy tools, one set of relationships is of particular interest here. Volumes of work in international relations have examined the effect of alliances on states' other foreign policies. A great deal of work has examined whether alliances make military conflict more or less likely, and as much work has been conducted on how alliances affect the defense-spending decisions of their signatories. We shall therefore focus briefly on presenting some of the conclusions our theory produces regarding the effects of alliances.

We approach this question by considering what we should expect in the aftermath of an alliance formation. We presume that when we observe the formation of an alliance, it had to be preceded by something that made at least one of the signatories willing to join an alliance that it had previously avoided. This would occur when the relative efficiency with which the alliance produces the desired composite good (change for a state aligning with a weaker power, maintenance for a state aligning with a stronger power) has increased. This implies that the act of forming the alliance serves to increase the amount of change and/or maintenance that can be produced by a joining state's foreign policy. (Referring back to figure 2.2, the production possibility frontier moves outward as a result of joining an alliance.) This leads to several conclusions regarding the effect of alliance formation on other policies.

In general, since the production possibility frontier has moved outward, we expect alliance formation to be followed by an overall increase in foreign policy activity. That is, alliances are liberating, not constraining, as is commonly presumed. Much of the existing literature treats the loss of sovereignty as a major cost of alliances. Our theory suggests that alliances actually give states more freedom of action by freeing resources that can be used in other ways. We acknowledge that some forms of action may be constrained. A signatory, particularly a state aligning with a stronger power, may commit to actions it would otherwise prefer not to do. This is the price paid for freeing resources to pursue other ends, however. We presume that if the benefits, in terms of freedom of action, did not outweigh the costs, in terms of constraints, the alliance would not be formed.

We do not expect an increase in all foreign policy behaviors, however. Recall that we expect a state finding itself able to produce more foreign policy goods will produce some additional change and some additional maintenance. Since the recently formed alliance provides one or the other (change for a state aligning with a weaker partner, maintenance for a state aligning with a stronger), we expect the state to reduce the resources it would otherwise devote to that good and shift them to the policy behaviors that produce the other good. Thus, a state joining an alliance that provides it maintenance would be expected to reduce at least one other maintenance-producing policy (defense expenditures, conflict reciprocation) and to increase at least one change-seeking policy (dispute initiation, foreign aid). Similarly, a state joining an alliance that produces change would be expected to reduce at least one other change-producing policy and to increase at least one maintenance-producing policy. This leads to a number of more specific, testable hypotheses.

H13:   States joining an alliance with stronger states will, in general, increase the frequency with which they initiate disputes, increase foreign aid donations, and devote a greater proportion of their defense budgets to force projection capabilities.

H14:   States joining an alliance with stronger states will, in general, decrease their overall level of defense expenditures and the frequency with which they reciprocate disputes.

H15:   States joining an alliance with weaker states will, in general, decrease the frequency with which they initiate disputes, decrease foreign aid donations, and devote a lesser proportion of their defense budgets to force projection capabilities.

H16:   States joining an alliance with weaker states will, in general, increase their overall level of defense expenditures, the frequency with which they reciprocate disputes, and the resources they devote to defending against covert operations.

Conclusion

In this chapter, we presented a non-formal version of our theory. We set forth our assumptions and we outlined many of the hypotheses to which the theory leads. In subsequent chapters, we show that our theory can be used to guide an understanding of specific foreign policy events, and we present the formalization of our theory. We present some illustrative case studies so that the reader may see how the two-good theory can be used. We do this because we want an understanding of the theory and the differences between it and other approaches to the study of international relations to be fully formed by the time we present our empirical analyses. And while we do not test all the hypotheses we have presented here, we do subject many of them to empirical tests.

We began this chapter by noting that one of the appeals of neorealism is that it offers explanations of international relations and foreign policy that operate at a number of different levels. We have offered a number of arguments suggesting that the conceptualization upon which this theory is based is superior. Furthermore, it can be seen from our argument to this point that our theory can provide general explanations for international behavior and can lead to fairly specific hypotheses associating key variables with one another. In the following chapter, we turn to an application of the theory to an explanation of specific foreign policy behaviors by a specific state (the United States) to show that our theory affords a superior basis from which to interpret such events.

3

American Foreign Policy since World War II from the Two-Good Perspective

IN THIS CHAPTER we aim to apply the two-good theory to the broad patterns of American foreign policy since 1945. There are two major reasons for this. Our goal in this book, of course, is to show how the two-good theory is useful in a variety of ways. The two-good theory tells us some interesting things about international relations generally, such as that the most powerful states in the system will tend to be the most change seeking. It allows us to analyze specific foreign policy decisions that other general theories such as realism have difficulty explaining, as we will show in the next chapter. It does these things while providing hypotheses that can be applied to specific policies such as conflict initiation and foreign aid allocation. It also provides insight into the relationships between and among different policies. In later chapters we will apply the theory's implications to some specific and seemingly odd foreign policy decisions and to statistical tests of the relationships between the variables anticipated by the theory. Since the two-good theory identifies the effects of specific variables on types of foreign policy behavior, one way in which the theory is useful is in explaining from a more general and scientific perspective the behavior of specific states in changing circumstances. We want to show in this chapter how that can be accomplished by looking broadly at the behavior of the United States in the post–World War II era. We hope to demonstrate throughout this book that much of the value the two-good theory lies in the breadth of its applications.

The second goal of this chapter is substantive. The two-good theory's interpretation of American foreign policy over the last fifty years differs significantly from many others. Many traditional examinations of American foreign policy argue that the United States was forced by circumstances into its role as world leader in the postwar years. In that role, American foreign policy was directed largely toward containing Soviet influence and maintaining global peace and security for its allies. It filled this role reluctantly, becoming much more active in world affairs than it traditionally had been, by adopting a more militarized foreign policy to protect its allies and interests and by establishing international institutions to promote peace and security in democratic countries. At base, traditional understandings of American behavior since World War II also emphasize the bipartisan consensus in the United States regarding the need to contain Soviet expansion, the politically divisive effects of the war in Vietnam, and the general lack of coherence in U.S. foreign policy over the last quarter of the twentieth century. Much of the understanding of U.S. foreign policy over the last half-century emphasizes the uniqueness of the American situation after World War II and the peculiarities of the American political system.

The two-good theory, on the other hand, sees the United States as using its unchallenged power in the immediate postwar years to bring about changes in the international system. The United States created economic, social, and political arrangements in Western European countries and in Japan, establishing international institutions such as the United Nations, World Bank, and International Monetary Fund that would aid in the development of rules of behavior desired by the United States. In the early postwar years its power was so great that the United States could simultaneously pursue these change-seeking policies while adopting other policies designed to protect aspects of the international status quo to its liking; the permanent stationing of troops in Europe and Japan and the containment of Soviet influence serve as prominent examples.

According to the two-good theory, the bipartisan consensus existed because both domestic actors who wanted changes in the international status quo and those who wanted the United States to protect the gains it had already realized could simultaneously be satisfied. American power was so great that widely varying preferences could be accommodated. As the power of the United States declined relative to its competitors and friends, the United States was less able to pursue change seeking. With increasingly limited resources, political disagreements became more apparent; Americans who wanted the United States to pursue change clashed with those who wanted to protect existing international achievements. Specifically, to provide an example, those who thought that the peaceful coexistence with the Soviet Union provided by the policy of détente gave the United States highly valued maintenance fought with the Reagan administration's attempts to target vulnerable and weak communist regimes, altering some aspects of the status quo in preferred ways. Still, U.S. power provided opportunities for both maintenance- and change-seeking behavior. The collapse of the Soviet Union provided the opportunity for both change and maintenance seekers to be satisfied with at least some parts of American international behavior, and the politicization of foreign policy that was observed with the end of the Vietnam War was tempered. Additionally, the unchallenged power of the United States in the post–cold war world allowed it to adopt change-seeking policies at a rate unseen since the end of the World War II. As we will argue, American foreign policy since the early 1990s has largely been designed to move important aspects of the world political scene to be in conformity with American preferences and that actions designed to accomplish this end are often taken unilaterally.

To show the two-good theory in operation in this case, we first lay out the fundamentals of the traditional understanding of American foreign policy since World War II. Our point in doing this is to present the "understanding" rather than the reality of the policy, because we want to show how the two-good theory's analytic framework provides a more coherent and scientifically based picture of the era. We then present the two-good theory's version of the same period. We hope, at the end, to have demonstrated the two-good theory's value as a tool for analyzing a specific state's policies under changing circumstances.

The Traditional View

The traditional interpretation of American foreign policy in the post–World War II era is easily summarized. Immediately after the war, the United States found itself the preeminent power in world politics. While other combatants suffered grievously—the Soviet Union lost about twenty million lives, Germany and Japan were utterly destroyed, and Britain was in economic ruin—the United States emerged from the war relatively unscathed.[1] As one observer captures it, "With 7 percent of the world's population in the late 1940's, America possessed 42 percent of the world's income and accounted for half the world's manufacturing output. American workers produced 57 percent of the planet's steel, 43 percent of the electricity, 62 percent of the oil, 80 percent of the automobiles" (Patterson 1996, 61).[2] With its overwhelming economic, political, and military power, and with the war's devastation leaving Europe and Japan at least temporarily unable to participate fully in international affairs, the United States could no longer rest comfortably in splendid isolation and found it necessary to assume a far greater role in world affairs. After intense domestic discussion, the United States broke with its isolationist tradition by taking an active role in the United Nations, by adopting global containment of the Soviet Union as its fundamental strategy, by joining a series of "entangling" alliances, by establishing a permanent presence of American troops in many foreign countries, and by involving itself in myriad activities throughout the globe (Bailey 1964; Spanier 1991; Ambrose 1993). The "lessons" provided by World War II forced Americans to realize that they had security interests beyond their borders and that active involvement abroad was the only way to

[1] The United States lost about 400,000 people in the war, on the order of 2 percent of the total number of Soviet fatalities.

[2] The Correlates of War Project has developed an indicator of the relative power of states that is a composite measure made up of six different capabilities indices. A state's overall score provides what is essentially the percentage of capabilities within the international system that it possesses. According to those data, in 1946 the United States had 35.4 percent of the global capability, a dominance that was relatively greater than Britain's during the nineteenth century, which saw its highest value of 32.3 percent in 1854.

protect one's interests.[3] The need to defend its interest by taking an active role was so widely shared within the country that a "bipartisan consensus" arose in which Americans agreed on the broad outlines of foreign policy (Roskin 1974; Holsti and Rosenau 1984; Destler, Gelb, and Lake 1984; Kasten Nelson 1987; Kegley and Wittkopf 1991).[4] The Soviet Union was seen as the major threat to American security,[5] and events everywhere were interpreted in terms of the Soviet-American relationship.

The general shared understanding—the bipartisan consensus—regarding the goals and purposes of American international activities lasted for a generation. To be sure, there were relatively minor disagreements between (and within) presidential administrations over a range of foreign policy issues, but little serious discussion was given to whether the United States should or could return to the days when it had a limited role in world affairs. Whatever disagreements did exist did not threaten the existence of the broad consensus. The question of the appropriate size of the U.S. defense budget was debated, for instance, without much serious support given for drastic cuts in that budget or (until Vietnam) for new restrictions placed on the use of American military power abroad. Similarly, how much military and political reliance should be placed on nuclear weapons was a question that permeated U.S. security policy throughout the cold war. There was little chance, however, that the United

[3] On the "lessons" of World War II, see Kolodziej (1966) and Neustadt and May (1986).

[4] Melanson observes that "from the late 1940s to the mid-1960s presidents offered foreign policies that apparently enjoyed substantial public and elite support" (1991, 2) but warns that the degree of bipartisan consensus can be exaggerated. He points out, for instance, that Neustadt and May (1986, 258–59) found "bitter, partisan, and utterly consensus-free debate about the loss of China, the long-term stationing of troops in Europe, the limiting of warfare in Korea, and whether a new war ought to be risked for Dien Bien Phu, Quemoy, or the Matsus" (29). Destler, Gelb, and Lake similarly point out that foreign policy was not immune from political debate: "The Korean War and rolling back Soviet influence in Europe were major campaign themes for Eisenhower in 1952. . . . Stevenson tried to make foreign policy a key issue in the 1956 campaign, and Mr. Kennedy succeeded in doing so in 1960" (1984, 17). Nonetheless, they conclude that "while politics was never in short supply, it was moderated by a near-consensus in elite and general public opinion" (ibid.). A wide "centrism and majorityship" dominated American foreign policy and the ideological extremes were not politically powerful. In his overview of the postwar foreign policy debate, Melanson is able to list seven aspects of a "policy consensus" regarding a "set of fundamental propositions about the nature of the international system, the requirements of American security, and the nation's proper orientation to the world" (1991, 4).

The foreign policy consensus may not have extended over every issue facing the United States, but it was real. Our emphasis, of course, is on the traditional interpretation of postwar American foreign policy and less on whether the perceived consensus existed.

[5] There was, of course, no unanimity of opinion on the expansionist nature of Soviet foreign policy, nor upon the role of ideology in determining the USSR's actions. The debates on these points were long and voluminous. For examples of discussion on these issues, see Shulman (1965), Zimmerman (1969), Gati (1974), Taubman (1982), Ulam (1983), and Cohen (1985). See also Gaddis (1987), Kasten Nelson (1987), Kissinger (1994), and McCauley (1995) for discussions of the role of the Soviet Union in American foreign policy.

States would seek nuclear disarmament, adopt a policy of "no first-use," or opt to deploy large numbers of conventional forces and downplay reliance on a nuclear deterrent. Nuclear weapons, in other words, played an important, even central, role in U.S. policy, and debates about those weapons were over tactical matters.[6]

According to the conventional understanding, the bipartisan consensus ended when American foreign policy experienced a sea change as a result of the Vietnam War (see Holsti and Rosenau 1979; Maggiotto and Wittkopf 1981; Rourke 1983; McCormick and Wittkopf 1990; Wittkopf 1990; and Jettleson 1992). According to the traditional understanding, the war in Vietnam had three major effects on American foreign policy. First, the failure to win the war forced Americans to accept that there were limits to what power—particularly military power—could accomplish. The optimism that came out of World War II—the belief that the United States could achieve whatever it set out to—was replaced by greater caution and skepticism. The United States had fit the conflict in Vietnam into its own worldview, had seen the problem as military rather than political, and had attempted to impose solutions crafted to fit American global interests and learned from World War II. The more guarded view of American capabilities that emerged after Vietnam was reinforced by the common perception that America's power was declining relative to many of its adversaries, particularly the Soviet Union. The United States must be more selective in choosing which policies to pursue and when to use force to achieve its ends.

Second, the belief that it was *proper* for the United States to attempt to create a just and moral international order (as Americans understood those concepts) was drastically undermined as a result of the war. In part, the tragedy of Vietnam was caused by American "hubris," and a conclusion drawn from the Vietnam experience was that the United States should not try to impose its values (at least by force) on others.

Third, the failure and costs of American involvement in the war in Vietnam eroded support for containment as the cornerstone of U.S. foreign policy. If the war followed from the policy of containment—as many held that it did—then obedience to that policy had to be tempered. Instead of viewing any actions that challenged the status quo as threats to American interests coordinated by a unified and coherent global communist movement, the United States began to back away from the strategy that created that image. A military response to instability in friendly nations—such as in Angola in 1975—was no longer automatic. And while adversarial relations with communist states continued, negotiations and closer relations with the Soviet Union and China became possible.

---

[6] Representative or instructive works on the topic of nuclear weapons and their role in U.S. foreign policy include Brodie (1946, 1959), Kahn (1960), Snyder (1961), Friedberg (1980), Mandelbaum (1981), Freedman (1982), and Jervis (1984, 1989).

The result of the various conclusions, drawn and debated, from the Vietnam experience was that the bipartisan consensus over the nature and goals of American foreign policy evaporated after Vietnam. No longer could presidents assume wide support for their foreign policies, nor could they use foreign policy to create agreement regarding domestic priorities. After Vietnam, even such basic issues as policy toward the Soviet Union became grounds for disagreement. Whether the United States should pursue arms control with the U.S.S.R. was widely debated; whether human rights constituted a valuable or even meaningful aspect of détente was questioned; whether most favored nation status should be granted to the Soviets remained an issue for years; indeed, whether détente was a fruitful policy to pursue at all was the subject of political and often partisan discussion.

Finally, in the traditional view, the breakdown of the bipartisan consensus was an abnormal state of affairs resulting from petty domestic political squabbles. A sense that politics *should* "stop at the water's edge" permeated the political scene. There were two senses in which this was the case. The first was based on the assumption of American exceptionalism. Most nations, in this view, do not allow foreign policy to be fodder for political discussion; instead definitions of what constitutes a country's "national interest" generally transcend politics and remained relatively constant over time, and the understanding of that national interest guides leaders' decisions, regardless of their political affiliation. The United States, on the other hand, has allowed foreign policy to be politicized, sometimes contradictory, and, certainly since the mid-1970s, inconsistent. In this view, extending back to the War of 1812, the United States has only infrequently had a foreign policy consensus: "The United States was always different, as the French observer Alexis de Tocqueville noticed more than a century ago. So pragmatic and stable in our internal politics we were, yet so ideological and quixotic in foreign affairs" (Destler, Gelb, and Lake, 1984, 28).[7] What the United States needed to do, according to this line of thought, is act more like a "normal state" in divorcing domestic and foreign policy. On the other hand, some believed that for the United States, consensus on foreign policy was the normal state of affairs, that the post-Vietnam foreign policy squabbling was abnormal for Americans, and the dissolution of consensus after Vietnam was unfortunate but reversible. After the American experience in Vietnam brought the viability of containment into question and after the demise of the Soviet Union left containment meaningless, the United States lacked a coherent guiding strategy around which foreign policy actions could be based. When an immediate and desirable goal is identified and accepted, according to this perspective, we can expect to see a new foreign policy

---

[7] Clearly, these eminent scholars and practitioners believe that consensus and the resulting stability during most of the cold war are preferred to the inconsistency that results from the politicization of foreign policy.

strategy to emerge and for the United States once again to have a generally accepted set of precepts about which there is general agreement.

Our brief summary of the traditional view of postwar American foreign policy is not meant to explain that policy; it is by no means analysis. We offer it only to present generally accepted understandings about the external factors that affected U.S. foreign policy and about the existence of widely shared beliefs regarding American goals and the proper role of the United States in international affairs. Some of our summary may be caricature. Like any broad summary of historiography, some details may be misleading or subject to varying interpretation. Nonetheless, we believe that the traditional understanding of postwar U.S. foreign policy contains the elements we have discussed. We have presented this survey so that we can show how the two-good theory's analysis of these events differs. We hope to show that the analysis of events from the perspective of the two-good theory provides a better and more useful approach.

The Two-Good Theory's View

The two-good theory allows us to offer a different interpretation of post–World War II American foreign policy. Our interpretation is based on a more general theory of foreign policy, which, among other things, means that we view the pattern of American postwar foreign policy as not unique. Rather, the theory tells us what the effect of certain factors—such as overwhelming power and then declining power—should be on a state's—any state's—behavior. The theory is also able to tie these factors to the changes in the nature or existence of the domestic debate over foreign policy. Essentially, the theory's interpretations and explanations are more scientific because they are derived from general expectations regarding the effect of important factors on the formation of foreign policy. The theory tells us that an explanation and interpretation of international behavior should be based on the observation of changes in those factors. Finally, the general theoretical approach tells us to consider the degree to which the observed policies fit the theory's expectations. If the expectations and observations match relatively well (as we think they do and as we will show), the two-good theory provides a better foundation from which to anticipate future trends. That is, because the theory tells us to focus on a limited set of variables and because the theory's predictions are directly tied to changes in those variables, we should be able to make general statements about the future of American foreign policy.

Our general theory leads to a number of predictions relevant to American foreign policy. First, our theory says that when a state experiences a significant increase in power we should expect it to increase its foreign policy activities substantially; that is, it should increase both its maintenance-seeking and

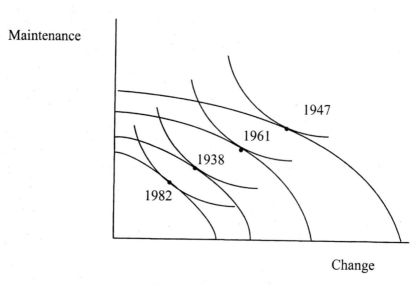

Figure 3.1. The U.S. Foreign Policy Portfolio—1938, 1947, 1961, 1982

change-seeking activities. There is no disputing the fact that the United States underwent a substantial increase in its relative power between the pre– and post–World War II periods or that it subsequently experienced a gradual decline in relative power. According to the Correlates of War (COW) Project's figures, the relative capability of the United States in 1938 was 16.5, rising dramatically to 29.9 in 1947, falling to 21.2 in 1961, and declining even further to 13.6 by 1982—a clear indication of the magnitude of the increase and subsequent decrease of American power. These four production possibility frontiers reflecting the growth and decline of American power are presented in figure 3.1.

Besides the four production possibility frontiers, the figure includes indifference contours that are associated with a state that values change and maintenance about equally.[8] From these contours and frontiers, of course, we can

---

[8] We do not insist that the United States cared equally about the two goods throughout the entire postwar era, as the figure's depiction assumes. It is possible that over the period the United States had a relatively greater preference for change, or for maintenance, than we have depicted. In either of those cases, the tangents of the production possibility frontiers and the indifference contours would be located differently—either higher and to the left if the United States was more maintenance seeking than we have portrayed it, or lower and to the right if the United States was more change seeking than we have assumed. It is also possible that the relative preference for these goods changed rather than remained constant as we've shown. Changes in administration or the threatened economic collapse of a close ally, for instance, might lead the United States to emphasize one good over the other for short periods of time. Our goal is to present the general expectations drawn from the theory, which precludes us from addressing the peculiarities that are exogenous to our model.

derive general expectations about the goals of American foreign policy as the country's power changes. Focusing for the moment on the immediate postwar years, the implications are clear. As the United States moved in relative capability from the 1938 to the 1947 contour, we would expect to see more of both kinds of foreign policy behavior; the United States was able to do much more than it had been able to previously. Recall from our discussion in the previous chapter that with increases in power more resources can be given over to foreign policy, so that more powerful states are expected to be more active internationally. And increases in power lead to increasing marginal production for change. This implies four important things: more powerful states should engage in more types of foreign policy behaviors of both types than weaker countries; more powerful countries will have relatively more change seeking in their entire foreign policy portfolios than weaker countries; increases in power will increasingly be directed toward change-seeking policies; and the greatest change-seeking behavior can be expected from powerful states getting more powerful. This implies that in the immediate postwar period we should notice the United States being more active internationally (a statement that is not surprising) and, most particularly, see a greater emphasis in American foreign policy on change-seeking behavior.

When we compare American foreign policy before World War II to that after, we see significant increases in all types of activities, as we expected. Many of the actions represent increases in maintenance seeking. Increases in overall defense spending and the creation of a centralized Department of Defense are prominent examples of maintenance-seeking policies. Military capabilities are generally associated with a desire and ability to protect an asset, territorial or political. After World War II, the United States took responsibility for the protection of many countries from external or internal threat, requiring that greater resources be given to the military. A comparison of military spending before and after World War II and after the cold war is striking. In 1938, the last year of world peace before the war began, American military spending as a proportion of gross domestic product (GDP) was about 1.5 percent (Cordesman 1998). By contrast, the *lowest* level of American military spending during the cold war (aside from a temporary fall in 1948) was 4.9 percent in 1979; that is equivalent to an increase in military spending of about 1862 percent in constant dollars. Even *after* the cold war, military spending fell only to 3.2 percent of GDP in 1999—which, again in constant dollars, is a military budget about 22 percent greater than in 1979 and almost 2300 percent greater than in 1938. The size and prevalence of the American military establishment are so evident to many Americans on a daily basis that they go without notice.[9] But we should note that American military power today and the omnipresence of its

[9] For an excellent academic approach measuring the effect of militarization on American society, we suggest Pat Regan's essay on war toys (1994).

establishment dwarf the situation of the interwar period. The increased size, rationality, and readiness of American forces were directed toward protecting the political and territorial gains the United States realized through the war and represented (and continues to represent) a reaction to the existence of the global interests of the United States.

A further example of a maintenance-seeking policy (one we investigate statistically in a later chapter) is the reciprocation—as opposed to initiation—of militarized conflict. The United States was attempting to protect the status quo in many of the more dramatic military confrontations of the early cold war period. Consider, for example, four prominent confrontations of the early cold war. The United States and British acted in concert by sending material and advisors to protect Greece from communist insurgents in the Greek Civil War from 1946 to 1947, stabilizing that country and the region and preventing clearly undesired changes in the status quo. Western actions during the Berlin blockade in 1948 were designed to maintain the Allied presence in that city, overcoming Soviet attempts to alter the situation fundamentally. President Truman's decision to send American troops to oppose the North Korean attack on South Korea in June 1950 was meant to protect not only the Korean peninsula but to counter threats to Japan. In the Taiwan Straights Crisis of 1954–55, the U.S. military presence was directed toward protecting the military capabilities of Taiwan, as well as its independence and sovereignty. American military activity in the years right after World War II should be seen as largely, even overwhelmingly, as directed toward the protection of the status quo. A brief perusal of the military incidents involving the United States analyzed in Blechman and Kaplan's *Force without War* is instructive. Of the twenty-five incidents they find involving U.S. military activity during 1946–49, the vast majority are clearly efforts to protect the existing political situation. We would categorize only three as motivated by change seeking: the attempt to bring about political change in Lebanon in 1946; involvement in Italian elections in 1948; and (much less obviously) actions related to the Arab-Israeli War in 1948. The undeniable and unsurprising point is that American efforts to protect the international status quo—military and other—increased dramatically after World War II.

What of the American pursuit of change in the immediate postwar period? In addition to efforts to maintain aspects of the status quo, change-seeking policies also became much more prominent in the immediate postwar years, when U.S. relative strength was at its peak. The two-good theory says that the power of the United States was so great that both maintenance and change could be pursued. Consistent with that prediction, the United States dramatically increased its foreign aid, pursued the formation of alliances with weaker states, initiated a larger number of militarized conflicts, and moved to a relatively more capital-intensive defense posture. Each of these policy changes is an example of change-seeking behavior. Taken together, they show that the

United States was constructing a foreign policy portfolio that emphasized much more change than had been the case before the war.

The perspective of the two-good theory and the specific conclusion drawn from the theory that very powerful states can add both change and maintenance to their foreign policy portfolios offer a more useful and empirically correct interpretation of early postwar American policy than does the traditional view. Typically, the shift in American foreign policy that resulted from its power advantage after World War II is characterized as a move from isolationism to internationalism (Schulzinger 1984; Lundestad 1990; Johnson 1991; Ambrose 1993). This shift toward greater international involvement and activity is generally attributed to the "lessons" of World War II; the war was thought to have resulted from the isolationism of the United States and the appeasement policies of the West generally. The change in policy toward greater international involvement was brought about primarily by a change in the attitude of the American public and decision makers, who concluded that the maintenance of a peaceful democratic world required greater American activity (Almond 1960; Caspary 1970; Klingberg 1983; Destler, Gelb, and Lake 1984; Holsti and Rosenau 1984; Melanson 1991).

There are a number of problems with this explanation for greater American involvement in foreign affairs. First, the direction of causation is difficult to determine in this explanation: did foreign policy change because of the internationalist mood of the American people, or did Americans become internationalist because the international situation and their policy had changed? Second, the interpretation does not allow us to forecast subsequent and future shifts in policy. Because it is solely descriptive and not general, we cannot identify the recurring factors that might lead to similar or different changes in policy. Third, while the interpretation explains why the United States became more active in world affairs, it does not explain the precise form of this activity. Broad descriptions of political strategy or of goals may be valuable, but better are statements that are more precise and that can point to specific policy changes that can be anticipated. Will foreign aid increase or decline? Will there be more or fewer alliances? Last, this explanation does not provide a theoretical basis from which to understand policies in other times and places. What do the changes in American policy in the postwar era tell us about Chinese foreign policy after the demise of the Soviet Union?

The two-good theory has more precise predictions about postwar American policy. For example, the theory says that an already strong state that becomes stronger will undertake significant changes in the institutional structure of the foreign policy establishment and in security policy. These changes would be designed more to facilitate the state's ability to produce changes internationally than to protect the status quo. In particular, we would expect the foreign policy establishment to expand, with more personnel being stationed overseas, making them better able to alter the behavior of the host countries.

We would also expect an increase in the use of covert operatives; we would expect the bureaucracy to grow to accommodate the personnel needed to oversee the expanded operations such as alliances and foreign aid. With respect to security policy, we expect to observe five major changes: a reorganization that places greater emphasis on projection of force rather than capabilities aimed more at homeland defense; a concomitant move to a more capital-intensive armament program, better at force projection and taking greater advantage of a substantial lead in technology; a change in military doctrine that emphasizes the use of technology and the use of rapid deployment and offensive strategies, reflecting the desire to have global capabilities to impose desired political and military changes; the formation of alliances with smaller countries; and the initiation of militarized disputes at an increased rate. The theory leads us to expect little domestic dissension regarding foreign policy, since foreign policy debates should occur chiefly over the proper mix of maintenance- and change-seeking policies. When a state undergoes a dramatic increase in capabilities, it should pursue both more maintenance and more change, and all domestic actors get more of what they want. This, according to our theory, is the source of the early postwar bipartisan consensus in American foreign policy. It was less a product of patriots setting aside differences to work for the common good than a function of the country's expanded capabilities permitting a foreign policy that could make both change seekers and maintenance seekers happy.

Each of these expectations conforms to the pattern observed in the United States after World War II (see Kennedy 1987; Cohen 1993). The foreign policy bureaucracy did expand considerably beyond prewar levels. In 1938 the Department of State had 963 employees; by 1948 this had grown to 4,198 (Campbell 1971). Furthermore, the foreign policy establishment underwent a major institutional restructuring, beginning with the creation, in 1947, of the Central Intelligence Agency (CIA) and the National Security Council (NSC), as well as the reorganization of the armed forces which, among other things, separated the air force from the army (Millis 1958; Huntington 1961; and Schilling, Hammond, and Snyder 1962). Many of these changes can clearly be seen as putting in place the machinery necessary to pursue more change. The information-seeking responsibilities of the CIA are certainly useful for both maintenance- and change-seeking policies, but the covert operations are useful almost exclusively for acquiring change. Among the examples of CIA activities that were change seeking are: Operation Ajax, designed to overthrow the government of Iran in 1953; support for anticommunist parties in Italy during the elections of 1948; and Operation Success, which overthrew the government of Guatemala in 1954.[10] Similarly, the air force serves to protect

---

[10] For discussions of CIA activities, see Ranelagh (1992), Prados (1991), Leffler (1992), Brands (1993), Warner (1994), and Andrews (1995).

American air space, but it also can be used to project force abroad.[11] In addition, giving the air force a prominent role is consistent with our theory's expectation that a greater emphasis would be placed on a technologically advanced military.

Other predominantly change-seeking agencies were also created. In 1948 Congress substantially increased the budget for the Voice of America (VOA), which had been founded in 1942, and began considering it as a "permanent" institution. Through VOA, and the United States Information Agency (which was also established during this period), the United States undertook a substantial propaganda campaign abroad.

Foreign aid is an aspect of foreign policy that is frequently change seeking. As we will argue in greater detail in chapter 6, foreign aid is generally given by one state as a reward or an inducement to another state to change its behavior in some regard. While other policies may also bring about desired change in behavior, foreign aid is, for its cost, very effective. A country gets a lot of change for the dollars allocated to foreign aid. To take one recent example, the United States in 2002 announced plans to triple its foreign aid allocation to developing countries over a period of some (yet to be determined) number of years. This intention was heralded internationally, providing the United States with increased international influence. The United States clearly saw this increased aid as bringing about desired changes in policies of other countries. Specifically, the United States wanted to see changes in the policies of other states and greater international coordination to aid in the American-led campaign against terrorism. The United States also wanted greater cooperation on a number of other fronts, including its efforts to curtail the global production of illegal drugs and further lower barriers to international trade. The annual amount of this increase, if realized, will be about $10 billion. By contrast, the Bush administration's requested increase in the American military budget from 2002 to 2003 was almost five times that amount, at $48 billion. Indeed, at the same time as these budgetary plans were being made, the U.S. Army, opposed by Secretary of Defense Donald Rumsfeld, wanted to procure a new Crusader howitzer, priced at a relatively modest $11 billion.[12] The main point,

---

[11] Leffler (1992, 56) points out that the supporters of an independent air force began pushing for a continued American military presence in the western Pacific as early as 1943. The lessons of both world wars were used to bolster arguments for an independent and greatly strengthened air force (Bernardo and Bacon 1955; Caraley 1966; and Borowski 1982). While some of this motivation was based on the concern that civilian populations would be at risk in future wars, decision makers also saw a widely dispersed air force as an efficient way to exert American influence. See also Brodie (1959).

[12] Ten billion dollars is also about what the annual increase in the American defense budget through 2010 is projected to be, assuming a 1 percent per person annual increase in military health care and minor increases in other aspects of the Pentagon's operations and maintenance budget (O'Hanlon 2001, 16).

to summarize, is that for its size, foreign aid buys the donor nation a tremendous increase in its change-seeking capabilities.

As predicted by the two-good theory, the United States undertook a substantial foreign aid effort after the war, altering the postwar recovery path in directions that the United States wanted to see. Most significant, of course, was the Marshall Plan, enacted in 1948. The Marshall Plan was the first major peacetime aid program and was designed to assist in the recovery of Western Europe but also to get the Europeans to adopt policies preferred by the United States; it was not solely an exercise in altruism. Before receiving aid, in fact, the recipient states of Western Europe had to agree to American provisions and to develop multilateral plans to execute those provisions. The economic and political goals of the plan can quickly be summarized. Economically, the Marshall Plan accomplished three main things. First, it restored financial stability to Europe by encouraging that price controls be removed, requiring balanced national budgets, creating central institutions, stabilizing exchange rates, and decreasing inflation pressures. Second, it demanded that the free market be allowed to operate throughout Western Europe: "As a condition for receiving Marshall Plan aid, each country was required to develop a program for removing quotas and other trade controls" (De Long and Eichengreen 1991, 49–50.) The free market was not obviously going to emerge from the destruction left by World War II in Europe; mixed economies were the standard in the interwar years, and socialist parties were ascendant in the immediate postwar period. The American policies designed to realize free trade clearly were contrary to the anticipated trend and in that way were change seeking. Last, the plan created a social contract, by which "workers would moderate their wage demands, management its demands for profits. . . . Higher investment and faster productivity growth would ensue, eventually rendering everyone better off " (De Long and Eichengreen 1991, 54). As Hogan notes, "These economic assumptions grew fundamentally out of the American experience at home, where a large internal economy integrated by free-market forces and central institutions had supposedly laid the groundwork for a new era of economic growth and social harmony" (1991, 116). The economic goals of the Marshall Plan were reason enough for the Eastern European countries to decline the offered participation in the plan; the communist states did not want their economic and political futures tied closely to an American vision.

The political goals underlying the Marshall Plan paralleled the economic goals. Fundamentally and generally, "American leaders envisioned an open international economy founded on the principles of liberal capitalism, such as free trade and economic opportunity. But they also equated these principles with democratic forms of government, [and] associated autarkic economic policies with totalitarian political regimes" (Hohan 1987, 26). More immediately, the plan was designed to decrease the attraction for the leftist—socialist and communist—parties in Europe by providing viable more centrist economic and social alternatives. Second, the United States desired a revitalized—particularly German—economy to aid in the prevention of Soviet political and military incursions into Western Europe. The Marshall Plan was to create "a unit coherent enough to harness Germany's industrial strength without restoring its prewar dominance and strong enough to countervail the Soviet bloc in Eastern Europe" (Hohan 1987, 54). Clearly, the Marshall Plan's purposes were to remake Europe in ways desired by the United States.[13] The destruction brought about by World War II provided the United States with the opportunity to realize its economic and political preferences. Other policies would be required if the United States were to achieve its desired outcomes in other areas of the world.

Finally, the Marshall Plan also allowed the United States to introduce American business techniques to European firms, meeting and generally overcoming varying levels of resistance (Kipping and Bjarnar 1998). This may have been one of the less central goals of the Marshall Plan, but the U.S. business community gained influence over European firms through this process. The Marshall Plan, to put it differently, altered a variety of aspects of the status quo to conform more to American preferences.[14]

Policies designed to alter policies in other areas of the world were also adopted shortly after the war. Truman's Point Four program was adopted in 1950 and provided aid to developing areas. In 1951 the United States started to coordinate technical assistance with military and economic aid programs through the creation of the Military Security Agency. In 1954 the International Cooperation Administration, located in the State Department, was given responsibility for the administration of foreign aid for economic, political, and social development. The amount of American aid provided to other countries and the number of aid programs continued to grow throughout the decade. This increased activism in foreign aid policy with its emphasis on changing the behavior of recipient states is explained well by our theory.

The two-good theory expects that a strong state getting stronger would significantly increase certain behaviors that we have identified as change seeking. The two-good model sees alliances between powerful and weaker states—what Morrow and we refer to as "asymmetrical alliance"—as involving a mutually beneficial transfer of goods. The weaker state is able to acquire some maintenance (or "security" in Morrow's terms and in common parlance) from the stronger state, while the stronger is able to gain some policy concessions from

[13] We do not wish to ignore the relationship between the Marshall Plan and the formation of the North Atlantic Treaty Organization (NATO) in 1949. Each tied Europe more closely to the United States, and each helped to realize American preferences in European social, economic, political, and military policies. An excellent discussion of NATO's institutionalization of the changes brought about in the Marshall Plan is provided by Latham (2001).

[14] For a less sanguine view of the successes of American business to reform their European counterparts, see McGlade (2001).

the weaker. Consider an alliance between the United States and New Zealand or between Britain and Portugal. In general, such alliances do little if anything to increase the security of the stronger state. Indeed, the more powerful country may be more likely to become involved in international conflict, protecting its weaker ally. The weaker state, on the other hand, has its ability to protect its interests—including its own existence—materially augmented. Why do large states enter into these odd but frequently observed arrangements? What do they gain? The benefit the more powerful state derives from these asymmetrical alliances is "autonomy" (Morrow's term) or "change" (to use our language). That is, the stronger state provides the smaller state some security (maintenance) and in return the smaller state gives some political or economic concessions to the more powerful state. (We explore this argument in greater depth in chapter 7.) Thus, the two-good theory leads us to expect a strong state getting stronger to increase its alliance commitments, particularly to weaker parties.

U.S. behavior conforms to this expectation. The fact that the United States had shunned peacetime alliances before World War II makes the vast network of alliances established after the war all the more impressive. The Rio Pact was signed in 1947 along with the Charter of the Organization of American States (OAS). Through these alliances the United States was able to coordinate the foreign policies of the member states to its benefit; this is perhaps most easily seen in the support the OAS has given to the United States in its long conflict with Cuba. The North Atlantic Treaty, signed in 1949, established NATO and tied the United States politically and militarily to Western Europe. The United States signed a mutual defense pact with the Philippines in 1951; in return for a promise to defend the islands if attacked, the United States gained basing rights at Subic Bay. That same year saw the formation of the ANZUS, the alliance among Australia, New Zealand, and the United States. (We discuss ANZUS in greater detail in the next chapter.) In 1952 the United States and Japan reached a mutual cooperation and security agreement. A mutual defense pact between South Korea and the United States was signed in 1953 at the end of the Korean War. The Southeast Asian Treaty Organization (SEATO) was agreed to in 1954 by the United States, Australia, Britain, France, New Zealand, Pakistan, the Philippines, and Thailand. (South Vietnam was a "protocol," or nonsignatory country.) Also in 1954, the United States signed a mutual defense treaty with Taiwan (Harkavy 1982; Lundestad 1990). Harkavy (1982) notes that the United States, while not a signatory, was involved with the Central Treaty Organization (CENTO) among Britain, Iraq, Turkey, Iran, and Pakistan.

All of these alliances were with smaller states and most of the new American allies were developing countries. With the possible exception of NATO, none of the new alliances should be seen as adding appreciably to American security, and in ANZUS and the OAS (at the very least), American interests were not threatened seriously by the Soviet Union (or anyone else). The alliances did

provide the United States a direct means of influencing policy in these countries, however. The OAS, for instance, served as a vehicle for the United States to
coordinate foreign policy with its southern neighbors; the security guarantees
provided for in ANZUS allowed the United States to get agreement from the
other two signatories regarding such things as support for a liberal peace treaty
with Japan and military cooperation in counterinsurgency actions in Southeast Asia. Even NATO, the least asymmetrical of the new alliances, was sometimes criticized as a way for the Americans to exert influence in Europe. The
United States used its predominance to sign treaties by which the United States
provided security to its new allies in return for political concessions.

Another policy that we generally consider to be change seeking is the initiation of militarized conflict. That is, when one state initiates a dispute against
another it is generally because it wants to bring about a change in the status
quo. (We explore this point in greater detail in chapter 6.) Therefore, again
drawing directly from the theory, we expect a strong state getting stronger to
increase noticeably its rate of dispute initiation. As the two-good theory predicts, the rate of dispute initiation by the United States increased substantially
in the early postwar period. According to the Militarized Interstate Dispute
(MID) data set (Jones, Bremer, and Singer 1996), the United States initiated
two militarized disputes in the 1930s and three in the 1940s after World War II.
This rose to eleven in the 1950s and to nineteen in the 1960s. (For a discussion
of the U.S. uses of force, see Blechman and Kaplan 1978.)

It is important to note that the motivation for much of the behavior being
summarized here is, in fact, what the theory claims. That is, during the postwar
period, particularly in the early years, the United States was largely endeavor-
ing to change the world more to its liking. As noted by Leffler (1992, 3), Americans soon after the war "expected to refashion the world in America's image
and create the American century. They intended to promote world peace and
foster international stability at the same time that they safeguarded national
security, perpetuated American power, and further augmented American prosperity."[15] Two examples make the point regarding American motives. In December 1945, the United States negotiated a loan agreement by which Britain
would be provided $4.4 billion at very low interest rates (effectively under 2
percent). While altruism and the desire to bolster an ally may have played a
role in this decision, it is interesting that the British, in exchange, agreed to reduce barriers to American trade in the British Commonwealth (De Conde
1963). Similarly, in 1954 President Eisenhower used the CIA to remove the
president of Guatemala and immediately followed this with $45 million in

---

[15] Leffler clearly was not thinking in terms of change and maintenance when he wrote this, and
he might reject the distinction we are drawing. It is clear from this quotation, however, that the
distinction is there. American policy was intended to protect what was already enjoyed and to
change things for the better.

military assistance to the new regime. These policies were clearly designed to reshape others' policies more to the liking of the United States.

Finally, we expect any state that undergoes a major increase in its relative capabilities to exhibit little domestic dissension regarding foreign policy. According to our theory, internal foreign policy disputes should occur chiefly over the determination of societal preferences that guide the state's foreign policy. That is, the focus of debate should involve the proper mix of maintenance- and change-seeking policies. When a state undergoes an increase in capabilities, we expect it to adopt a new policy portfolio that produces more maintenance and more change. Thus, all domestic actors should perceive an improvement—everyone is getting more of what they want. As J. Snyder argues, "Foreign policy consensus and harmony . . . were achieved by giving both internationalists [our change seekers] and nationalists [maintenance seekers] what they wanted on issues they cared about most" (1991, 257). This, according to our theory, is the source of the early postwar bipartisan consensus in American foreign policy. The great power of the United States allowed those who wanted change and those who wanted maintenance to get what they wanted. This holds true particularly when attention is given to the institutional structure of American foreign policy making. Elsewhere (Morgan and Palmer 1998) we have argued that the American president serves as an agenda setter in foreign policy. He has the responsibility for proposing the policy portfolio while the function of Congress is to approve or disapprove of suggested changes. The postwar increase in American power provided the president the opportunity to make dramatic shifts in policy. With the possibility frontier pushed so far out, virtually any policy he suggested would be seen as an improvement by most of Congress and, therefore, be approved.

Policy debates did occur, however, and it is not a stretch to see them as focusing on the proper balance of change and maintenance. To a large degree, one can interpret the isolationist versus internationalist clash of the immediate postwar years in these terms. Isolationists were generally those who valued maintenance almost exclusively. Their main point was that the United States should focus its resources and energies toward protecting what it had already achieved rather than attempting to change those things, and that attempts to foster desired changes in the world brought with them risks to what Americans already enjoyed. Isolationists did not think that spreading democracy, increasing profits from trade, and making the world better for everyone were bad goals, only that attempts to achieve these goals brought danger. Only those things in the international system that represented a direct threat to the United States itself, not to its allies or other global and artificial interests, should be countered. Internationalists, on the other hand, typically believed that Americans were morally bound to make the world a better place. They believed that spreading democracy, wealth, and civil liberties were worth running risks, and they felt that the United States should devote some of its resources to achieving these goals. Besides bringing desired changes, actions such as spreading democracy and capitalism would help generate lasting peace in the world. To be sure, some internationalists were maintenance seekers who believed that an active involvement in world affairs was necessary to protect what America already had. These people believed that American internationalism should be measured, however, and that it should be driven solely by considerations of maintenance. We have in mind here staunch realists such as George F. Kennan and Hans Morganthau, both of whom strongly supported an active foreign policy designed to contain the Soviet Union and to maintain a global balance of power favorable to the United States. Kennan and Morganthau felt the United States should be internationally active (Kennan 1954; Morganthau 1951, 1952) and that it should focus its resources on areas of the world that were capable of threatening real American interests. Southeast Asia was not an area where genuine American interests were present or threatened. For this reason, to the surprise of many, Kennan and Morganthau were among the earliest opponents of U.S. involvement in Vietnam (see Morganthau 1965b; Myers 1988). Their support of an active hard line against the Soviets did not extend to a change-seeking engagement that they saw as producing more risks than benefits.

Let us turn to the effects of diminishing relative capability on U.S. policy. The capability of the United States relative to the rest of the world declined after the beginning of the cold war through the collapse of the Soviet Union. The two-good theory does a good job of predicting and explaining the effects of a relative decline in power on American policy. The most salient expectation coming out of the theory is that any state undergoing such a decline should be cutting back its foreign policy activities. More interesting conclusions involve the specific decisions making up these changes. If we assume that the United States acted in accordance without regard to domestic factors, there is a second salient conclusion. For a strong state such as the United States, the cutbacks resulting from diminished capabilities should occur primarily in change seeking with a smaller decline in maintenance-seeking activities; the ability of the state's power to produce change is decreasing more rapidly than is its ability to produce maintenance.

Domestic political considerations alter this second expectation somewhat, however. The American president is the agenda setter in foreign policy and is thus able to establish the terms of debate and to propose the policies or set of policies that will be adopted. Other domestic actors can either accept or reject the president's proposals, but the president initially proposes the policies. If a president addresses a decline in capabilities in accordance with the general theory and cuts back both types of activities, she or he is going to make change seekers and maintenance seekers alike unhappy. Instead, the theory expects a declining state, such as the United States, to cut back overwhelmingly in one area or the other so that the president can maintain the support of at least one segment of the population. The result, following from the theory, is that foreign policy should become increasingly subject to public debate as the relative power of the country declines and as the president's proposed policies necessarily favor one action over another. Different groups, supporting specific policies, see their preferred policies as requiring increasingly scarce resources. The debates generally can be seen as focusing on whether reduced foreign policy resources should be devoted to changing the world or protecting what we already have. Of note is the fact that the most serious disputes involved change-seeking activities. During the 1960s and 1970s, as American power eroded relative to that of others, foreign aid and covert activities were the object of significant domestic opposition. During the same period, Congress asserted greater control over covert activities. Domestic political battles raged over other specific activities, such as the issue of intervention in Angola, and usually resulted in less change-seeking behavior.

The theory, putting domestic politics aside, predicts noticeable cutbacks in change-seeking policies and relatively few in maintenance-seeking policies. The theory leads us to expect the United States to continue high levels of defense spending, for example. Additionally, symmetrical international relationships, requiring fewer resources being given to the protection of others (with less maintenance being traded for change, in the theory's terms), should become more prominent. Also, we would expect to see the United States, while declining in relative power, to reciprocate more military actions that are taken against it. We also expect to see fewer change-seeking policies: asymmetrical alliances—those between the United States and significantly weaker states—will be eschewed in favor of the formation of closer ties with strong countries. According to the theory, the United States would cut back existing commitments, saving the resources required to achieve the resulting maintenance. We would also expect a reduced rate of dispute initiation, another policy most closely associated with change seeking. During periods of decline in relative capabilities, there should be a slower pace of technological advancement in the military; we expect a reduced level of foreign aid, and reductions in the use of covert activities to influence others abroad should also decline.

Again, the actual pattern of behavior is consistent with our expectations. The United States, through détente, attempted to protect the status quo by coordinating policy with the Soviet Union, and it established relations with China. The relative growth in the capabilities of these two former adversaries made such maintenance-enhancing activities by the United States more appealing. After the withdrawal from Vietnam was completed, U.S. spending on the military continued to increase and, as we have noted, continued to go up even after the demise of the Soviet Union: compared to 1979, military spending twenty years later was 22 percent higher in real terms. And when others took military action against the United States, America responded, as in the *Mayaguez* incident. In other words, maintenance-seeking behaviors did not suffer an appreciable decline. We do notice in this period, however, a considerable cutback in change-seeking behavior. There was a reduction in efforts to align with weaker powers and some existing commitments were reduced. The frequency of the initiation of international disputes fell. The rate of adoption of technological advances in the military also declined, and for much of the period of the 1970s through the 1990s there was a reduction in naval and air forces.

We want to turn to a brief description of U.S. foreign policy in the post–cold war era, as the predictions of the two-good theory are borne well by the record. We also want to give some attention to American policy since September 11, 2001; the perspective of the two-good theory offers a different set of explanations for U.S. behavior than is generally used in public debate. We hope, therefore, that a quick investigation of recent American foreign policy will both illustrate the uses of the two-good theory and offer a valuable analytic approach.

U.S. Foreign Policy since the End of the Cold War

Since 1990, two significant events are seen as defining the American role in the world—the collapse of the Soviet Union in 1991 and the attacks on the World Trade Center and the Pentagon on September 11, 2001. The collapse of the Soviet Union in 1991 meant that the policy of containment was no longer meaningful. The guiding precept of U.S. policy for almost fifty years had been abruptly removed, the primary adversary had disappeared, and new foreign policy opportunities were presented. The attacks of September 11 required an immediate reorientation of American policy in order to combat a nonstate actor using terrorism as its primary weapon. The American responses to these two very different events have, of course, encompassed a range of foreign policies from encouraging the expansion of NATO, carrying out a bombing campaign against Serbia over its policies in Kosovo, to invading Afghanistan and Iraq. It would be a mistake to see the American responses to these events as predetermined and the specific actions somehow devoid of choice. Instead, these actions can be explained in the context of our more general theory.

The two-good theory is useful in explaining the general nature of American foreign policy since 1991, and an application of the theory further illustrates its simplicity and its benefits as a tool. The primary factor that affects state international behavior, according to the theory, is the state's relative capabilities. The political preferences of leaders certainly affect policies adopted, and differences certainly exist between the Clinton and George W. Bush administrations. Nonetheless, by focusing solely on the most important environmental variable—relative capability—and applying the model, we can say quite a bit about general tendencies in U.S. foreign policy.

Table 3.1 shows each of the seven major powers' percentage of their combined

TABLE 3.1
Percentage of Combined Gross Domestic Product in Major Powers, 1985–2003

	1985	1991	1997	2003
United States	37.7	41.4	44.1	47.3
Japan	26.3	24.3	23.1	18.8
Germany	12.7	12.4	11.3	10.4
Great Britain	6.0	7.2	7.1	7.8
France	8.5	8.5	7.5	7.6
China	1.8	2.6	4.8	6.1
Russia	7.0*	3.6	2.2	1.9
Total	100%	100%	100.1%	99.9%

* Soviet Union

GDPs from 1985 through 2003.[16] As the table shows, the United States has been the most powerful state throughout the period. Its capabilities relative to these most powerful states have been increasing: the American GDP was a little less than 38 percent of the major powers' combined GDPs in 1985, rising to more than 47 percent by 2003.[17] The United States clearly has been able to reverse the decline in its relative capability in 1947–82 that we discussed earlier. The United States is far from declining in its capabilities; it is a powerful state becoming relatively more powerful. It may be the case that American hegemony will erode at some point in the future. Currently, however, American dominance is undeniable and shows no immediate indication of weakening.

As noted above, the two-good model has predictions for the behavior of powerful states with increasing capabilities: such states can be expected to be making greater efforts to alter the status quo in desired ways. Resources allocated toward maintaining the status quo should also be increasing, though not as rapidly as resources given to change-seeking policies. A brief tour of American international behavior since 1991 in four policy arenas lends support to these expectations.

With the demise of the Soviet Union, many observers expected to see NATO disband. The primary purposes of the alliance, after all, had been to deter a Soviet attack on Western Europe and, more generally, to provide a balance to Soviet power. If one sees alliances as aggregating capabilities and

[16] The data are taken from the World Bank and are available at http://devdata.worldbank.org/dataonline.

[17] Closer inspection reveals an even greater increase in relative capability: in 1985 the U.S. GDP was about 43 percent greater than the Japanese GDP; by 2003, it was 152 percent greater. In 1985 the U.S. GDP was almost the same as the combined GDPs of the two next most powerful states; by 2003 it was *greater* than the combined GDP of the next *four* states.

providing security to all its members, this expectation is entirely reasonable and understandable. This, however, is not what asymmetrical alliances—those between or among great and small powers—do, according to the two-good theory. Asymmetrical alliances such as NATO are mechanisms for the less powerful states to gain maintenance while the more powerful states gain change. To put it simply, more powerful states gain policy concessions from smaller states in return for providing protection—maintenance—from threats to valued things. The United States has reasons to desire the continuation of NATO; the alliance is one of the political frameworks through which it persuades European states on political matters. More, with the increased American capabilities, we would have expected to see the United States seek NATO's expansion. The maintenance and formation of asymmetrical alliances (as we argue more fully in chapters 4 and 7) require resources: the smaller members will want something provided by the more powerful in return for their policy concessions, and the United States currently has the capability to meet those expectations. By adding Poland, the Czech Republic, Bulgaria, Estonia, Latvia, Lithuania, Romania, Slovakia, and Slovenia and moving toward including Albania, Croatia, and Macedonia, NATO allows the United States to exert greater influence in Europe. Specifically, the United States has had a preference for stable democratic institutions in Europe (and globally), and NATO provides one way for the United States to move toward realizing that goal. Policy coordination on other issues, such as economic integration, is more easily achieved with NATO in place and with broader participation. NATO's expansion is clearly anticipated by the two-good theory.

A second policy arena where the two-good theory leads us to have expected the allocation of greater resources is foreign aid. This is a policy that we see primarily directed toward realizing changes in the behavior of recipient states. As such, states seeking greater change are expected to increase their foreign aid. And as expected, the United States has increased its foreign aid significantly. According to the World Bank, from 2000 to 2003, U.S. economic aid as a proportion of its GDP has risen from about 0.10 percent to about 0.14 percent. Further, policy statements indicate that the United States intends to increase its foreign aid even more. We have already alluded to President Bush's 2002 announcement that the United States will triple its aid in the future. This aid is expected to bring policy concessions from recipient states on the fight against terrorism, efforts to limit drug trafficking, and lowering of trade barriers.

The initiation of conflict is the third policy used by states seeking change. The two-good theory would predict that the rate at which the United States has initiated interstate conflict should have risen over the period since 1985 as its capabilities have increased. The MID data set (Jones, Bremer, and Singer 1996; Ghosn, Palmer, and Bremer 2004) records all instances from 1816 through 2001 where one nation-state has threatened, displayed, or used force against another. It also records which state (or side, in the case of multilateral actions) initiated the military conflict. In three five-year periods—1987–91, 1992–96, and 1997–2001—the yearly average number of such conflicts initiated by the United States was 1.6, 2.0, and 2.6, respectively. In other words, there is a clear increase in the rate at which the United States begins interstate conflict.

American involvement in large-scale military conflict, the fourth policy arena, has also increased. Some of this conflict was designed to increase maintenance, and we expect to see states getting stronger to increase their pursuit of both kinds of goods. The U.S.-led war against Iraq in 1991 following that country's invasion of Kuwait, for instance, was meant to reinforce an internationally recognized status quo. Much of this large-scale conflict was designed to alter the world, however. Over a four-year period starting in 1999, the United States was involved in three massive military operations. First, the United States and its NATO allies waged a seventy-eight-day bombing campaign against Serbia in 1999 over the status of Kosovo. In 2001, following the terrorist attacks of September 11, the United States led a force from fifteen countries in attacking Afghanistan, overthrowing the Taliban regime and attempting to find Osama bin-Laden. Finally, in 2003, the United States, with significant help from Great Britain,[18] invaded Iraq to eliminate the regime of Saddam Hussein. Each of these operations was designed to bring about significant changes in the international status quo. They are, individually and as a set of behaviors, the type of actions expected of a powerful state gaining capability.

The predictions of the two-good model that we have laid out here are based solely on the relative capability of the United States and increases in that capability and have nothing to do with the specific American president or his party. While the Clinton administration and George W. Bush administration may have had different policy goals, they each were able to draw on the increasing might of the United States in pursuit of those goals. In recognizing and acknowledging the differences between the two administrations, we should not ignore the common strains. The two-good theory says stronger states increasing in capability will pursue their preferences more actively; it does not purport to say what those preferences are. It is clear that both administrations pursued its particular goals—whether for greater democratization or for more complete diplomatic isolation of "rogue states"—with greater alacrity; and pursuit of those goals sometimes was criticized for ignoring the preferences of the international community. For instance, the Clinton administration chose not to sign the 1997 Land Mine Treaty, which banned the use of land mines. The United States remains (with Latvia) one of only two NATO states that has not signed the treaty. In 2001 the Bush administration announced that it would not participate in discussions to implement the 1997 Kyoto Protocol,

---

[18] Troops from Australia and Poland also participated in the invasion. Naval forces from Australia, Denmark, and Spain played smaller supporting roles.

the international treaty to reduce emissions of gases that are often held to be largely responsible for global warming. The invasion of Iraq in 2003 was undertaken despite widespread international criticism. And American actions in responses to September 11 more generally have served to irritate much of the world.

The pattern and content of American foreign policy since 1991 matches well the two-good theory's predictions. The most powerful state in the world has been increasing in capability. The theory says that one would expect to see that state allocating a greater proportion of its resources to attempts to change the status quo. While some approaches would see a very powerful state as largely status quo oriented and would have a difficult time explaining American behavior, that behavior is consistent with the two-good theory's expectations.

Summary

Our goal in this chapter has been to show how a simple and direct application of the two-good theory to the foreign policy of the United States since World War II can lead to interpretations that differ from traditional understandings. The two-good theory is a general and generalized approach. That is to say, the theory identifies specific variables that affect international behavior, and based on our observations of the values those variables take we can make statements about expected behavior. Once the theory has done the work for us by pinpointing the important variables—such as relative capability and the direction of change in that capability—we are able to see easily what the effects should be. The exercise we have carried out in this chapter is to apply the broad lessons gleaned from the theory to well-known, if not universally accepted, interpretations of U.S. foreign policy. The chapter is not meant to present a complete history of American foreign policy interpreted through the lens of the two-good theory; such an effort would take volumes. Instead, we wanted to show what the implications of the two-good theory are in, we hope, a fashion that suggests that those implications can lead to novel and valuable lessons.

The theory argues that the strongest countries are generally the most change seeking, ceteris paribus. From this vantage point, the two-good theory sees American international efforts in the postwar period as being directed in large part toward altering the international status quo in ways preferred by the United States. The international regimes established at Bretton Woods in 1944 represent examples of attempts by the United States to bring about changes in the functioning of the international system. The attempt to establish a viable, functioning, and self-sufficient noncommunist regime in Vietnam is another example of change-seeking behavior. And in more recent years, no other country in the world has made greater attempts to change the foreign and domestic policies of Iraq, North Korea, and Cuba than has the United States.

The orientations of these three countries comprise some of the more obvious deviations between international outcomes and American preferences.

This chapter does not subject the two-good theory to test; we will do that in later chapters after we have given a more rigorous presentation of the theory. Our purpose has been to show how the theory can be used in one way. In the next chapter we apply the two-good theory to two less well-known (at least to American audiences) specific decisions—the Bolshevik decision to accept the Brest-Litovsk treaty, ending Russian involvement in World War I, and New Zealand's decision to require the United States to verify that its visiting naval vessels did not carry nuclear weapons. We also use the two-good theory to analyze in a quantitative and more rigorous fashion Chinese international behavior since 1949. This next chapter, much like the present one, is aimed at showing the wide range of use to which the two-good theory can be put.

4

Three Applications of the Two-Good Theory

ONE OF THE advantages of a general theory of foreign policy is that it can be (and should be) applied broadly. Because it is general, there are few restrictions to the theory. It does not, for instance, explain only the conflict behavior of states, or the pattern of their foreign aid, or how foreign policy is changed by membership in a new alliance. The restrictions that we need to place on a situation before we can apply the theory in order to understand the foreign policy of a state are few. Indeed, while our model is developed largely to explain international behavior, we think that the two-good theory may be useful in understanding political behavior beyond international relations.

The decisions of appellate judges, for instance, may be analyzed through the two-good theory. Judges are generally affected by two prominent motivations. First, they are strongly motivated to follow precedent in their decisions—to be guided by similar and applicable decisions that were reached in the past. In following precedents, judges minimize the likelihood that their decisions will be subsequently overturned; that is, they are playing it safe and protecting an established understanding of the law's meaning within a specific context. Second, however, judges are motivated to apply the law to achieve justice, however each judge understands that concept. In other words, judges may use the law and their positions to make the world a better place. In doing this, of course, the judges must be careful to define their new understanding of law carefully, so that it can withstand the scrutiny of more senior colleagues. In our view of politics, the first type of behavior is "maintenance," and judges who follow precedents exclusively are almost always protecting some aspect of the status quo that they find attractive. Using our terminology, the second motivation is for "change," and judges are bringing about desired changes in some part of the legal, social, and political world when they try to establish new legal understandings.

Our emphasis, of course, is on foreign policy and how our general theory can explain a variety of international phenomena. Since the implications of our theory are broad, we should be able to apply it to explain a wide range of behavior, and here we will look at three different examples of foreign policy behavior. These examples were purposively selected to have little in common in order to better illustrate the power of the two-good model.

We will be looking, first, at the Russian decision to accept the Brest-Litovsk treaty that ended Russia's involvement in World War I, even though it contained exceptionally harsh German terms. This treaty required Russia to give up approximately one-third of its industrial capacity and about 25 percent of its population in return for an immediate cessation of hostilities. The treaty's terms were so harsh that the Bolsheviks had an extensive and heated debate before accepting it. Our model will be useful in explaining the decision and in framing the positions of the debate's factions.

Second, we will investigate New Zealand's behavior toward the United States in the mid-1980s regarding American warships visiting New Zealand's ports. New Zealand wanted assurance that any visiting warships were not carrying nuclear weapons. The United States was unwilling to provide such assurance, and after some negotiations the United States withdrew security guarantees from New Zealand, essentially throwing New Zealand out of the ANZUS alliance. Seldom in international relations do small countries make such strong demands on larger allies that the larger country will end an alliance, especially when the two remain basically friendly toward each other, as New Zealand and the United States have. Our theory helps understand this odd behavior.

In the third exercise, we apply the model to Chinese foreign policy since 1949. The motivations behind the behavior of the People's Republic have been ascribed to a variety of things, many of them peculiar to the Chinese historical, cultural, or ideological experience or situation. We want to show that China, while unique in many respects, has a foreign policy that is consistent with that of many other countries, and that it conforms to the expectations of our model. Certainly, knowledge of Marx-Lenin-Mao Tse-tung might contribute to a full understanding of Chinese behavior, and indeed China's political revolutionary experiences since 1949 might serve as a potent explanation for much of its foreign policy behavior. Chinese experiences with the Western powers during the nineteenth century, when the imperialist countries divided large parts of the country among them, can be useful in achieving insight into Chinese concerns about the West; and an understanding of China's social structure may add flavor to any analysis of the country's actions. The application of our theory to China, however, is meant to show how applying a general theory of foreign policy even to countries with such distinct characteristics and experiences as China can be useful.

The third application is meant to show how the theory can be used to explain broad patterns of foreign policy behavior as well as specific decisions. Unlike our qualitative overview of American foreign policy in chapter 3, this analysis of Chinese foreign policy provides quantitative tests of several hypotheses. It is unusual in works of this nature to place a quantitative analysis of one country's foreign policy behavior after two case studies of odd decisions. We make this unusual combination intentionally to highlight the disparate nature of the phenomena that can be addressed and explained by the two-good theory.

We have chosen these three cases because they represent a desired mixture on a number of dimensions. First, the cases capture variance in the dependent variable: included are one state's decision to seek additional change; one state's increased desire for maintenance; and one state's attempt to increase each over time. Second, the states analyzed have different political arrangements: New Zealand is a parliamentary democracy; Soviet Russia was a dictatorship striving to survive in the midst of revolution; and China had become an established dictatorship. Third, the threat posed to these states varied greatly: in the early 1980s, New Zealand faced a less aggressive Soviet Union and China; in 1918 the very survival of Soviet Russia was by no means certain; and the People's Republic has gone from having its existence challenged to becoming a stable and accepted member of the international community. Finally, the national capabilities of the states were changing in different ways: New Zealand's power was relatively stable; Soviet Russia was rapidly losing its ability to wage war against Germany; and China's capabilities have fluctuated since 1949.

Let us turn now to our first case, the Bolshevik decision to accept the German terms of the Brest-Litovsk treaty in 1918.

The Treaty of Brest-Litovsk

On January 18, 1918, German negotiators presented their Russian counterparts with the final set of German demands to be included in the Treaty of Brest-Litovsk, formally ending the war between the two countries.[1] The German demands were extreme, and encompassed independence for large sections of western Russia, including eastern parts of Poland, most of the Ukraine, and Courland (much of current-day Latvia). The German terms set off a debate within the Bolshevik leadership as to whether, as Lenin suggested, agreeing to this "miserable peace" was preferred to a continuation of war (the Left Communist position) or to a policy of "neither war nor peace" (Trotsky's suggestion). Each position had explicit beliefs about the value of protecting the status quo and the value of attempts to further the goals of the revolution, which would significantly alter parts of the international status quo. Eventually Russia agreed to the German terms, accepting one of the harshest peace settlements in modern history. Why would a major power agree to give up so much? Why were the alternatives to acceptance of the demands not pursued? The debate within the Bolshevik hierarchy over the Brest-Litovsk treaty can be understood by our general theory, and the arguments illustrate many of the aspects of our model.

The military and political situation prior to the treaty is quickly summarized.

---

[1] Russia had not incorporated adjustments to its calendar that were made in the West in the Middle Ages. By 1917 Russian dates were thirteen days behind the West. The new regime soon adopted the Western calendar, and the dates as we present them are the "Western" dates.

Aside from Germany, perhaps no country was more affected by the experience of World War I than was Russia. After entering the war in support of Serbia in 1914, about 1.7 million Russian soldiers were killed in battle, a greater number than that of any other country, except for Germany's 1.8 million battle deaths. Another five million soldiers were wounded. Civilian deaths numbered about two million, the vast majority of which resulted from disease and hunger (Small and Singer 1982; Clodfelter 1992). And in March 1917 Tsar Nicholas II was overthrown, ending the Romanov dynasty that had headed Russia since 1613. By November, the Bolshevik (Communist) Party assumed a measure of control and, after consolidating power in a long and bloody civil war, remained in power until 1991.

After the overthrow of the tsar, the provisional government led by A. F. Kerensky faced an extremely difficult political situation domestically and a rapidly worsening military situation, due in part to the newly established workers' and soldiers' councils ("soviets"), which disputed its authority. Despite this, the Kerensky government decided to abide by what it saw as its international obligations to the Western allies and to continue Russia's war effort. There was a partially successful offensive launched against the German forces in July, though that offensive quickly turned to a rout.

Germany, meanwhile, had determined that war in the west could not be won without a major adjustment in the military situation on the eastern front. Germany adopted what can be called a reverse Schlieffen Plan. That plan, used in 1914 to begin the war, sought to avoid a two-front war by first defeating France and then moving German troops to the Russian frontier. By 1917 the dangers to Germany of the dreaded two-front war had been fully realized. Now, Germany was determined to knock Russia out of the war. If this could be done, Germany would be able to move large numbers of troops to the western front, and accomplishing this became the major German military goal. After it repelled the Russian offensive in July, the German army was in a position to attack Riga, which it did in September, to land troops in Estonia (begun in October), and to gain control of most of Latvia. Germany began to prepare for a general advance along the front, expecting that advance to lead to a Russian surrender.

The Russian military situation was certainly precarious. The Russian army's fighting ability had deteriorated badly since the "bourgeois" revolution of March 1917 and, most particularly, since the Bolshevik revolution in November. Indeed, the Russian army as a fighting force had largely vanished after the November revolution, which had wide support among the soldiers at the front.[2] Soldiers were quick to "vote with their feet" after the Bolsheviks seized

---

[2] In the elections to the Constituent Assembly—held November 25–27, 1917—the Bolsheviks received 63 percent of the vote of the Baltic fleet, 56 percent of the vote from the soldiers on the northern front, and 67 percent of the vote on the western front. On the southern parts of the front, far removed from Petrograd, Bolshevik support was smaller, reaching only 15 percent on the Romanian frontier (see Hough and Fainsod 1979, 71–72).

power, as Lenin immediately moved to expropriate land and redistribute it to the peasants, many of whom were now in the army. Also, the Bolsheviks worked against standard military discipline by calling for the troops to fraternize with the Germans, which, it was hoped, would hurry the proletarian revolution in Germany (Ulam 1974, 56).

The new regime also lacked the political desire to further prosecute the war. After all, it had been the tsar's regime that had tied Russia so disastrously to the Western powers, and Kerensky's ineffective bourgeois government had continued to follow that bankrupt policy. The new government would make no such mistake. On November 8, the day after the Bolsheviks seized power, the new regime declared its intention immediately to cease hostilities with the German army and to open negotiations to achieve a "just and democratic peace" (Wheeler-Bennett 1963, 67–70). By this the Bolsheviks meant that a final peace treaty would not include any annexations or the imposition of any indemnities.

Lenin announced the unilateral cessation of hostilities on November 26. The Germans waited, apparently with an understandable mixture of confusion and hope[3] for official word from the regime regarding the opening of armistice negotiations (Wheeler-Bennett 1963, 77–83). At the end of the month, the Russians and Germans agreed that negotiations would begin December 2, and the terms of the armistice were quickly agreed to and signed on December 15. The armistice was to last four weeks, automatically prolonged unless a warning of one week was given by either side; no German troops were to be moved (to the western front) unless they had already been sent or ordered there; and supervised fraternization between German and Russian troops was allowed (Wheeler-Bennett 1963, 88–90). The armistice also included a provision that final peace talks were to begin shortly. This armistice agreement was remarkably one-sided. As Adam Ulam points out, "[T]he non-transfer agreement cost the Germans nothing: because of its phrasing it could always be claimed that the troops being sent westward had been so ordered before the armistice was signed. On the issue of fraternization, [German major general Max] Hoffmann was [correctly] confident . . . that supervised contacts between the Russian agitators and the German soldiers would not do too much harm" (1974, 58).

With the armistice in place, on December 22 the two sides set about negotiating a peace treaty that would formally end the war. Adolph Joffe led the Bolshevik delegation. Joffe, while an important member of the Bolshevik Party, was not a member of the inner circle, showing that the Russian leadership thought that reaching final peace terms with the Germans would be a relatively simple and quick task. Lenin and the other members of the party elite were required in Petrograd, where their attention was needed to protect the revolution.

---

[3] Lenin had been escorted into Russia in the spring of 1917 by the Germans in the hopes that his policies would lead to Russia's withdrawal from the war. See, particularly, Wheeler-Bennett (1963) and Pipes (1954).

Representatives from Germany, Austria-Hungary, Turkey, and Bulgaria made up the opposing side, with the Germans clearly acting as senior partner. The armistice had allowed Germany to begin the transfer of troops from the Russian to the western front, and the winter months meant a relatively quiet front in the west. The Germans, consequently, were in no great hurry to conclude the peace treaty.

Although the armistice terms had been reached with relative ease, it soon became clear that the German position for peace terms was much harsher than had been anticipated by the Russians. The demands included that Russian Poland and the Baltic states be given independence. Large, though as yet unspecified, tracks of the Ukraine were to be transferred to Poland. The extreme demands caught the Russians by surprise and one of the Russian negotiators, Mikhail Pokrovsky, "broke down and wept" upon hearing them (Ulam 1974, 60).

During a break in the negotiations, the Bolsheviks decided that higher-level attention to the negotiations was required, and so the Russian negotiating team was reconstituted. When negotiations resumed on January 9, 1918, Leon Trotsky was the new head of the Russian side. Trotsky, of course, was one of the two primary members of the Bolsheviks, Lenin's "right hand." It was Trotsky who had served as the main party leader inside Russia before Lenin's return following the March revolution. Indeed, while Lenin was absolutely essential for the party's existence, the revolution without Trotsky is almost unimaginable. That Trotsky was now sent to the negotiations, away from the daily events in Petrograd, meant that the Bolsheviks realized the longer-term significance of the peace negotiations for Russia's future. Simply to give in to the harsh German demands without offering a credible counteroffer might endanger Russia, even assuming that the Bolshevik revolution survived. On the other hand, Germany not only had an overwhelming military advantage, but because it wanted to move its troops facing the Russians to the western front, it had a strong incentive to end the negotiations quickly and could be expected to force the issue. The negotiations were not going to be easy.

Trotsky was to demonstrate the Russians' seriousness at the negotiations, with the hope that his presence might lead the Germans to moderate their demands. His primary task, however, was to delay an agreement. There were two main reasons for this. First, Trotsky believed that Germany and Austria-Hungary would be anxious to conclude the peace treaty for military reasons, and the longer the negotiations could be dragged out, the more favorable the terms that Russia might expect. Those countries, Trotsky thought, desperately needed access to raw materials (particularly grain) that could be supplied by the Russians (Wheeler-Bennett 1963, 142–44). To continue the war in the west required a final peace in the east. Second, more important to all the Bolsheviks were the beliefs and hopes that "the eagerly awaited revolution might break out in Germany before any critical decision had to be taken by the Soviet

Government" (Carr 1953, 31).[4] German soldiers and workers were carrying out demonstrations in Germany's major cities, and the Bolsheviks believed that the proletariat revolution was a matter of days or weeks away. Trotsky, in fact, held to the hope that very soon the German army would simply melt away as its soldiers returned to Germany and that the revolution would lead to the ultimate collapse of the German and Austria-Hungarian Empires.

The delaying tactics were not successful, however. On January 18, the Germans provided the Russian delegation with a map that contained the details of the German demands. Before the Russians demobilized, the Germans would remain in occupied territories. Specifically, the German demands "left virtually the whole of Polish, Lithuanian and White Russian territory" under German control and "divided Latvia in two" (Carr 1953, 31–32). After seeing the details of the German position and "[f]aced with something like an ultimatum" (32), Trotsky requested that negotiations be adjourned so he could take the demands back to Petrograd and the Bolsheviks could discuss them fully.

The Bolshevik Party was deeply divided on whether to accept the German terms, and the division of opinion makes this case useful for our purposes. Three positions became apparent, which remained unchanged during the debate. The first was that of the Left Communist faction, led by Nikolai Bukharin. Bukharin was motivated by pessimism about the regime's ability to survive (a pessimism that was widely shared, even beyond the Left Communists), as well as a belief in the likelihood of the revolution in Europe (a belief that was not as widely shared). The Left Communists opposed not only the treaty but had even been against the opening of peace negotiations with Germany (White 1994, 179). Bukharin believed that the European revolution was imminent and that without it the Bolshevik regime could not long survive: "The Russian revolution will either be saved by the international proletariat or it will perish under the blows of international capital. . . . Everything depends on whether or not the international revolution is victorious . . . the international revolution—and that alone—is our salvation" (quoted in Cohen 1980, 66).

How could the international revolution be encouraged and hastened? Two possible methods were available. First, the Left Communists argued for "breaking off negotiations with imperialist Germany, the immediate creation of a volunteer revolutionary army and the commencement of a ruthless war against the bourgeoisie of the entire world in the cause of international socialism" (White 1994, 179). The second method of achieving the revolution would be used should the unlikely Russian military victory fail to be realized: "Bukharin was confident that if the German army did advance any farther into

---

[4] Trotsky's delaying tactics may also have been motivated by concern about the Constituent Assembly, which was scheduled to meet in Petrograd on January 18 and which was immediately disbanded by Lenin (Ulam 1974, 62). Trotsky wanted no peace agreement until the difficulty of the assembly had been dealt with.

Russia, this would encourage the development of the international workers' movement. He was encouraged by the appearance of a strike movement in Vienna" (White 1994, 167; see also Cohen 1980, 66; Williams 1987, 55; and Goemans 2000, 252–58). To sign the peace treaty would not only betray the revolution but also serve to invite the destruction of the new regime.

The second position was Trotsky's own and is summarized in the slogan "No War—No Peace." Trotsky found the German terms of Brest-Litovsk unacceptable, and he proposed that the Russians "announce the termination of the war and demobilization without signing any peace. . . . The Germans will not be able to attack us after we declare the war ended . . . if they attack us, our position will be no worse than now" (quoted in Wheeler-Bennett 1963, 185). Like Bukharin, Trotsky expected that the "German working people" would constrain the German army, either through revolution directly or by pressuring the German government to avoid widening the war: "The Germans would not dare to advance on Petrograd. It would cause a revolution in Germany" (quoted in Wheeler-Bennett 1963, 226). Unlike Bukharin, though, Trotsky believed the new regime could survive even without the revolution in Europe. While he thought it unlikely, if the German army were to advance further into Russia, Trotsky argued that "we would be compelled to sign the peace" and be no worse off than in agreeing to the Brest-Litovsk terms immediately (quoted in Wheeler-Bennett 1963, 188). Indeed, Trotsky felt that not signing the treaty would benefit the European revolution, because agreeing to the treaty allowed the Germans the opportunity "to proclaim and declare us agents of England and of [President Woodrow] Wilson" (quoted in Wheeler-Bennett 1963, 185).

The final position was taken by Lenin, the party leader. Lenin, of course, was the most powerful member of the Bolshevik Party, but he did not often act without agreement among the members of the Central Committee, and he was unwilling to impose his position on important issues without wide discussion within the party elite. (While he allowed debate on this and other issues, Lenin generally believed that once the party's position had been determined, it was the duty of all members to abide by that position. This was the principle of "democratic centralism.") Lenin argued strongly for accepting the German terms without delay. Simply put, Lenin believed that there was no alternative. To Lenin, Bukharin's idea of a revolutionary offensive against the Germans assumed a Russian fighting capability that was nonexistent. What Russians soldiers did Bukharin imagine would take the fight to the Germans? The Russian army was melting away, and to launch a major offensive against an essentially victorious German army would lead to its complete destruction. Further, while both Trotsky and Bukharin included the political influence of the German workers in their calculations, Lenin was not as quick to pin the regime's hopes on them; he saw little evidence that the European proletariat was about to rise up in support of the Russian revolution. To base the survival of the Bolshevik revolution on unreal military and political expectations was naive. To argue (as

Bukharin did) that the Russian revolution should fight for the liberation of Poland, Lithuania, and Courland was anti-revolutionary: "No follower of Marx can deny that the interests of Socialism are higher than the interests of the national right to self-determination" (quoted in Tyrkova-Williams 1919, 476). Lenin saw signing the Brest-Litovsk treaty as trading land for "breathing room," time to consolidate the gains of the revolution. Once the fruits of the revolution in Russia were secure, the Bolsheviks could concern themselves with the European proletariat. Until that time, however, it was the Bolshevik duty to protect the gains of socialism.

Let us turn to an analysis of these three positions using the two-good theory. The three can be distinguished on two related dimensions. The first issue that separated the factions dealt with the relative preference for the survival of the new regime or for the furtherance of the proletarian revolution in Europe, particularly in Germany. In our theory's terms, this question is one about the value of the status quo. To put it differently, the issue can be framed in terms of the preference for maintenance: how strong was the preference for the preservation of the regime? The second question had to do with the expected course of military operations at the front if the peace treaty was not accepted. This question regards the estimate of Russian power, particularly its military capability: if the revolution were to be pursued on the battlefield, what would be the likely results? In our theory, a state's power is a major determinant of its preference for change or maintenance: the stronger the state, ceteris paribus, the more likely it is to be change seeking. By putting the two issues together, we are able to determine the actors' *relative* preferences for the two goods, and the usefulness of our approach may be demonstrated.

The differences between the three positions can be summarized by reference to figures 4.1a and 4.1b. Figure 4.1a presents examples of the indifference contours over maintenance and change for each of the three leaders' positions. For the actor's position that is described by a contour, the actor is indifferent between any two points on each of the lines. The Bukharin position (the nearly vertical indifference contour) illustrates that Bukharin placed virtually no value on maintenance; no increase in the regime's ability to protect the status quo was worth giving up any change. Bukharin was willing to see the Bolshevik revolution die rather than forego the potential to further the European revolution.[5] In contrast, Lenin held a strong preference for maintenance: the newly achieved status quo must be preserved at any price, and he was willing to give up any ability to change the political situation in Europe to protect the

---

[5] In late February 1918, the Western powers offered the Russians assistance in warding off the advancing German army. Bukharin wanted to reject this aid, arguing that it "was absolutely inadmissible for [the Bolsheviks] to make any compromise with imperialism of any sort; to accept assistance from the Entente was as treasonable to their revolutionary principles as to negotiate with the Germans" (Wheeler-Bennett 1963, 254).

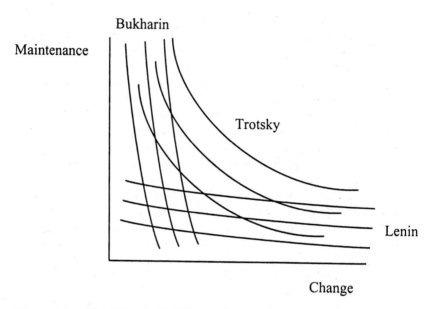

Figure 4.1a. Bolshevik Leaders' Indifference Contours

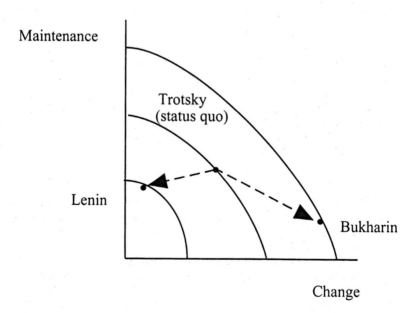

Figure 4.1b. Estimates of Production Possibility Frontier

revolution. Lenin's indifference contours are thus nearly horizontal, reflecting the preference for maintenance. Finally, Trotsky's complicated position attempted to achieve the maintenance of the revolution while supporting the workers' movement in Europe. The policy of "No War—No Peace" was meant to protect the new regime and (by refusing to sign a treaty with Germany) encourage the European workers with the Bolshevik commitment to the revolution. In our terms, Trotsky's position revealed a preference for both maintenance and change, and this is reflected in his indifference contour: for any mixture of the two goods, Trotsky would be willing to give up some maintenance for change, or vice versa, depending on the circumstances.

The second distinguishing difference between the three positions has to do with the Russian military capability. In figure 4.1b we present three production possibility frontiers, which represent the amounts of maintenance and change that the regime could pursue if it chose. To illustrate the figure's use we begin with Trotsky's position. Trotsky believed that should the Russians sign the Brest-Litovsk treaty, the Germans would probably not press their offensive, but that if they did so, the Russians could quickly agree to the German peace terms. In other words, Trotsky held that the status quo was preservable with the power available to the new regime. Trotsky's position regarding the Russian power is represented by the middle production possibility frontier, and the retainable status quo is on that frontier. Bukharin thought the Russians were stronger than did either Trotsky or Lenin, holding that a Russian revolutionary army could defeat the Germans; this belief is reflected in the northeastern production frontier. In combination with Bukharin's strong preference for change, Bukharin's position can be represented by a proposed move from the status quo downward and to the right (toward the southeast), reflecting a proposal that the regime pursue greater change while giving up maintenance. Finally, Lenin's position is given by the innermost production possibility frontier and is based on his position that the Russian army had ceased to exist as a viable military force; the Russians would be unable to stop a German advance. Given his preference for maintenance over change, this implies that Lenin's proposal was for a move to the left in figure 4.1b, which would be an attempt to maximize the Soviets' maintenance by giving up all efforts toward change.

The debate within the leadership regarding the correct response to the German peace terms was heated, but its particulars go beyond our current task. Trotsky's "No War—No Peace" proposal was adopted by the Bolsheviks on January 22, with specific instructions that he delay as long as possible. Finally, after eleven days of negotiating, on February 10 Trotsky announced the Bolshevik position: "Russia, while refusing to sign an annexationist peace, for her part declares the state of war with Germany, Austria-Hungary, Turkey and Bulgaria at an end" (quoted in Carr 1953, 38). The Germans were left confused by this peculiar end to the matter and engaged in some internal discussions about how to proceed.[6] On February 17 the Germans renounced the armistice and informed the Russians that military operations would recommence. The Bolsheviks immediately restarted their internal debate. After Lenin threatened to resign, they decided to sign a peace treaty with Germany to end the war. On February 23 Germany presented the Russians with their newer, even harsher demands. On March 3, after more discussions, the Russians accepted the German terms. In the final Treaty of Brest-Litovsk, the Russians gave Germany "three-quarters of [its] iron and steel, 26 percent of her railway network, 26 percent of her population, and much of the most fertile soil of the empire" (Williams 1987, 56). For our interest in the episode, the German advance demonstrated to the Bolsheviks that both Trotsky's and Bukharin's estimate of Russian power was dramatically wrong: "Lenin alone had seen the light, had plumbed the grim situation to its darkest depths of impotency" (Wheeler-Bennett 1963, 186). Given the inability of the Russians to pursue change-seeking policies, there was little choice but to adopt Lenin's maintenance seeking and to agree to the German terms. The weakness of the Bolshevik regime did not allow for any alternative.

We turn now to an illustration of how our theory can be applied to alliance politics. In this case, a democratically elected government will reverse a long-standing policy, in a clear example of choosing a change-seeking policy over the maintenance seeking that had typically marked membership in the alliance.

New Zealand and ANZUS

The 1985 New Zealand decision to require the United States to verify that American ships visiting New Zealand were not carrying nuclear weapons brings together several elements of our theory. The decision is an odd one, because the United States clearly was unhappy with the widely anticipated New Zealand action and made its unhappiness known. After some discussions (and threats) between the two countries, the United States broke security arrangements with New Zealand, essentially throwing them out of ANZUS. It is interesting here that a small country made such extreme demands (from the American perspective, at least) on a large ally that the larger ally broke the alliance. Since a number of years have passed since the incident without a re-forming of the alliance, apparently each country is relatively happy with the new arrangement. New Zealand evidently prefers that there be no alliance between the two

---

[6] According to Carr (1953), there was support, particularly among German civilians, for accepting the Russian position. The Austrians were opposed to reopening an offensive against Russia, and a quick acceptance of the Trotsky formulae would allow Germany to move its troops immediately to the western front. More traditional heads prevailed, however, and Trotsky's position was treated as an end to the armistice.

countries and no American security guarantees, rather than belong to an alliance operating under the "old rules." The United States, on the other hand, prefers that the alliance be terminated rather than operate under "new rules." How did this situation arise? A traditional realist perspective of international relations has a difficult time explaining this turn of events. Our general theory, we believe, offers a good explanation for this strange outcome by bringing together several elements of the model and facts of the situation. We want to illustrate how our theory works in this case by looking briefly at the effects of the nature of asymmetrical alliances, the perception of a diminishing international threat, and changing national preferences.

We begin with a discussion of the nature of alliances. According to the two-good model, alliances are entered into by states that may wish to increase the amount of change or maintenance contained in the foreign policy portfolios.[7] Small countries frequently seek alliances with stronger countries in order to acquire greater amounts of maintenance from them. The stronger countries, in return, receive some benefits in the form of change from the smaller states. In other words, many alliances bring together states with different goals.[8] In general, asymmetrical alliances are those where one state (or states) gains maintenance in exchange for change. In alliances that consist of countries of different capabilities the larger state gets change in return for supplying the smaller with maintenance.[9]

This approach differs significantly from the power-accretion model, which fundamentally maintains that alliances form to increase the security of or power available to the members (see, for instance, Osgood 1968; G. Snyder 1997). One of the main difficulties with the power-accretion model is its inability to explain why a stronger state would want to form an alliance with a weaker one. From a purely power perspective, why would the United States, for instance, be willing to establish and remain in the OAS or NATO? How is American security enhanced through U.S. membership in either of these alliances? For instance, consider the American alliance with Asian states through

---

[7] A relatively extensive literature using this perspective has developed in recent years. For prominent examples, see the seminal Morrow piece (1991); Palmer and Souchet (1994); Bennett (1997); Morgan and Palmer (1998); and Palmer and David (1999).

[8] Some alliances are symmetrical. That means that all the allies are seeking the same good through membership. Symmetrical alliances, for the most part, contain states that are of the same or similar relative capability. Examples of symmetrical alliances would include the Arab League (which consists of many relatively small states) and the 1939 nonagression pact between Nazi Germany and the Soviet Union.

[9] An early and good example of a treaty that transfers change for maintenance is God's Covenant with Moses. In return for an alteration in the behavior of the Israelites, including abiding by the Law (change), God provided them with maintenance. In the Book of Genesis, God sends an angel to Moses: "Pay heed to him and obey him. Do not defy him . . . since My Name is in him; but if you obey him and do all that I say, I will be an enemy to your enemies and a foe to your foes" (Gen. 23:21–22).

the now defunct SEATO. That alliance, which also included Britain and France, is generally explained as a signal of military commitment to American allies sent to the Soviet Union and other American adversaries, designed more to deter aggression against those allies than to achieve any hope that the allies will contribute to American security directly (see, for instance, Gaddis 1982, 153).[10] The power-accretion model explains what benefit the smaller, more threatened states may derive from the alliance but, using the model, the precise motivation for the United States is more difficult to locate. If the security of the allies (in Southeast Asia, for example) is vital to American interests, no alliance should be necessary to demonstrate that to any potential adversary. On the other hand, if the formation of the alliance itself is meant to increase American commitment and to raise the probability of an American protective response, then the formation of the alliance commits the United States to undertake an action that may be contrary to its immediate interests.[11] Explanations for this behavior that are based on security calculations require a logic that, in the end, is circular: the United States wants to protect its allies because not to protect them harms America credibility, and that credibility is what allows the alliance to be meaningful in the first instance. Enhanced credibility allows the alliance to be formed and is simultaneously the purpose of the alliance.

Our model more readily explains the motivation of major powers that join asymmetrical alliances than do more power-oriented approaches. Asymmetrical alliances are agreements where one state gains maintenance while another state benefits from changes in the first state's policies. Each state prefers this arrangement to one where there is no alliance at all, and the arrangement will last as long as that remains true. As soon as one state finds the costs of the arrangement too high compared to the benefits, the alliance will end. For a small state, this probably means that the value of the maintenance it receives from the alliance is not worth the price of changing its policies. That small state then will seek to restructure its arrangement with the larger state so as to increase the maintenance it receives or to decrease the change it gives up. If the level of threat emanating from the international system is high, the first path will be chosen; if it is low, the second will probably be selected. Our task now is

---

[10] Indeed, SEATO's terms required the United States to come to the defense of the signatories only if they were attacked by a communist power. Hence, India's attack on Pakistan (a SEATO member) did not raise U.S. obligations. Illustrating the asymmetry of the obligations of the alliance's terms is the fact that other states were obligated to protect U.S. interests—for example, American troops—if those interests were attacked in Southeast Asia only. We thank Ashley Leeds for providing these specifics.

[11] This is precisely the form of argument presented by, among others, Schelling (1960) and Osgood (1968). The formulation has been attacked from different perspectives by, among others, Walt (1987), Morrow (1994), Sorokin (1994), and Morgan and Palmer (1998). For a model that centers on the importance of domestic politics in the formation of alliances, see Siverson and Starr (1994).

to see how that general idea applies to New Zealand's alliances and, in particular, describes its dealings with the United States.

First, New Zealand's security arrangements with Great Britain and the United States provide excellent examples of asymmetrical alliances. Neither British nor American security interests were directly served by their alliances with New Zealand, yet each major power benefited from their arrangements. In each case, New Zealand gave up change in return for maintenance. The value of the maintenance provided by Britain declined as the European struggle moved away from the Asian theater from the late nineteenth century onward; and the value of the American-supplied maintenance diminished as the Soviet/communist threat to New Zealand decreased after the end of the Vietnam War. Eventually, in 1985, New Zealand concluded that a continuation of its participation in ANZUS was too costly and that the maintenance it received from the United States was not worth the cost of the required policies. We trace the nature of New Zealand's alliance participation with each country to illustrate this.

In its security dealings with Britain from the end of the nineteenth century onward, New Zealand gained maintenance in return for change. Specifically, New Zealand received "pledges by the Royal Navy to protect them from putative threats by France, Germany, Russia, and the United States, considerable weaponry . . . and logistical and training support" (Hoadley 1994, 30). In return, New Zealand's exports were directed almost exclusively toward Britain, and in the early part of the twentieth century New Zealand supported British proposals for a council of the British Dominion (Laking 1988, 44; Hoadley 1994). We can see, then, that both countries benefited from their alliances, New Zealand by gaining greater maintenance, and Britain by getting change. Through the creation of ANZUS in 1951, a similar asymmetrical alliance was formed that benefited both the United States and New Zealand, though even at the beginning of ANZUS its benefits to New Zealand were negligible to some. New Zealand's prime minister in 1951, Sydney Holland, felt that the United States was getting the better of the new arrangement, since an invasion of Australia or New Zealand by the Soviets seemed highly unlikely. Nonetheless, the new alliance with the United States provided some security benefits to New Zealand. And in return, New Zealand adopted some policies the United States wanted it to. For example, after World War II New Zealand's (and Australia's) involvement in Asian military affairs included British Commonwealth planning in Malaya in 1948, fighting in the Korean War, military involvement in Malaya in 1955 and in Borneo (to counter Indonesian aggression) in 1955, and action during the Vietnam War. Additionally, the Americans used ANZUS to convince Australia and New Zealand to "agree to liberal terms in the peace treaty with Japan" (Gardner 1988, 207).

New Zealand's disenchantment with ANZUS began to take form in the mid-1970s, when a popular anti-nuclear movement within the country led "to an extensive campaign aimed at persuading municipal authorities to declare their areas nuclear free zones" (Camilleri 1987, 132).[12] "Public attention shifted somewhat from French underground testing to visits by nuclear-powered [warships] to New Zealand ports" (132; see also Jackson and Lamare 1988). Popular opposition to the visits increased from 1978 to 1985, and several small parties adopted stringently anti-nuclear positions. The relatively small Values Party, the Social Credit Party, and the New Zealand Party all took radically anti-nuclear positions. The largest opposition party, Labour, took the lead in representing these views nationally, though its position was more moderate than those of the other anti-nuclear groups. The ruling National Party accepted the visits by the nuclear warships and wanted to maintain the existing ANZUS arrangements, though at least through 1980 the party preferred to achieve "a more independent stance with the ANZUS alliance" (Camilleri 1987, 134). Just before the election of July 1984, David Lange, leader of the Labour Party, "reiterated his intention to exclude all nuclear weapons systems from New Zealand . . . and indicated he would 'seek to convince the nuclear powers to respect the wishes of the Pacific peoples to keep the Pacific nuclear free'" (Camilleri 1987, 135–36). In the election, "the anti-nuclear parties gained 64 percent of the vote," with the Labour Party and Lange capturing the prime minister's office (135). The stage was now set for New Zealand's confrontation with the United States.

The new government sought a reinterpretation of ANZUS that would allow it to require the United States to certify that visiting ships did not carry nuclear weapons. This position ran counter to the American navy's policy to "neither confirm nor deny" the presence of nuclear weapons on any specific vessel. To do so, truthfully, would mean that the navy would be communicating not only to New Zealand but also to its adversaries which of its ships were carrying those weapons. This is something the navy was not willing to do. To accede to New Zealand's request, the United States also argued, would encourage other allies to ask the navy to adopt the same policy toward them. If the United States adopted the "no nukes" policy toward New Zealand would Australia follow? The Philippines? Japan? Quite obviously, the United States felt it simply could not accept the New Zealand position without some significant modifications.

Prime Minister Lange may have preferred the new policy to take effect within the structure of ANZUS; that is, Lange did not want the United States

---

[12] Public support of a nuclear-free Pacific, including New Zealand's policy regarding the visits of nuclear-capable warships, was not restricted to the country:

A 1982 survey of the views of the major non-governmental organizations with specific policies on peace and disarmament found overwhelming but predictable support for . . . the establishment of a nuclear-weapons-free zone, especially in the South Pacific. . . . New Zealand was seen as well placed to take such steps, and in particular to terminate all existing involvement in nuclear activities. (Camilleri 1987, 132–33) to dissolve the alliance. In the terms of our model, we would say Lange wanted to win back a measure of change while maintaining the same degree of maintenance New Zealand received from the Americans. The United States, however, indicated on several occasions that this was not possible: the status quo could not survive these demands for a new arrangement. Two days before New Zealand's election, for instance, two members of the U.S. House of Representatives, Stephen Solarz and Joel Pritchard, visited Wellington. Both served on the House Foreign Affairs Subcommittee on East Asia and the Pacific, Solarz as the committee's chair. Their message was that "the United States could impose . . . trade sanctions . . . if Mr. Lange persisted in his party's policy" (Landais-Stamp and Rogers 1989, 62). An ANZUS council meeting only two days after the elections described "access by allied aircraft and ships to ports and airfields of ANZUS members as 'essential to the continuing effectiveness of the alliance'" (Camilleri 1987, 140). At a press conference after that meeting, Secretary of State George Schultz argued that there was no need to renegotiate ANZUS and openly wondered, "What kind of an alliance is it if the military forces of the countries involved are not able to be in contact with each other?" (quoted in Landais-Stamp and Rogers 1989, 64). The U.S. position was clear: there would be no pledges regarding the nuclear status of visiting American warships.

The situation came to a head in January 1985 when the United States formally requested that New Zealand allow a visit by the U.S.S. *Buchanan*, a ship that was capable of carrying nuclear weapons. The Americans did not say that the *Buchanan* was carrying nuclear weapons, but neither would they say that it was not. The Lange government rejected this and offered, instead, "to receive a substitute warship"—one that could not carry nuclear weapons (Camilleri 1987, 139).

After this rejection, the United States adopted a number of policies designed to demonstrate its unhappiness with New Zealand's position. It immediately cancelled a planned joint military exercise, withdrew an invitation to have New Zealand troops participate in an exercise in Korea, opened congressional hearings to discuss suspension of U.S. defense obligations to New Zealand, cut visits by senior U.S. defense personnel, terminated the training of New Zealand personnel in the United States, and withheld classified intelligence (see McMillan 1987; Albinski 1988; Camilleri 1987; and Pugh 1989). Despite these clear signals of American displeasure, New Zealand maintained its policy of not allowing nuclear-capable ships to call at its ports. In August 1986 the United States rescinded its promise to provide security to New Zealand.

New Zealand's actions are, from our theory's perspective, change seeking: New Zealand altered the status quo and, in effect, traded the maintenance provided through ANZUS for this change. Our theory suggests that in a parliamentary democracy, policy changes occur with changes in government, as is the case here. The 1984 election that resulted in the Labour Party's assumption of power is, of course, critical to the subsequent events. Further, one of the motivations to seek this change when it did was the diminution of the Soviet threat to New Zealand's sovereignty. From the beginning, the alliance with the United States had been seen as providing security for an extremely unlikely event: an attack on New Zealand. The decline of the Soviet threat, the fissures between China and Vietnam, and the continued courting of China by the West all served to decrease the value New Zealand placed on the American security guarantee. Our theory predicts that the perceived level of threat from the international system affects the relative preference for maintenance and change. In this case, the international threat was declining, leading to a fall in the value of the maintenance New Zealand received from ANZUS and increasing the relative preference for change. In addition, the Reagan administration's policy of confrontation with the Soviet Union was not popular in New Zealand, and continued support for the U.S. military strategy was increasingly politically expensive. The cost of continued acquiescence to American policy was prohibitive. The combination of the change in government and the decline in the perceived threat allowed for the conditions whereby New Zealand took actions that led to the end of its alliance with the United States.

Our last case is an application of our model to the general pattern of a specific state's foreign policy. Rather than look at specific decisions, we want to see how insights from our model allow us to understand, in a general way, a country's foreign policy behavior. We apply our model to the People's Republic of China.

Chinese Foreign Policy since 1949

China is an alluring and fascinating country to study. Many foreign policy scholars and practitioners who study the country work from the premise that Chinese philosophy, society, culture, and history create a unique combination of factors that require a thorough familiarity with the Chinese history and people before any true understanding can be achieved.[13] Of course, they are correct: China *is* unique. But that is a long way from concluding that no general theories, gleaned from studying other areas of the world, at any time, can tell us anything of value about China or any other country.

In our discipline, we often share the assumption that different and seemingly unique historical periods nonetheless have things in common with other periods and that we often learn general things from studying one specific thing. For example, academic references to Thucydides, who described and

---

[13] Indeed, many regional specialists start with the assumption that the area they study is unique. Middle East specialists, in particular, are at times moved to argue that without a complete immersion in the languages, religions, and histories of the peoples of the region, any claims to understanding the sources of that region's problems and situations are vacuous.

analyzed the Peloponnesian Wars of 431 through 403 BC, are common. Clearly we believe the behavior of the Greek city-states is related to the behavior of modern states. While many aspects of life in ancient Greece were fundamentally different from modern living, there are sufficient commonalities to make the lessons drawn from the study of the Greek city-states relevant to our times. To provide another example, one well-respected research project, led by Claudio Cioffi-Revilla at George Mason University, studies the conflict behavior of the Chinese warlords from 7200 to 722 BC (see Cioffi-Revilla and Lai 2001). The assumption of this project, which we share, is that the actions of the warring states of China can be used to test some of the theories developed to explain the behavior of contemporary international relations. Again, the starting point of this research is that whatever the unique characteristics of a specific historical time and place, there are common factors that link them.

What we want to do in this section is, in a manner of speaking, work backward. Rather than deriving broad generalities or theories from the study of a particular time and place, we want to apply our general theory to a specific country. Since our general theory has very few restrictions to its application, we should be able to do this.

To analyze China's international behavior, we concentrate on three components of foreign policy: conflict involvement, alliance participation, and foreign aid. Each of these components is a widely recognized and discussed aspect of a state's foreign policy. We first look at China's involvement in international conflict.

In our view of international relations, the role of militarized conflict initiation is simple: states initiate militarized conflict in an attempt to change the status quo. That is, the initiation of conflict is change-seeking behavior.[14] To be sure, change seekers have a range of other policy options available, but the probability of conflict initiation is greatest in countries highly motivated to alter the status quo in a direction they favor—specifically, in relatively strong countries increasing in power. Since China is a relatively strong country, we expect it to initiate conflict when it is increasing in capability. We subjected this expectation to analysis. We used the MID data set, which records all threats, displays, or uses of military force by one nation against another (Jones, Bremer, and Singer, 1996). We focus, of course, on the disputes that involved China; from 1949 through 1992 (the last year for which we have complete dispute data) China was involved in 118 military conflicts. To capture the relative power of China, we used two measures, both derived from the widely used Correlates of War Project. The first is China's share of the world's economic

---

[14] As we have argued, the initiation of a militarized conflict may on occasion be a maintenance-seeking act designed to preempt an attack by another country. While we think it more likely that the initiator of a particular conflict is the state most interested in altering the status quo, the exceptions to this make our model harder to prove but they do not invalidate the empirical applications of it.

TABLE 4.1
Effect of Economic Factors on the Likelihood of the Initiation of Militarized Disputes,
China, 1950-1992

China's share of the world economy	−0.373***
	(0.090)
Change in China's share of the world economy	−1.45*
	(0.770)
Interaction of share and change in share	0.462**
	(0.193)
Constant	1.67***
	(0.301)
Log-likelihood Full Model	−58.80
Log-likelihood Null Model	−67.67
Chi-square	21.33
Significance	0.0000
N	43

Dependent variable: initiation of militarized dispute
One-tailed significance levels reported (* $p < .10$; ** $p < .05$; *** $p < .01$)
Standard errors in parentheses.

production, measured by a combination of iron and steel production and energy consumption.[15] We use this because China's recent growth in power (and
its conceivable decline) is most manifest to its political leaders in the economic
realm, and we are trying to tap the leaders' perception. Our model predicts
that as a state grows in capability, it will initiate more militarized disputes in an
attempt to alter the status quo, and that the relationship increases with greater
power. In other words, this slope increases exponentially. Here, we focus on an
analysis of China's involvement in international disputes to see if our model's
general expectations are confirmed. In this analysis, the dependent variable is
the number of times in a particular year China initiated the use of force against
another state. Since this is a count variable, we use Poisson regression. We use
three explanatory variables: China's share of the world's economy; the change
from one year to the next in that share; and an interactive variable formed by
multiplying the first two variables together. The results of the analysis are displayed in table 4.1.

The results show that all three independent variables have significant effects
on the likelihood of China's initiating the use of force against another state.
The size of China's share of the world economy has a negative effect on the
likelihood of China's initiating militarized disputes, as does the change in that
share. However, the positive coefficient on the interactive variable has a strong

[15] China's share of the world's economy using this measure is around 15 percent though it has
grown dramatically in the last ten years, at least according to Chinese accounts.

TABLE 4.2

Five Hypothetical Situations of China's Economic Growth and the Effect on the
Likelihood of the Initiation of Conflict

Growth in Chinese Economy	Growth in World Economy	Probability of the Initiation of No Conflicts	Probability of the Initiation of 1 Conflict	Probability of the Initiation of More than 1 Conflict
9.86%	3.6%	~0	0.001	0.999
15%	3.0%	~0	~0	~1.0
6.0%	3.0%	0.82	0.17	0.01
3.0%	3.0%	0.98	0.02	~0
0%	3.0%	0.99	~0.01	~0

effect on the predicted likelihood of initiation of conflict, such that the more
China's share of the world economy grows, the more likely it is to initiate conflict with other countries.

We can use these results, derived from the application of our general theory,
to make some predictions about China's future dispute involvement. To illustrate the effect of a growing Chinese economy on the likelihood of China's initiating international conflict in a particular year, we construct five hypothetical situations. These five alternatives present different possible growth rates
for the Chinese and world economies. In the first, the Chinese economy grows
at 9.86 percent while the world's economy increases 3.6 percent, both numbers
representing the averages for the years 1994–98, according to the International
Monetary Fund (1998). As table 4.2 shows, with these growth rates, there is a
very high probability (approaching 1.0) that China would initiate more than
one militarized dispute in a year. The other four cases present the Chinese
economy growing at different rates while the world economy grows at 3 percent. The probability of initiating at least one dispute increases rapidly once
the Chinese economy grows faster than the world's, and the probability that
China would initiate more than 1 dispute becomes significant once the Chinese economy grows at a rate faster than 6 percent.

Applying our model to China indicates that should China's economy continue to grow at a pace faster than the world's economy, it is very likely that
China will initiate militarized conflicts with other states. Some of those conflicts may escalate, while the majority are likely to be at a relatively low level of
hostility. We do not see, for instance, a significant probability that China will
initiate a major war in the near future. But we do predict that China will make
greater efforts at altering the status quo in directions it favors and will do so, in
part, through the exercise of the threat or use of military force. Should China's
economic growth slow to something like 5 percent a year or less, on the other

hand, we can anticipate a relatively nonassertive China, at least in terms of the initiation of international conflict is concerned.

The second area of Chinese foreign policy we investigate is alliance membership. As we saw in our story of New Zealand's dealings with the United States, states join and remain in alliances in order to gain either maintenance or change more efficiently than they could without the alliance. Our model implies that strong states, particularly strong states getting stronger, are more likely to form asymmetrical alliances with smaller states. By doing that, the stronger states are able to gain change. Through the cold war, China's foreign policy was remarkable for its very few formal allies. China had a defense pact with North Korea, in force since 1961, and bilateral neutrality pacts with Guinea, Afghanistan, and Burma (each since 1960), with Ghana since 1961, with Tanzania since 1965, and with Japan since 1978. The Soviet Union, of course, had a defense pact with China from 1950 to 1961. After the cold war, China signed nonaggression pacts with Mongolia and Ukraine, both in 1994.

One of our model's direct implications is that China will continue to attempt to form more asymmetrical alliances with smaller states as it becomes more powerful. Indeed, we predicted an expansion of China's alliance ties several years ago (Morgan and Palmer 1999). We present here some of what we wrote then:

> Any observed alliance represents a jointly preferred arrangement over no alliance. If China (as our model suggests) gains *change* through the formation of an asymmetrical alliance, it must provide *maintenance* to its new partner, and that partner must be willing to allow Chinese influence over its domestic and/or foreign policies. This will require one of two changes in situation. First, China's demands on a potential new ally must be modest enough to be acceptable to the new ally. This will mean, most centrally, that China make no demands for fundamental alterations in the political or economic structure of its new partner. Smaller and less extreme demands are more likely to be acceptable. Second, the international situation may become increasingly threatening to one of China's potential allies, such that it may come to value an alliance with the People's Republic. Until either of these two conditions is realized, new Chinese alliances are unlikely. (52–53)

Since we wrote that paragraph, China has formed alliances in the form of nonaggression pacts with Kyrgyzstan (in June 2002) and Kazakhstan (December 2002).[16] Each conforms nicely to our expectations. In each case, China achieved a modest change in policy: both Kyrgyzstan and Kazakhstan accepted China's longstanding position that "there is but one China and that Taiwan is a part of China." What did the smaller countries receive in return? First, in each alliance both sides promised to make no territorial demands on the other, something of value for both Kyrgyzstan and Kazakhstan as they

---

[16] We thank Ashley Leeds for providing us with these examples.

seek to demarcate and delineate their borders with neighboring countries in the wake of the collapse of the Soviet Union. Second, the Chinese promise not to use force against them allows each to pursue their other policy goals more vigorously.[17] Specifically, Kyrgyzstan has an ongoing border disagreement with Uzbekistan and another with Tajikistan, and Chinese support, or at least promises of nonaggression, will prove useful. Kazakhstan has the largest oil reserves in the Caspian Sea region (about two-thirds of the current daily production in the area). Kazakhstan's relations with its neighbors—Russia, Turkmenistan, and Azerbaijan in particular—are expected to be complicated by uncertainty regarding control of the Caspian seabed, shared oilfields, pipeline routes, and resulting environmental issues. Chinese political support in its relations with these countries is clearly worth the small price associated with adopting the Chinese position on Taiwan.

As China continues to grow in capability, we can anticipate that it will seek new allies. The two-good model can address the effects of new ties on both China and its new allies. To illustrate these anticipated effects, we consider the ramifications of China's hypothetical formation of bilateral alliances with Pakistan and Laos. In particular, we can predict the effects of the formation of a new alliance on China's subsequent conflict behavior and on its defense spending.[18] In making these predictions, we assume that Laos's and Pakistan's current relative capabilities are approximately what they were in 1992, the last year for which we have complete data; we assume that neither is increasing its capability significantly; and we assume that China is increasing its power at about 6 percent per year.[19] Under the assumptions we have made about Chinese bilateral alliances with Laos or Pakistan, should those or similar alliances be realized, the probability that People's Republic will initiate an international dispute will increase by slightly more than one-third. Additionally, the probabilities that either of those two countries will initiate a dispute increase by about 20 percent.

Next is our estimate of the effect of the new alliances on China's defense expenditure. Simply, as we will show in chapter 7, our model shows that joining new alliances with weaker allies has the effect of increasing a state's defense spending. (Weaker states' spending goes up more than stronger states' spending, other things being equal.) China's military spending increased at an average rate of slightly less than 2.8 percent per year from 1991 through 1995, according to the World Military Expenditures and Arms Transfers (1996).

---

[17] In chapter 7 we will present at greater length the argument that smaller states, having achieved maintenance in their alliances with more powerful states, will subsequently pursue change through their foreign policies more actively.

[18] The statistical model we use to derive these predictions is presented in Morgan and Palmer (1999).

[19] This, of course, may be far too conservative an estimate. As we just showed, the stronger Chinese economic growth, the more likely is conflict initiation, and that likelihood would increase exponentially.

Should it join a new alliance, we expect China's military spending to increase at about 7.1 percent per year for the subsequent five years, leading to an increase of about 41 percent over five years.[20] According to our model's general empirical findings, that spending is likely to be seen largely in capital-intensive areas of the military establishment, such as a deep-water navy. A greater ability to project force would result.

The last area of Chinese foreign policy we investigate is foreign aid. In our model of foreign policy, states give foreign aid in order to extract concessions from the recipient nation (see Palmer, Wohlander, and Morgan 2002). Foreign aid can, depending on the precise circumstances, serve maintenance- or change-seeking ends, but by and large it is given in order to alter policies in the recipient. Indeed, foreign aid is one of the most effective change-seeking policies available to a state. Our model therefore sees aid as given more by large states than by weaker states and more by large states increasing in power. When we apply our model to China, we might expect to see that China's foreign aid has increased dramatically as its economic situation has improved. That, however, is not the case.

We undertook a series of statistical analyses of the major economic and political causes of changes in Chinese foreign aid from 1956 through 1987, the last year for which we have reliable aid data. In brief, we found no statistical relationship between changes in Chinese aid and any political or economic factors that we normally associated with the donation of foreign aid. Rather than being defined and largely determined by structural factors, Chinese foreign aid appears to be an aspect of foreign policy that is strongly affected by political considerations and that is easily manipulable.[21] There are few domestic interest groups that push for continued or increased foreign aid, while other institutional actors (primarily the People's Liberation Army) have significant political clout. Chinese aid has never reached very high levels, indicating that its effectiveness has never been terribly great.

But that is not the end of our story. Our general theory can be applied to the

---

[20] If Laos were to ally with China, we would expect its military spending to increase about 12.3 percent per year for five years. A new alliance with China would lead Pakistan to raise its military expenditures approximately 12.0 percent a year for five years.

[21] One analyst took note of a large decline in Chinese foreign aid in the late 1970s and sought to explain that drop. His primary explanation fits our model of foreign policy extremely well: "[B]y the mid-1970s China had already achieved the goals that had promoted it to increase its foreign aid program in the first place: it was a member of the United Nations, it had diplomatic relations with most developing countries, and it was regarded as a major force in the Third World" (Harding 1981, 275). In our words, the use of foreign aid as a change-seeking aspect of foreign policy had succeeded, and China moved to deemphasize that goal.

Our model provides for states to change their foreign policy orientation if they are satisfied with the status quo, but we do not want to use changes in policy to reveal that satisfaction to us. To do that would make our model and arguments circular: "China reduced foreign aid because it was satisfied, and we know China was satisfied because it cut foreign aid."

TABLE 4.3
The Effects of Dispute Involvement on Changes in Foreign Aid

Change in China's Share of the World Economy	−4.32
	(34.70)
China's Involvement in an International Dispute? (1 = yes; 0 = no)	−701.00***
	(143.55)
Constant	680.61***
	(142.37)
R^2	0.446
F-Statistic	12.06
Significance	0.0001
N	37

Dependent variable: yearly change in foreign aid
Two-tailed significance levels reported (* $p < .10$; ** $p < .05$; *** $p < .01$)
Standard errors in parentheses.

phenomenon of foreign policy substitutability. Essentially, as we will argue in greater depth in chapter 7, when a state seeks to pursue one of our goods, change or maintenance, it has a set of policies that are better able to accomplish that relative to some other group of policies. When it pursues a particular good, for instance, change, by increasing emphasis on one policy, such as foreign aid, we expect to see a subsequent decline in the emphasis on another policy that is generally used for pursuit of that same good. However, we expect little effect on policies that are better at achieving the other good. We have applied these general expectations and found that they are well supported (Morgan and Palmer 2000). It appears that some policies are substitutable for each other, while others are not.

Two policies our model identifies as relatively efficient at pursuing change are foreign aid and conflict initiation. We looked at those two policies to determine whether a change in emphasis on foreign aid is associated with the involvement in conflict. We applied ordinary least squares[22] to an equation where the dependent variable was change in Chinese foreign aid from one year to the subsequent year, measured in millions of U.S. dollars. Two independent variables were used: the first measured the change in China's share of the world economy and the second was a simple dummy variable that captured whether China was involved in a militarized interstate dispute in a particular year. The results are shown in table 4.3.

As the table shows, involvement in interstate disputes has a significant and strong effect on Chinese foreign aid: in years when the People's Republic is involved in militarized conflict, its foreign aid allocations are about $700 million

[22] Ordinary least squares was appropriate for this particular analysis, as there was little serial correlation in the error terms. The Durbin-Watson statistic using the OLS equation was 2.06.

less than in years when it is not involved. We have strong evidence that involvement in conflict and foreign aid allocations are substitutable policies. Each policy is efficient at the production of change. When the Chinese decision makers emphasize conflict, fewer resources are allocated to aid; when conflict is absent, more is allocated to aid.[23]

In summary, the allocation of foreign aid is not affected directly by changes in China's economic well-being, or by any other large factors. Instead we find, consistent with our theory of foreign policy substitutability, that there is a direct, significant, and large trade-off between China's conflict involvement and its foreign aid allocations.

One particularly interesting result of applying the two-good model of foreign policy to an evaluation of Chinese foreign policy is our finding that since the early 1980s, the Chinese have engaged in far less change-seeking policy behaviors than one would have expected, given their level of capabilities. They have initiated few militarized disputes, they have formed few alliances with smaller countries, they have provided little foreign aid, and their ability to project force remains underdeveloped relative to other states that have been in similar positions with regard to capability. The evidence we have is consistent with the inference that the Chinese, at least since 1980, have been remarkably maintenance seeking, considering their capabilities. This is not to say that they have sought no change or that the amount of change sought is unrelated to increases in capabilities. Furthermore, we cannot be absolutely certain that this will continue into the future, particularly as China undergoes changes in leadership.

That the Chinese are unique is no surprise to China experts, but it is interesting to note that their patterns of behavior still conform to the general model in spite of this uniqueness. In fact, the theory we offer provides a parsimonious way of characterizing their unique attributes. If we assume that the pattern of preferences over change and maintenance holds, however, we can conclude that the Chinese are not the significant threat to international stability that many seem to fear. The Chinese are maintenance oriented and will defend their interests, but they are not likely to seek a large number of significant international changes. To speculate on a specific example (and we note that this goes beyond what the model tells us), we would not expect the Chinese to attempt to force the reintegration of Taiwan with the mainland. However, if there appears to be an effort to change the status of Taiwan in a way contrary to the mainland's wishes (for example, independence), we would expect them to react vigorously. In short, if the United States, or anyone else, treats them as an enemy, they are likely to become one, but this enmity is not an inevitable result of Chinese preferences.

---

[23] Note also that changes in China's share of the world economy have no significant effect on changes in foreign aid allocation. That is consistent with other the findings in other analyses that we undertook: structural factors seem not to affect foreign aid decisions.

Conclusion

In this chapter we have applied our model to three cases. These applications have not been designed to test the theory. Instead, our purpose has been to show that the general theory is really that: general. It can be used to explain a variety of different behaviors. Specific decisions as well as general patterns of behavior can be fruitfully analyzed using the theory. We have looked at two state actions that are difficult or impossible to explain using more standard theories of international behavior. That a powerful state would surrender large tracts of land, segments of its population, and industrial capacity when it had not been fully defeated militarily is something that a realpolitik approach finds hard to explain. That a small state allied with a more powerful one would press a demand to the point where the larger one disbands the alliance is an action that appears baffling at first. We think the two-good theory does a reasonable job of providing understandings for each of these cases. In analyzing Chinese foreign policy, we have shown that the model can be valuably applied to a specific country and some interesting insights can be gained.

In the next chapters we take a different approach. We turn in chapter 5 to a more formal presentation of our theory, making explicit the assumptions and the logic of the theory. We then test some of the hypotheses we presented in chapter 2, focusing in turn on two basic questions. In chapter 6 we look at the effect of environmental factors on single policies. In that chapter and in chapter 7, we investigate more fully the implications of the two-good theory for foreign policy substitutability. That is, we look at the relations among various policies to see how they affect one another. We will show that the two-good theory is useful in explaining not only individual policies but also how the desire of states to construct their most preferred set of polices—given their relative capability—helps us explain the relations among those policies.

5

The Two-Good Theory Formalized

CHAPTER 2 WAS devoted to a non-formal development of our theory. We identified the major concepts upon which the theory is based; we presented and justified our main assumptions; and we specified some of the primary hypotheses that follow from the model. We then demonstrated that our theory provides a foundation from which to explain historical patterns and real world events in foreign policy. Here, we turn to the development of the formal, mathematical version of our theory. This will serve to make our assumptions more precise and will make the logic by which we reach our hypotheses more explicit. It will also provide a more rigorous guide for the systematic, large-N tests of many of our hypotheses that are presented in subsequent chapters.

Since we have discussed our concepts and assumptions earlier, we keep such considerations to a minimum in this chapter. It is worth reiterating, however, that we adopt a number of common assumptions. We assume that international relations consists of a multidimensional issue space consisting of the outcomes (or status quo) on all the issues upon which states in the international system hold divergent preferences; we assume that all states want to change the outcomes on some of the dimensions and want to maintain the outcomes on others. We assume as well that actors behave as if they are rational, in the sense that they have connected and transitive preference orderings, and that they are expected utility maximizers. Furthermore, we assume throughout that states are unitary actors with respect to carrying out foreign policy. The model does not require this assumption and, in fact, is designed to provide a means by which we can incorporate domestic politics into our analyses (see Morgan and Palmer 1998). For our purposes here, however, it is sufficient and much simpler to assume that domestic actors' preferences have been aggregated into a single preference ordering for the state.

The two-good theory, as we will shortly show, is meant to explain what states consider when making foreign policy decisions. Specifically, the two-good theory has states attempting to form and to protect the most desired set of outcomes within this multidimensional issue space that they can, given the limits of their capabilities. How they approach this matter of choice is the model's subject.

The Basic Model

The first assumption of our theory is that states attempt to produce two composite goods, change and maintenance, through their foreign policies and that these goods can be produced in greater or lesser amounts. The quantities of these goods, which we denote as Q_m and Q_c, are the outputs of foreign policy. This is a special case of a more general model that we presented elsewhere (Morgan and Palmer 2000). The more general model allows for states to pursue any number of goods through their foreign policies; it generalizes neorealism (which assumes states pursue one good, security) as well as the theory presented here. From our discussion here, it will be fairly easy to see how this theory can quickly generalize to more than two goods.

We further assume that a state's utility derived from foreign policy is a function of the quantity of each of the two goods produced. In particular, we specify

$$U = Q_m^{\pi_1} \times Q_c^{\pi_2} \qquad\qquad \{\text{Eq. 1}\}$$

The π parameters represent, in essence, how salient each of the goods is, relative to the other, for the state. Large values of π on Q_m, for instance, would imply that the state strongly values maintenance relative to change. We would expect such a state, acting to maximize the utility it derives from its foreign policy portfolio, to act largely—though not exclusively—to protect aspects of the status quo that it likes.

Next, we assume that each state has some amount of resources available to devote to foreign policy. These resources can be economic (capital, labor, raw materials) or political (time, attention, moral suasion). We further assume that the amount of resources a state has for foreign policy is largely dependent on the total resources available to the state—that is, big, rich states that are well endowed with natural resources devote more to foreign policy than do small, poor states. Presumably, no state devotes all of its resources to foreign policy; some are retained for domestic consumption and investment. The proportion of a state's available resources that are devoted to foreign policy is thus dependent on the preferences of the state for foreign policy goods as well as on the exigencies of the international environment. We label the amount of resources available to a state for dedication to foreign policy actions as b.

An example of this model is depicted in figure 5.1. The vertical axis represents the amount of maintenance and the horizontal axis represents the amount of change that the state produces through its foreign policy portfolio. Points in the space are associated with the production of specific amounts of

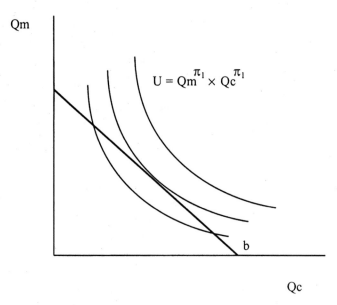

Figure 5.1. The Basic Two-Good Model

each good.[1] Curve b represents the production possibility frontier (PPF), or the maximum amount of foreign policy that can be produced, given the budget available for foreign policy and the various constraints (environmental, technological) facing the state. The other curves are the state's indifference contours, which reflect its preferences over maintenance and change. The state always prefers more of either good to less, but it must often make trade-offs over the two goods. The state is indifferent among all combinations of maintenance and change that fall on a given curve, and it prefers any combination on a curve farther to the northeast to any combination on a curve farther to the southwest. The state in this example values maintenance and change about equally, but the model can reflect, through the π parameters, cases in which a state places far greater salience on one of the goods.

The primary foreign policy decision for a state involves determining how much of each good to produce. Clearly, the state will adopt some portfolio of policies that places it on b. It does not have sufficient resources to produce quantities of maintenance and change beyond b, and it would be wasting resources if it adopted a portfolio that placed it beneath b. Since the state seeks to

[1] Note that a point in the space is not necessarily associated with a specific portfolio of foreign policies. Since several policies produce maintenance and several policies produces change, several combinations of policies can produce any particular combination of the two goods.

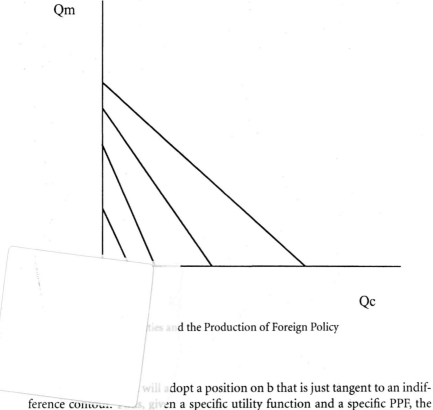

Qm

Qc

ies and the Production of Foreign Policy

will adopt a position on b that is just tangent to an indifference contour. Thus, given a specific utility function and a specific PPF, the model provides a precise equilibrium prediction regarding the amounts of change and maintenance the state will produce through its foreign policies. These amounts will change as conditions affecting the PPF change, providing us the means to derive hypotheses associating various factors with changes in foreign policy behavior.

Recall from chapter 2 that we assume b changes as the state's capabilities increase (or decrease). Obviously, increasing capabilities will move b outward; states with more resources to devote to foreign policy will produce more foreign policy goods. We also assume, however, that a state's ability to produce change increases at an increasing rate as capabilities rise. This is depicted in figure 5.2. Several PPFs are shown in this figure. Note that as we move farther from the origin, the amount of change that can be produced increases faster than the amount of maintenance that can be produced.

At this point we can derive a number of hypotheses relating changes in capabilities to changes in foreign policy. To accomplish this, we must state our assumptions mathematically. A state's indifference contours are defined by equation 1, which captures our assumption that the state's utility is a function of the quantity of maintenance and change produced by its foreign policy portfolio:

$$U = Q_m^{\pi_1} \times Q_c^{\pi_2}. \qquad \{\text{Eq. 1}\}$$

Next, we define the PPF as

$$Q_m = b - \Omega Q_c, \qquad \{\text{Eq. 2}\}$$

which can be rewritten as

$$Q_m + \Omega Q_c = b. \qquad \{\text{Eq. 3}\}$$

Here, b captures the maximum amount of foreign policy goods the state can produce. Increases in capabilities (or decreases in environmental, technological, or other constraints) are reflected through increases in b. Our assumption that the state's ability to produce change increases at an increasing rate as capabilities rise is captured by Ω. We assume that as b increases, Ω decreases.

Two things regarding the mathematical statement of our assumptions are worth noting. First, we have not incorporated the assumption that the state's ability to produce maintenance increases at a decreasing rate as b increases. As will be seen, we can derive our hypotheses in this treatment without that assumption. We omit it for simplicity. Second, we have defined a PPF that is linear. Our conceptualization of the model is more general, incorporating any non-convex PPF. We restrict the generality of the formal derivation of our hypotheses to simplify the mathematical treatment. The argument and fundamental, substantive conclusions do not change in the more general treatment, and they are *much* easier to follow with the assumption of a linear PPF. We restrict the generality of our formal treatment to clarify the exposition of our argument.

Returning to our discussion, the expectation is that the state will adopt a foreign policy portfolio that produces the mixture of change and maintenance that maximizes U, subject to the constraint imposed by b. This is determined by finding, for a PPF of a particular b, the indifference contour that is just tangent to the PPF. Thus, we want to maximize $U = Q_m^{\pi_1} \times Q_c^{\pi_2}$ subject to $Q_m + \Omega Q_c = b$.

We accomplish this by setting up the Lagrangian

$$L = Q_m^{\pi_1} \times Q_c^{\pi_2} + \lambda(b - Q_m - \Omega Q_c). \qquad \{\text{Eq. 4}\}$$

Since we can maximize U by maximizing $\ln U$, we solve

$$L = \ln Q_m \times \pi_1 + \ln Q_c \times \pi_2 + \lambda(b - Q_m - \Omega Q_c). \qquad \{Eq.\ 5\}$$

Taking the partial derivative of L with respect to each good, setting this equal to zero, and solving for the good, gives

$$\frac{\partial L}{\partial Q_m} = \frac{\pi_1}{Q_m} - \lambda = 0;$$
$$Q_m = \frac{\pi_1}{\lambda} \qquad \{Eq.\ 6\}$$

and

$$\frac{\partial L}{\partial Q_c} = \frac{\pi_2}{Q_c} - \Omega\lambda = 0;$$
$$Q_c = \frac{\pi_2}{\Omega\lambda}. \qquad \{Eq.\ 7\}$$

Since

$$\frac{\partial L}{\partial \lambda} = b - Q_m - \Omega Q_c$$
$$b = \frac{\pi_1}{\lambda} + \frac{\Omega \pi_2}{\lambda\Omega}$$

and

$$\lambda = \frac{\pi_1 + \pi_2}{b}. \qquad \{Eq.\ 8\}$$

Thus,

$$Q_m = \frac{\pi_1 b}{\pi_1 + \pi_2} \qquad \{Eq.\ 9\}$$

$$Q_c = \frac{\pi_2 b}{(\pi_1 + \pi_2)\Omega}. \qquad \{Eq.\ 10\}$$

Equations 9 and 10 specify the optimal quantities of maintenance and change that can be produced by a state's having a utility function of the specified form (that is, $U = Q_m^{\pi_1} \times Q_c^{\pi_2}$) and constrained by a PPF of the form $Q_m = b - \Omega Q_c$. It is a straightforward exercise to use these equations to determine how foreign policy, in terms of the amounts of maintenance and change produced, will respond to variations in the parameters making up the model. First, if π_1 increases relative to π_2, indicating that the state has a higher salience for maintenance, the production of maintenance will increase and the production of change will decrease. Thus, states that place a greater emphasis on maintenance than change are expected to devote a greater proportion of their foreign policy resources to the production of maintenance and should engage in more behaviors intended to produce maintenance, on average, than do states that place a greater emphasis on change. Of course, the converse is true if π_2 increases relative to π_1.

Second, since b is in the numerator of both ratios, we can conclude that as the resources available for foreign policy increase,[2] states will produce more of both goods. In other words, we expect strong states to engage in more of all types of foreign policy, on average, than do weak states. Similarly, we expect any state experiencing an increase in capabilities to increase its production of both change and maintenance.

Finally, Ω decreases as b increases, which captures our assumption that the ability to produce change increases at an increasing rate as capabilities rise. Since Ω is in the denominator of the ratio determining Q_c, we can see that the production of change will increase at a rate faster than that for the production of maintenance as capabilities increase.

These conclusions are captured graphically in figures 5.3a and 5.3b. In figure 5.3a, we have a single PPF with three utility functions. In the first utility function $\pi_1 > \pi_2$, indicating that maintenance is of higher salience for the state than is change. In the second $\pi_1 = \pi_2$, indicating that the state cares about maintenance and change equally. In the third $\pi_1 < \pi_2$, indicating that change is more important than is maintenance. It is easy to see that, holding the resources available for foreign policy constant, these differences in preferences produce very different foreign policy portfolios. Simply put, the more one cares about a particular foreign policy good, the more of that good (and the less of the other good) one will produce. Figure 5.3b depicts three PPFs representing different capability levels for the state, and three corresponding indifference contours, over which π_1 and π_2 are held constant. Here, we can see that as capabilities increase, the amount of both goods produced also increases but that the production of change increases at an increasing rate and the production of maintenance increases at a decreasing rate.

---

[2] Similar effects are produced when technological improvements or reductions in the constraints imposed by the international environment make given capabilities more efficient.

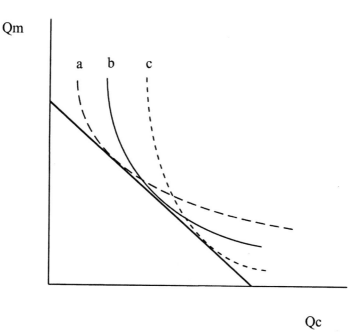

Figure 5.3a. Preferences and the Production of Foreign Policy

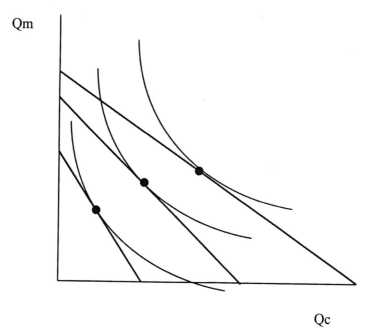

Figure 5.3b. Capabilities, Preferences, and Foreign Policy

These conclusions are sufficient to produce the first set of hypotheses presented in chapter 2. Basically, as capabilities increase we expect all types of foreign policy behaviors to increase. We expect the use of behaviors intended to produce maintenance (defense spending, dispute reciprocation, alliances with stronger powers) to increase at a decreasing rate. We also expect the use of behaviors intended to produce change (dispute initiation, foreign aid, alliances with weaker powers) to increase at an increasing rate.

Some of these conclusions are, in general, not too surprising. That states devote more resources to the production of the good they value more and that states with more resources engage in more foreign policy activities are intuitive findings. We would doubt any model that produced other conclusions.

That states tend to be more change seeking as capabilities increase, regardless of preferences, is not intuitive. In fact, this hypothesis is directly contrary to the assertions of some well-known and widely accepted perspectives on international relations. Power transition theory, for example, is premised on the notion that strong states are likely to be "satisfied" and therefore status quo oriented, while weak states are likely to be "dissatisfied." Our model suggests that the strong will make, on average, many more attempts to change the status quo than will the weak.[3]

This conclusion will not be surprising to those who adopt some other perspectives. It is, for example, very similar to the common realist dictum that "the strong do what they will, the weak do what they must." There are important differences, however. First and foremost, we do not assume that preferences are constant across all states. A weak state whose preferences weigh heavily toward change (that is, $\pi_2 \gg \pi_1$) can engage in more change-seeking behaviors than a strong state whose preferences weigh heavily toward maintenance. Second, we do not assume that preferences are associated with capabilities. The conclusion here, in other words, is not driven by an assumption that strong states prefer change more than weak states do. The conclusion is instead based on holding individual states' preferences constant over varying capability levels and assuming that there is no systematic relationship between capability level and preferences across states. Thus, while this conclusion is similar to that advanced by some other perspectives, we believe it is based on a simpler and more elegant logic.

The conclusions presented to this point lead to hypotheses associating variations in state environmental situations—particularly pertaining to a state's relative capabilities—with broad variations in state foreign policy portfolios.

---

[3] Keep in mind that our notion of the status quo is different from that used in the power transition theory. Nevertheless, our conclusion is contrary to what one would conclude from the power transition theory.

The model also leads to conclusions regarding the relationships among various foreign policy actions. We now turn to an analysis of these questions.

The Instruments of Foreign Policy

Foreign policy decisions, in this model, are essentially decisions over how to allocate available resources, characterized by the parameter b, among policy inputs. These inputs are the behaviors that analysts normally observe and attempt to explain: arms expenditures, alliances, dispute behavior, foreign aid, and so forth. Engaging in these behaviors consumes resources and produces outputs in terms of the foreign policy goals, Q_m and Q_c. We denote the amount of resources devoted to a particular input by I_i, and we assume that the entire foreign policy budget is used, so

$$b = \sum_{i=1}^{m} I_i. \qquad\qquad \{\text{Eq. 11}\}$$

These inputs combine to produce particular outputs according to a relevant production function, which we specify as

$$Q_m = I_1^{\alpha_1} \times I_2^{\beta_1} \times \cdots \times I_m^{\omega_1} \text{ for maintenance, and}$$
$$Q_c = I_1^{\alpha_2} \times I_2^{\beta_2} \times \cdots \times I_m^{\omega_2} \text{ for change.}$$

$$\{\text{Eq. 12}\}$$

The exponents represent the efficiency with which the associated inputs contribute to the production of a particular good.

Most questions addressed by foreign policy analysts center on attempts at explaining the sorts of behaviors we identify as the foreign policy inputs: How do we account for the level of arms expenditures in a particular country? What accounts for the decisions states make regarding whether to form an alliance? How do we explain decisions to initiate or escalate a dispute? From the perspective of the theory advanced here, each of these questions basically focuses on the decisions states make regarding how they allocate their foreign policy resources among policy alternatives and is motivated by a desire to understand why changes in these allocations come about.

In the preceding section, we showed that for any given value of b and for any given set of parameters specifying the utility and production functions, there exist amounts of maintenance and change that maximize U. Here, we focus on the allocation of b over the available I that produces these amounts of change and maintenance and we determine how this allocation varies with changes in the parameters. We present this derivation for a case in which there are four inputs, or policies, available to the state ($m = 4$). Once this is accomplished, it is quite easy to see how the result generalizes to cases of any m (and for any number of foreign policy goods). Generically, we label the foreign policy inputs as I_1, I_2, I_3, and I_4. To further simplify, we stipulate that I_1 and I_2 are used in the production of Q_m while I_3 and I_4 are used in the production of Q_c.[4]

Recall equation 1:

$$U = Q_m^{\pi_1} \times Q_c^{\pi_2}. \qquad \text{\{Eq. 1\}}$$

For this four-policy case, we have

$$Q_m = I_1^{\alpha_1} \times I_2^{\beta_1} \times I_3^{\gamma_1} \times I_4^{\varphi_1}, \text{ which reduces to}$$
$$Q_m = I_1^{\alpha_1} \times I_2^{\beta_1}, \text{ and} \qquad \text{\{Eq. 13\}}$$

$$Q_c = I_1^{\alpha_2} \times I_2^{\beta_2} \times I_3^{\gamma_2} \times I_4^{\varphi_2}, \text{ which reduces to}$$
$$Q_c = I_3^{\gamma_2} \times I_4^{\varphi_2} \qquad \text{\{Eq. 14\}}$$

subject to the constraint

$$b = I_1 + I_2 + I_3 + I_4. \qquad \text{\{Eq. 15\}}$$

Our problem is to find the allocation of the budget over the policy inputs that maximizes U subject to the constraints imposed by the equations specified. We solve this by substituting the equations for Q_m and Q_c into the equation for U, and setting up the Lagrangian

$$L = (I_1^{\alpha_1} \times I_2^{\beta_1})^{\pi_1} \times (I_3^{\gamma_2} \times I_4^{\varphi_2})^{\pi_2} + \lambda(b - I_1 - I_2 - I_3 - I_4). \qquad \text{\{Eq. 16\}}$$

[4] Note that this is not required by the formal model and, as will be seen, the generalization is straightforward. This is a fairly important point for potential future developments of the model. Recall that we assume that each foreign policy action contributes to the production of only one good (for example, foreign aid is assumed to produce change), even though we recognize that this is probably not the case. It is possible, within the existing framework of the model, to relax this assumption and allow each policy to contribute to the production of both goods. There is a fairly severe empirical problem in doing this, however. It would require that we determine how much each action contributes to the production of each good. Rather than tackle this particular problem at this stage, we have opted for simplicity.

Since we can maximize U by maximizing $\ln U$, we solve

$$L = \ln I_1 \times \pi_1\alpha_1 + \ln I_2 \times \pi_1\beta_1 + \ln I_3 \times \pi_2\gamma_2 + \ln I_4 \times \pi_2\varphi_2$$
$$+ \lambda(b - I_1 - I_2 - I_3 - I_4). \qquad \text{\{Eq. 17\}}$$

Taking the partial derivative of L with respect to each input, setting this equal to 0, and solving for the input, gives

$$\frac{\partial L}{\partial I_1} = \frac{\pi_1\alpha_1}{I_1} - \lambda = 0;$$

$$I_1 = \frac{\pi_1\alpha_1}{\lambda} \qquad \text{\{Eq. 18\}}$$

$$\frac{\partial L}{\partial I_2} = \frac{\pi_1\beta_1}{I_2} - \lambda = 0;$$

$$I_2 = \frac{\pi_1\beta_1}{\lambda} \qquad \text{\{Eq. 19\}}$$

$$\frac{\partial L}{\partial I_3} = \frac{\pi_2\gamma_2}{I_3} - \lambda = 0;$$

$$I_3 = \frac{\pi_2\gamma_2}{\lambda} \qquad \text{\{Eq. 20\}}$$

$$\frac{\partial L}{\partial I_4} = \frac{\pi_2\phi_2}{I_4} - \lambda = 0;$$

$$I_4 = \frac{\pi_2\phi_2}{\lambda}. \qquad \text{\{Eq. 21\}}$$

Now, since $\frac{\partial L}{\partial \lambda} = b - I_1 - I_2 - I_3 - I_4$, we can replace the inputs with the above terms and get

$$b = \frac{\pi_1\alpha_1}{\lambda} + \frac{\pi_1\beta_1}{\lambda} + \frac{\pi_2\gamma_2}{\lambda} + \frac{\pi_2\phi_2}{\lambda}. \qquad \text{\{Eq. 22\}}$$

Solving for λ gives

$$\lambda = \frac{\pi_1(\alpha_1 + \beta_1) + \pi_2(\gamma_2 + \phi_2)}{b}. \qquad \text{\{Eq. 23\}}$$

Replacing λ with this value in the equations above enables us to specify each input in terms of the variables included in the theory.

$$I_1 = \frac{\pi_1 \alpha_1 b}{\pi_1(\alpha_1 + \beta_1) + \pi_2(\gamma_2 + \phi_2)} \qquad \{\text{Eq. 24}\}$$

$$I_2 = \frac{\pi_1 \beta_1 b}{\pi_1(\alpha_1 + \beta_1) + \pi_2(\gamma_2 + \phi_2)} \qquad \{\text{Eq. 25}\}$$

$$I_3 = \frac{\pi_2 \gamma_2 b}{\pi_1(\alpha_1 + \beta_1) + \pi_2(\gamma_2 + \phi_2)} \qquad \{\text{Eq. 26}\}$$

$$I_4 = \frac{\pi_2 \phi_2 b}{\pi_1(\alpha_1 + \beta_1) + \pi_2(\gamma_2 + \phi_2)} \qquad \{\text{Eq. 27}\}$$

These equations constitute the core of our formal model. The key questions in an analysis of foreign policy are concerned with explaining or predicting specific behaviors, such as conflict initiation, alliance formation, arms expenditures, or foreign aid donations. Equations 24–27 specify the amount of resources devoted to each such policy as a function of the variables included in our theory. That is, the amount of any particular behavior by a state is determined by the foreign policy resources available to that state (b), the preferences of that state regarding the appropriate mix of maintenance and change (π_1 and π_2), and the efficiency with which each policy produces change or maintenance ($\alpha, \beta, \gamma, \varphi$). Our main hypotheses follow directly from a simple examination of these equations—we can easily determine the expected relationship between any of our independent variables and any foreign policy input.

Before turning to the derivation of our hypotheses, we wish to note that generalizing the model in several ways is quite straightforward. Note that this set of equations specifies the proportion of the state's foreign policy budget that is devoted to each input and then multiplies these proportions by the overall level of the budget. We can increase the number of inputs incorporated in the model easily. Each additional input would have an associated efficiency parameter that would appear in the numerator of that input's equation and in the denominators of all equations. Furthermore, we do not have to assume that each input contributes to only one output. Thus, I_1 may produce Q_2 as well as Q_1. If, for example, I_1 represents arms expenditures and this contributes to two goods (perhaps protecting the state's borders and projecting force abroad), we can assume that there are two armament inputs, one contributing to the production of each good, and that the overall level of arms expenditure is represented by the sum of these inputs: $I_{1_a} + I_{1_b} = I_1$.[5] Finally, it is easy to expand the model to allow for foreign policy to produce more than two goods or to capture the essence of realism by assuming that foreign policy serves to produce only one good (see Morgan and Palmer 2000).

Let us return to equations 24–27 to see what hypotheses can be derived from them. We can determine the effect of a given variable on a particular instrument of policy by seeing whether an increase (or decrease) in the parameter associated with the variable leads to an increase or decrease in the relevant I.[6]

Our first set of hypotheses is straightforward and, to be honest, obvious. Note that b, the amount of foreign policy resources available, appears in the numerator of every equation. Thus, every I will vary directly with b. That is, as the resources available for foreign policy increase, we expect an increase in every type of foreign policy activity. States with great capabilities should, on average, engage in more conflict, belong to more alliances, spend more on defense, provide more foreign aid, and simply be more involved in international affairs than are states with fewer capabilities. These comparisons can be taken as either cross-sectional or cross-temporal. That is, states with greater capabilities should engage in more activity than states with lesser capabilities; as a single state increases its capabilities, it should increase the amount of foreign policy activities in which it engages. Recall that the hypotheses do refer to general expectations. Some weak states may engage in more of some activities than do some strong states. However, this should not be the case, on average.

Second, the formal model also shows that preferences affect policy choices in a straightforward and intuitively obvious way. Recall that the state's relative preferences for maintenance and change are reflected in the πs. As the state's valuation for maintenance over change increases, π_1 increases, relative to π_2.

---

[5] Alternatively, we could assign an efficiency parameter for this input to each of the foreign policy goods. This would allow us to consider that the expenditure of a particular foreign policy resource is contributing, in some measure, to the production of both goods simultaneously. (Thus, for example, a foreign aid donation could be intended both to stabilize a government and to ease suffering.) This would, perhaps, lead to a more accurate theory, descriptively. It would definitely complicate the theory considerably, both mathematically and conceptually, however. For this reason, we have chosen to adopt the simplifying assumption that each input serves to produce only one good.

[6] Technically, we are engaged in comparative statics analysis. A complete formalization would require that for each variable and policy, we calculate the partial derivative of the equation with respect to the parameter representing the variable of interest. This is not really necessary in this case because the equations are quite simple. It is easy to determine whether there should be an increase, or decrease, in the policy by considering whether the variable appears in the numerator or denominator of the right side of the equation.

Consider the effect of increasing π_1 on I^1, an input that produces maintenance. From equation 24 we can see that π_1 appears in the denominator and in the numerator. We can also see that as π_1 increases, the value of I^1 must increase because the numerator will increase faster than the denominator. Thus, as state preferences vary in favor of maintenance, the resources devoted to a policy that produces maintenance will increase. We can easily see that this is the case for all policies—states will devote more resources, on average, to policies that produce the good they value most. As a state increases its valuation of maintenance over change, it will increase the resources devoted to defense spending, dispute reciprocation, and alliances with stronger powers while reducing the resources devoted to conflict initiation, foreign aid, alliances with smaller powers, and other change-seeking policies.

Third, the model shows that the efficiency with which a foreign policy input produces a foreign policy good affects the use of that input in a predictable way. Consider I^1 and I^2, the inputs that produce maintenance, for example. The α_1 and β_1 parameters reflect the efficiency with which I^1 and I^2, respectively, can be translated into maintenance. Suppose that I^1 refers to defense expenditures and I^2 refers to alliances with stronger powers. If some technological change improves the effectiveness of arms, a given amount of resources devoted to arms production would produce more maintenance than was previously the case. This improvement in the efficiency of I^1 would be reflected through an increase in α_1, relative to β_1. Note that the parameters representing the efficiency of each policy input are included in the denominator of equations 24–27. Each is also included in the numerator of the equation specifying the proportion of resources devoted to the policy input I with which it is associated. Thus, as the efficiency of a given input increases, relative to the other inputs, more resources will be devoted to that policy and fewer will be devoted to other policies.

Considered singly, these conclusions are intuitive. Clearly, states with more resources to devote to foreign policy will do so and states will produce more of the good they value the most. That states would allocate their foreign policy resources across policies in a way that would produce the most of what they want from foreign policy seems obvious. That they would adjust their allocation of resources in response to changes in the efficiency with which various policies serve their intended purposes is also intuitive. To our knowledge, however, no previous theory of foreign policy has incorporated all of these obvious conclusions as central derivations. Furthermore, these aspects of the model provide a means for explaining some findings that have struck many as perplexing. We will discuss several of these points in subsequent chapters as we present our empirical analyses. In the next section, we turn briefly to a discussion of foreign policy substitutability to show how our theory both accounts for empirical results that have confounded many and significantly refines our expectations regarding substitutability.

Foreign Policy Substitutability

The concept of foreign policy substitutability was developed by Most and Starr nearly two decades ago (1984, 1987). They noted that many empirical studies attempting to explain variations in the frequency with which foreign policy instruments (for example, dispute initiation) are used produced surprisingly weak results. They suggested that this could be the result of researchers ignoring the real possibility of foreign policy substitutability. That is, if a decision maker can address any specific foreign policy problem with any of several instruments (arms or alliances), we are unlikely to find significant, simple relationships explaining the variation in the use of any foreign policy tool. Further, if any particular instrument can be used to address several problems—that is, the motivations for initiating a policy can vary—investigations of the effects of any one policy on a particular issue are similarly unlikely to produce impressive findings.

Many scholars have found Most and Starr's argument compelling. Several attempted to test the argument by determining whether substitution between policies does occur. The primary hypothesis guiding these studies is that if two policies (for example, arms and alliances) are substitutes, then we should expect to observe an inverse relationship in their use. Unfortunately, these studies consistently found that the expected inverse relationship does not exist. The theory presented here can speak directly to the question of foreign policy substitutability. It suggests that the hypothesis guiding previous empirical work on substitutability is not correct and provides a more refined set of expectations.

Essentially, the search for substitutability involves examining how the use of one instrument of foreign policy affects the use of another instrument. For example, if a state joins an alliance, what effect does that have on that state's defense expenditures, on the likelihood that it will initiate a dispute, or on its foreign aid allocations? Existing empirical studies of substitutability are based on the notion that there will be an inverse relationship between policies that are substitutes for one another. That is, if a state increases the resources given to one policy, it must decrease the resources for substitutable policies. From the perspective of our theory, the effect on the use of other policies that is produced by an increase in the use of one policy depends centrally on why that increase occurred in the first place. Our model shows that there are three general factors that can lead a state to adjust its use of any given instrument of foreign policy, and that each factor has different implications for the state's use of other instruments.

Recall that equations 24–27 specify a state's usage of each instrument (input) of foreign policy as a function of the factors incorporated into our theory. Our hypotheses on substitutability follow from these equations. First, we again note that b, the amount of resources available for foreign policy, is in the numerator of each equation, suggesting that as the resources available for foreign policy go up, the use of every foreign policy instrument will increase. Thus, if we observe an increase in the use of one instrument of policy and that increase is the result of an increase in the resources available for foreign policy, we should expect a concurrent increase in the use of *all* other policies. We should expect there to be a strong tendency for variations in the use of different instruments of foreign policy to be related positively.

Second, a state should reallocate the resources it devotes to various policies in response to changes in the relative values of π_1 and π_2. These parameters capture the relative salience of the two goods produced by foreign policy, maintenance and change. Note in equations 24–27, these parameters appear in the denominator of all four equations, but each appears in the numerator of only those equations for the inputs that produce the good with which the parameter is associated. Thus, if the salience for one of the goods increases, relative to that for the other good, we should expect an increase in the use of *all* policies that produce that good and a decrease in the use of *all* policies that produce the other good.

This second factor that may cause resources allocated to policies to change is not something that is provided for in neorealist approaches to substitutability because under neorealism, states do not pursue more than one goal; security is the only thing states want. Thus, there is no need for parameters that capture how much the state values two different goals, nor are any changes in state preferences—in the relative values of the πs—important in investigating substitutability.

The two conclusions we have presented thus far are sufficient to account for many earlier empirical results on substitutability. They suggest that the use of substitutable policies should vary directly, when changes in policies are brought about by changes in the resources available to foreign policy or by changes in the salience of the two foreign policy goods. Since these factors are likely to account for a significant proportion of policy adjustments, we should expect that any study examining a simple association between substitutable policies should fail to find a negative relationship.

Our third factor does identify the conditions under which the use of substitutable policies should vary inversely. The third set of parameters in the equations consists of α_1, β_1, γ_2, and φ_2, which capture the efficiency with which their associated inputs produce the relevant foreign policy good. Note that each appears in the denominator of every equation and in the numerator of only the equation for its associated policy. Thus, if the efficiency with which a policy instrument produces one of the foreign policy goods increases, the use of that instrument will increase and the use of all other instruments that produce that same good will decrease. It is important to highlight that the relationship between this more efficient policy and the policies that produce the other good will not change. The resources allocated to substitutable foreign policies will vary inversely only when the reallocation to policies is brought about by a change in the efficiency in the use of one of those substitutable policies.

Clearly, our theory significantly refines what we mean by foreign policy substitutability and what we should expect to observe in any substitutable relationship. It leads us to conclude that the empirical results produced by earlier studies are what we should expect if foreign policy substitution occurs, and it provides the basis for additional empirical work that could address the question more directly. We also believe that this better captures the flavor of Most and Starr's original argument than does any other theoretical treatment that has served as the basis for empirical analyses.

Conclusion

Our purpose in this chapter has been to present the formal version of the two-good theory of foreign policy. We have expressed our assumptions mathematically and we have shown the conclusions to which these assumptions lead. In subsequent chapters, we draw on these arguments to develop more precise hypotheses that are then subjected to empirical tests.

6

Tests of The Two-Good Theory
Conflict, Foreign Aid, and Military Spending

THE GENERAL EXPECTATIONS that we derived from the model in the previous chapter can be subjected to tests in a number of different policy areas. The two-good theory is meant to be general and its applications numerous and diverse. In other words, while many theories focus on the effect of one environmental factor on one aspect of foreign policy, the strength of the two-good theory is that it can explain a wide variety of policies under a range of circumstances. The theory does not, for instance, focus solely on the effect of the distribution of capabilities between rivals on the likelihood of their escalating the conflict to war, though we have learned much from such work.[1] Similarly, we do not look at the effect of a variety of factors (such as power distribution, geographic proximity, alliance patterns) on one policy (conflict escalation),[2] nor do we analyze one factor's influence (such as the health of a country's economy) on a number of policies, for example, growth in military spending, involvement in international conflict, and the imposition of trade barriers.[3] The tests we conduct of the theory's expectations do not rely on the results of any one given analysis but instead on a series of tests over a breadth of issues. In this chapter we test the model's expectations about the effects of environmental factors on three different foreign policy areas: the initiation and reciprocation of international conflict; the allocation of foreign aid; and the determination of a state's military expenditure. Each test concentrates on how states

---

[1] This, indeed, may be the single most commonly addressed question in international relations, and it has been the object of study for centuries, at least since Thucydides described the Peloponnesian War. The issue has been addressed by such prominent figures as Morgenthau (1965a), Claude (1962), Wright (1942), Blainey (1973), and Organski (1968). Other, more contemporary investigations into and discussion of this issue include Wagner (1986, 1994), Kugler and Lemke (1996), Powell (1999), and Tammen et al. (2000).

[2] Just to provide a small sampling of the work on escalation, we refer to Snyder and Diesing (1977), Maoz (1983), Bueno de Mesquita, Morrow, and Zorick (1992), Leng (1993), Fearon (1994), Dixon (1994), Carlson (1995), Senese (1996, 1997b), Signorino (1999), Bueno de Mesquita, Morrow, Siverson, and Smith (1999), Prins and Sprecher (1999), A. Smith (1999), Schultz (1999), Reed (2000), Wagner (2000), Palmer, Regan, and London (2001), and, of course, Herman Kahn (1965).

[3] This topic spans fields, and any summary we provide is bound to be biased. However, see Wallerstein (1979); Keohane (1984); Kennedy (1987); Rasler and Thompson (1983); Mansfield (1994); Weede (1996); Przeworski and Limongi (1997); and Gilpin (2001).

with different amounts of resources—strong and weak states—are expected to behave. The tests are designed to determine whether the simplest and most immediate expectations of the theory—stronger states generally seek change while weaker states generally seek maintenance—are correct. We will show that they are. These tests are directed by some simple and some surprising hypotheses, and the results demonstrate that the theory is headed in the right direction.

We also have some more demanding and more difficult tests of the theory, specifically addressing the implications of the theory for foreign policy substitutability. Chapter 7 is devoted to a full investigation of issues related to substitutability and alliances. To prepare for that analysis, in this chapter we investigate how policies adopted to pursue one goal affect other policies, designed to accomplish either the same or different ends. Our attention there will specifically be focused on how foreign policy substitutability affects foreign aid allocations. Our first step, however, is to establish that the general direction of our theory is sound. To do this, we turn our attention to separate investigations of dispute initiation, foreign aid, and military spending.

Dispute Initiation and Reciprocation

The general hypotheses that we derive from the model include the prediction that strong states are more likely to engage in change-seeking behavior than are weak states, and that states gaining in power are more likely to be change seeking than states whose power is declining or stable. Weaker states, on the other hand, are more likely to engage in maintenance seeking. Our first test is to apply these general expectations to the initiation and reciprocation of militarized interstate disputes.

We see dispute initiation as an attempt by the initiating country to bring about some change in the status quo. Discussions aimed at altering the status quo in the direction a state prefers often precede the introduction of military force, and we do not believe that the first use of force represents the first and only attempt to bring about some alteration in the existing situation. But should attempts to reach agreement through negotiations fail to lead to an outcome the state finds satisfactory, the state may be willing to use force to achieve its goals. States that are relatively satisfied with the status quo will be less willing to pursue change through the use of force. Consider the attempt by the United States, through NATO and the United Nations, to get Yugoslavia under Slobodan Milosevic to alter its policies in the province of Kosovo in 1998–99. The United States, and much of the West, wanted Yugoslavia to remove its troops and other personnel from Kosovo. Those troops were active in removing Kosovars from their homes, creating tremendous human suffering. Further, the political situation in the Balkans was increasingly becoming a concern outside the immediate region, as Albania, Greece, Turkey, and many other

Muslim countries were sympathetic to the plight of the refugees. After extensive negotiations, no compromise that the West and the United States found acceptable was reached. Finally, unwilling to allow the situation to deteriorate any further, the United States used force in an attempt to see its goals realized, and after a seventy-eight-day bombing campaign Yugoslavia agreed to withdraw its troops from Kosovo. The United States did, eventually, realize its goals by changing Yugoslav policy, but only after using force. The episode is generally consistent with our theory: stronger states are more likely to introduce military force in an attempt to get what they want. In our words, stronger states are able to produce change more efficiently than are relatively weaker states.

Note that in this case, as in many, the use of force was not the first policy chosen to meet the West's goals. The use of force is a policy choice that is often politically and economically expensive, and even frequently ethically difficult to justify. States commonly resort to the force of arms only after other, less demanding policies have failed or are expected to fail to achieve the desired end. Even Adolf Hitler, who seldom shied away from the use of force, preferred to achieve his goals through intimidation rather than the direct use of force. Some of Nazi Germany's goals, such as the remilitarization of the Rhineland, the Anschluss with Austria, and the gaining of the Sudetenland, were achieved without the direct use of force. Only the extreme extent of German demands made the use of force necessary. It is worth pointing out that the use of force, even for Hitler, was politically expensive. For instance, there was little German popular support for the invasion of Poland in 1939, much to Hitler's surprise and disappointment, and bolstering German popular morale throughout the war, even as things went well for Germany, was always an important and politically necessary undertaking. Also, German generals were steadfastly against the use of force against Czechoslovakia in 1938 and were unenthusiastic about the invasion of France in 1940 (see Taylor 1961; Mearsheimer 1983). Our point here is that states that want to alter some aspect of the status quo need not resort to the use of force to do so; since the use of force is a costly endeavor, there must be relatively large benefits to justify it. Those benefits generally are associated with a valued change in the status quo.

Having said this, there are times when the initiation of international military conflict is maintenance seeking. Certainly, the initiations of some military conflicts are preemptive and are attempts to protect the status quo; that is, the initiation of some disputes is maintenance seeking rather than change seeking. For instance, in our terms, Japan's attack on the United States at Pearl Harbor in 1941 was "maintenance seeking." Throughout 1941, the United States was attempting to convince the Japanese to remove its troops from East Asia, including parts of China. The American embargo on Japan was designed to achieve this goal. Japan, on the other hand, wanted American pressure lifted and wanted the United States to accept Japan's economic, political, and military presence through the Greater East Asia Co-Prosperity Sphere. The war against the United States, from our theory's perspective, was aimed at protecting Japanese gains, and the initiation of conflict was thus maintenance seeking.

Another example may be instructive. Some argue that Israel's decision to attack Egyptian, Jordanian, and Syrian forces in the 1967 Six-Day War was pre-emptive, motivated by the expectation that Israel was itself about to be attacked by the Arab forces. That is, this initiation of war was not designed to bring about change in the status quo in the Middle East but to protect it. Such an approach would label the Israeli initiation of warfare as a maintenance-seeking action. This is not how our model and our analysis address this situation, however. The dispute that culminated in Israel's attack on June 5, 1967, began much earlier. Leading up to the war, for one, Syria and Israel exchanged fire a number of times, beginning some six months before the war. Their dispute over periodic Syrian shelling of Israeli farms under the Golan Heights and subsequent Israeli retaliation did not begin on June 5. On the other front, Egypt, making the first serious use of force in the crisis, moved troops into the Sinai on May 14 and followed that by requesting that the United Nations remove peacekeeping troops from the peninsula two days later. The last straw, from the Israeli perspective, may have been Egypt's closing of the Strait of Tiran on May 22 (Quandt 1977, 39–41). As can be seen, in this conflict Israel was not the first to introduce the use of force. According to the MID data set, the first action of the conflict that culminated in war took place on December 16, 1966, when Syria threatened to declare war on Israel. This was followed by a series of clashes and raids between Syria and Israel before the Israelis launched their attack on June 5. What all this means is that the initiation of the military conflict was not undertaken by the Israelis but by its Arab enemies. When we analyze the initiation of militarized conflict, we ask which country first introduced a threat, display, or use for force, not which side escalated matters to "war." In this particular case, the historical record informs us through our theory that the Arab states were change seeking. They introduced the use of force because no other policy was as likely to achieve the desired ends.

In our view, to summarize, the initiation of interstate conflict is usually a change-seeking action. But it takes at least two states to have a conflict. Sometimes states do not fight back when attacked. The Czech capitulation to the Soviet Union's invasion in 1968 is one such example. The decision to resist or reciprocate a military action by another is a policy decision to which we can apply our theory and that we want to analyze.

States, of course, can choose either to ignore a threatened use of force or to respond to it. We assume that the reciprocation of a conflict, that is, responding militarily to a threat, display, or use of force, is maintenance-seeking behavior, as was the case with Israel in 1967.[4] As such, our model says that relatively weaker states are more likely to reciprocate disputes in which they become involved than are stronger states. This may seem a counterintuitive, even odd conclusion, but it follows from our model. That is, because weaker states are relatively more efficient at producing maintenance than are stronger states, we expect them to do it more frequently. Allow us to illustrate the point. According to the MID data set, since 1945 Peru and the United States have been involved in six militarized disputes, all initiated by Peru. (Many of these were Peruvian seizures of U.S. fishing vessels.) In none of those six cases did the United States respond with military force. In that same period, Peru and Ecuador faced each other in nine disputes, and in all but one there was a reciprocated use of force. That is to say, Ecuador was much more likely to respond to Peru militarily than was the United States. This is not to say that the United States is indifferent to the issues, while Ecuador places high salience on its issues. The United States probably has greater resources to use to address the issues involved in a militarized dispute with another state such as Peru, while Ecuador's alternatives are much more limited. The United States can, for instance, use foreign aid or the threat of trade sanctions as inducements to alter Peru's behavior; Ecuador does not enjoy the luxury of a wide range of policy options and is more likely to find itself in a position where it must respond to a military situation with the use of force itself.[5]

A somewhat unusual military conflict between unlikely opponents helps illustrate our argument. A militarized dispute between the United States and Canada began on August 28, 1979, when Canada seized eight American tuna boats off the British Columbia coast. Canada argued that the fishing vessels (and several others it confiscated a week later) were violating Canada's 200-mile territorial limit. The United States recognized the 200-mile limit, but the Americans argued that the territorial limit did not apply to migratory fish such as tuna. The United States wanted Canadian policy changed to allow American boats to fish (at least for tuna) in their waters, but it did not use military force to compel the Canadians to accept the American position. Instead, after lengthy negotiations, the two countries signed a treaty in July 1981. The agreement allowed each country's boats to fish in the other's waters. The agreement also allowed the fishing vessels to sell their catch in either Canadian or American

---

[4] The initiation or reciprocation of disputes, clearly, is sometimes not change or maintenance seeking, respectively. This simply means that our assumption that initiations are change seeking and reciprocations are maintenance seeking makes our tests more demanding but does not invalidate them. What the occasional misclassification of cases means is that statistical results may not be as strong as we would like. That is, our model would actually be "more correct" than the data analysis would show.

[5] Our position is similar to Karl Deutsch's, introduced in his *Nerves of Government* almost four decades ago.

ports. This last condition made the agreement acceptable to Canada, as the American market is much greater than the Canadian market. The tool the United States used to bring about the change in Canadian policy was economic rather than military and constituted a "reward" for agreeing to accept the American preference. Essentially, the United States won on this particular issue, succeeding in bringing about a change in Canadian policy but without resorting to the use of force. The stronger country chose not to respond militarily to the use of force by a weaker country.

These anecdotes serve, we hope, to illustrate how the theory views the initiation and reciprocation of conflict. Conflicts are generally initiated, we argue, by states seeking to alter the status quo; that is, it is a change-seeking policy. Reciprocation, on the other hand, is generally a maintenance-seeking device. These anecdotes are not, of course, tests. We want to apply more rigorous statistical analyses to the model's expectations. Specifically, we want to test three main derivations from the theory. The theory tells us that stronger states are more likely to pursue change than are weaker states; that states increasing in power (more able to alter the status quo in directions they favor than formerly) will be more likely to be change seeking and to initiate the use of force; and that weaker states will dedicate a greater proportion of their resources to maintenance than will stronger states.

Hypothesis 6.1: The amount of power a state has is positively associated with the likelihood that it will initiate a militarized dispute.

Hypothesis 6.2: States increasing in power are more likely to initiate militarized disputes than are states that are decreasing in power.

Hypothesis 6.3: Weaker states are more likely to reciprocate the military action than are stronger states.

To test these simple hypotheses, we use the COW Project's MID data set (Jones, Bremer, and Singer 1996). The data set records all instances where one state threatened, displayed, or used force against another from 1816 to 1992. It records whether a state initiated a dispute or was the target of the dispute. It also indicates whether the target state responded militarily to the initiator. We also use the project's Composite Index of National Capabilities (CINC) for the measure of power (Bremer 1980). We take the log of this measure, as the distribution of the variable is very skewed. (The results of the analysis are substantively unchanged if we do not take the log of power.) Our tests are straightforward. We want to determine whether states' power is *positively* related to the probability that it will initiate a dispute in a particular year, and whether that power is *negatively* related to the likelihood that it will reciprocate a dispute provided it is the target of another's military action. When testing the hypothesis about initiation, we use all nation-years from 1816 to 1992 for which there are data. Dispute initiation is coded as being observed for bilateral and

TABLE 6.1
Dispute Initiation and Reciprocation

	Dependent Variable: Dispute Initiation (1 = yes; 0 = no)	Dependent Variable: Dispute Reciprocation (1 = yes; 0 = no)
Log Power	0.44***	−0.19***
	(0.01)	(0.06)
Constant	−1.07***	0.22***
	(0.03)	(0.08)
Log-likelihood Full Model	−5064.08	−881.46
Log-likelihood Null Model	−5717.22	−875.72
Chi-square (1)	1306.29	11.48
Significance	0.0000	0.000
N	11274	1272

Two-tailed significance levels reported (*** $p < .01$).
Standard errors in parentheses.

multilateral disputes.[6] When we analyze the reciprocation of conflict, the analysis is done only on the target in a bilateral dispute, and we want to know whether that target reciprocated the conflict or not. We exclude multilateral disputes from analysis, as the decision to respond to force or not is seldom solely up to the original target.[7] As our dependent variables are both dichotomous, we use logit analysis. The results are shown in table 6.1.

The table shows two results, pertaining to the initiation and reciprocation of disputes. We find, consistent with the expectations, that power is positively related to the likelihood of dispute initiation. A state with average power (a value of 2.05, as measured throughout the period) has an estimated probability of 0.17 of initiating a dispute in any year; increasing that by one standard deviation almost doubles the estimated probability to .33. The results of the analysis (that more powerful states initiate disputes more frequently than do weaker states) are not terribly surprising, but it would be disappointing if these simplest of expectations were not supported. But the strength of the model is its applicability to a variety of different foreign policy areas, and as we proceed, we will meet increasingly demanding tests.

Second, as we expected, we find that power is negatively related to the likelihood of a state's reciprocation in a dispute. While stronger states initiate

---

[6] Frequently, the side that initiates the dispute does not know whether more states will join the dispute or not, and it is that original decision that we are interested in.

[7] We could, of course, include in the analysis disputes that began as bilateral disputes but then became multilateral. But doing that would bias our tests, as such disputes clearly escalated. And in some sense, that is the very phenomenon we want to test for.

conflict more frequently, relatively weaker states reciprocate conflict more. This is a surprising finding, because conflict is at times portrayed as occurring between two powerful states, vying over an issue of importance to each. While large-scale conflict, such as World War II, involves major powers, much of the world's conflict involves military clashes between relatively weaker states, such as the recent war between Ethiopia and Eritrea. And it is worth remembering that World War II itself began as a conflict between a relatively strong state (Germany) and weaker one (Poland), where the weaker one chose to fight back rather than capitulate. In any event, the statistical results support the theory's expectations.

The finding that weaker states generally are more likely to reciprocate is consistent with Peter Partell's work, which found that the relatively weaker states *within a dispute* are more likely to respond than are the stronger states (Partell 1997). Similarly, Partell and Palmer (1999) found that disputes were more likely to escalate through early stages (from threat to display, and from display to use of force) when the target was weaker than its opponent rather than when the target was stronger. Bruce Bueno de Mesquita and David Lalman found that the probability that states they called "pacific doves" (which prefer to engage in negotiation rather than force their opponent's capitulation, and prefer their own capitulation to war) use force in a dispute decreases as the state's relative capability increases (1992, 107–11). In other words, weaker "pacific doves" are more likely to use force than stronger ones, once a dispute begins. Our argument, which focuses on the state's level of power and *not* its power relative to the adversary in the dispute, implies that the behavior may be more general than the Bueno de Mesquita and Lalman model allows and is applicable to a wider variety of states.[8]

Last, we test whether increasing power is related to the likelihood of dispute initiation. Here, we used the COW measure to determine whether or not in a particular year a state had increased its power over what it had five years before, and related that to whether that state initiated a dispute. The result is shown in table 6.2. As the table shows, there is a significant positive relationship between whether a state increased its power and whether it initiated a dispute. States increasing in power are about 20 percent more likely to begin conflicts than states that are decreasing in power: when a state was *decreasing* in power, it initiated a dispute in a year about 20.9 percent of the time; a state *increasing* in power started a conflict about 24.8 percent of the time.

We have found support for our three simple hypotheses regarding the initiation and reciprocation of conflict. We are encouraged by those results. We turn now to the second area of foreign policy to which we want to apply our theory's expectations, the sources of foreign aid allocation.

---

[8] The analysis regarding the reciprocation of disputes is drawn from Morgan and Palmer (1997).

TABLE 6.2
Change in Power and Dispute Initiation

	Change in Power (over five-year period)	
	Increasing	Decreasing
Initiate dispute	1103	836
	(24.8%)	(20.9%)
Do not initiate dispute	3350	3167
	(75.2%)	(71.9%)

Tau-b = .046
Chi-square (1) = 18.06
Prob. = .0000

Foreign Aid

The second area for foreign policy we investigate is the allocation of foreign aid.[9] The allocation of resources to foreign aid, particularly to development assistance, is an excellent example of change-seeking foreign policy behavior. Foreign aid, whatever its other purposes and merits, is a tool of foreign policy— states give it because they believe it encourages recipients to take desired actions. Foreign aid is a reward or an inducement.

It is certainly possible, and indeed is often the case, that states give aid for humanitarian reasons. Such humanitarian concerns, however, are change seeking: if State A wants State B to decrease its human rights violations, it may achieve that end through giving aid to B. Or State A may want to see greater nutrition for the people living in State B and may give foreign aid to realize that preference. In this case, State A, again, is pursuing change.

We assert that foreign aid is an efficient tool for bringing about desired changes in the international status quo.[10] Its efficiency is, of course, relative to other available tools for realizing change. And should states want to keep some aspects of the status quo intact, other policies are more suitable. This, of

---

[9] This section is drawn from Palmer, Wohlander, and Morgan (2002).

[10] The degree to which aid is motivated by the national interest of the donor versus the needs of the recipient is one of the primary debates in the field today. A related debate has to do with the role of human rights violations in affecting foreign aid, particularly for the United States. To provide but a sampling of the material on this topic, we refer the reader to the following: Wittkopf (1973); McKinlay and Little (1977, 1979); Carleton and Stohl (1987); Cingranelli and Pasquarello (1985); Lebovic (1988); McCormick and Mitchell (1988); Zahariadis, Travis, and Diehl (1990); Kegley and Hook (1991); Poe (1992); Travis and Zahariadis (1992); Poe and Sirirangsi (1993); Blanton (1994); Hook (1995); Poe and Meernik (1995); Regan (1995); Schraeder, Hook, and Taylor (1998); and Wang (1999).

course, is a general statement, and there may be occasions where the allocation of foreign aid has as its primary purpose maintenance.

While we believe that foreign aid is generally change seeking, we are particularly convinced this is true of developmental aid, which we analyze here. Development assistance, organized by the Organization for Economic Cooperation and Development (OECD), is designed to encourage recipient nations to adopt policies favored by donor states. Recipients of this aid are restricted to poor states or states in rapid transition, with applicability determined by specific thresholds established for income, economic diversification, and social development. The purposes of developmental assistance are to encourage "sustainable economic and social development" (OECD 1997b), such as the adoption of political institutions and economic systems similar to those of the donor states. The fact that development assistance is given with the stated intention that recipients orient their future policy choices in the direction preferred by donors makes clear that this type of foreign aid should be conceived of as change seeking. Indeed, there is growing resistance worldwide to the demands placed by some organizations (notably the World Bank) as a precondition to the granting of aid. That the donors require sometimes painful policy changes in many ways illustrates our point: foreign aid is designed to elicit changes in behavior. Generally speaking, aid allocation is designed to change the recipients' behavior.[11] Because this may be an unfamiliar perspective, we provide an extended example.

In the immediate post–World War II years, the United States adopted an active role in the rebuilding of a non-communist Western Europe. There was probably no more important goal to the United States than excluding Soviet influence from a democratic and economically rehabilitated Europe. To achieve this, two dimensions of the international status quo had to conform to American preferences, and two different means were used to do that. First, the United States needed to prevent the Soviet Red Army from taking more of Europe than it had won during the war, when it occupied most of Eastern Europe and the eastern part of Germany, including Berlin. This goal was designed to protect an existing outcome and was clearly maintenance seeking. To accomplish this, the United States retained large numbers of troops in Germany and the rest of Europe, even after American demobilization and before the formation of NATO in 1949.[12] Second, the United States needed to revitalize the European

---

[11] Ken Organski early argued that foreign aid is a method of rewarding states for doing what the donor desires. Organski maintained that using power was costly, and states would choose the most efficient and effective methods for achieving desired outcomes. He also observed that rewards as a method of exercising power were often used between states that were "fundamentally friendly." His perspective fits nicely with our own (1968, 111–18).

[12] The Soviets may have been able to defeat the American conventional forces in Europe for an extended period after 1945 (and even after 1949), but the Americans believed that fear of a large-scale war with the United States might deter Soviet aggression. The American troops, capable of defeating the Red Army or not, were in Europe to maintain an existing political outcome.

economy with stable democratic states, clearly a departure from the situations of either 1932 or 1938, when totalitarian regimes threatened to dominate the continent, or of 1945, when the social and economic situation in Western Europe was in rubble. No long-run American foreign policy strategy was viable without a democratic and thriving Western Europe.[13] To accomplish this, the United States donated approximately $12 billion in aid to war-ravaged states in Western Europe through the Marshall Plan. This huge aid package was designed to guide the development of the postwar economic and political order in Europe in a way consistent with the preferences of U.S. leaders. Indeed, the Marshall Plan was originally offered to the newly formed Communist states in Eastern Europe, and to the Soviet Union itself. The offer, not surprisingly, was turned down: the Communist leaders were not willing to integrate their economies with those of capitalist Western Europe. In the immediate postwar period, the protection of Western Europe—the maintenance of the region free from direct Soviet military influence—was accomplished through the use of American military capability, both threatened and actual. On the other hand, the change in the social and economic situation was realized through the donation of massive amounts of aid.

We provide just a few more examples of the use of aid as a change-seeking policy. During the cold war, the Soviet Union donated large amounts of economic aid to several African countries, particularly Ethiopia and Tanzania. This aid encouraged and rewarded these nations as they nationalized their economies and entered a period of close relations with the USSR, providing it with needed raw materials and a sphere of influence in Africa. Japan has used foreign aid to improve its international standing throughout the post–World War II era (Arase 1995), giving large amounts of aid, even while keeping its military establishment very small.[14] Japanese donations of development assistance, such as the construction of the Eastern Seaboard project in Thailand, exemplify its use of aid to improve ties with the Association of Southeast Asian Nations (ASEAN) and open relations with Asian socialist states, such as Mongolia and North Korea. This project in particular shows the political nature of these goals—both the World Bank and the Asian Development Bank discouraged Japan from pursuing the project, yet Japan did so to gain influence in the region. And Newnham (1998) argues that states use economic aid to purchase diplomatic recognition for themselves and hinder the recognition of other states. For example, West Germany successfully used economic aid to prevent non-communist states from recognizing East Germany until the late 1960s.

---

[13] For a while after World War II, some Americans argued that the United States should adopt an isolationist policy and remove itself from European affairs. This position, largely identified with Senator Robert Taft of Ohio, was never terribly popular and was essentially defeated with Eisenhower's nomination for the presidency by the Republican Party in 1952 (see Gaddis 1982).

[14] Japan is able to dedicate such a large portion of its foreign policy resources to foreign aid in large part because the United States provides for its security needs.

There are more specific and contemporary examples of foreign aid being used as a change-seeking policy. In 2002, as the United States began its withdrawal from Afghanistan following the military campaign against the Taliban in that country, the question of a residual peacekeeping force became important. The United States itself was not interested in assuming the role. After some negotiations, the United States persuaded Turkey to take command of the international peacekeeping force around Kabul. The main inducement for achieving this change in Turkish policy, according to one report, was $228 million in foreign aid, only $28 million of which was directly tied to the costs of the effort.[15] (Another American reward for Turkey's new policy was backing for Turkey's entrance into the European Union.)

A second example from that same year concerns Yugoslavia's cooperation with the international war crimes tribunal in The Hague. The United States supported the work of the tribunal and wanted Yugoslavia to capture and extradite individuals indicted for war crimes who were close associates of the former leader, Slobodan Milosevic, and to allow investigators access to government papers. Some Yugoslav leaders resisted, feeling that cooperation with the tribunal, particularly in the absence of a formal agreement, was a threat to Yugoslav sovereignty and demeaning. On April 1, 2002, the United States moved to freeze $40 million in financial aid. Immediately afterward, Yugoslav officials changed course, promising to work with the international tribunal. The United States asked for not just promises but for action. On April 11, Yugoslavia passed a law that would allow Yugoslav war suspects to be sent to The Hague. Secretary of State Colin Powell responded by saying that his office would wait to see how fully Yugoslavia cooperated with the tribunal before acting to reinstate the aid.[16] Within weeks, two former close aide's to Milosevic surrendered and were sent to The Hague while another committed suicide. Serbia shortly thereafter indicted a number of other Milosevic associates, accepted the surrender of four of them, and prepared to hunt down the remaining eighteen thought to be hiding in Serbia. On May 21, the United States announced that it was resuming aid to Yugoslavia, in recognition of the actions the Yugoslavs had taken and were still planning to take.[17] It is interesting to note that the U.S. decision to resume aid was criticized by Human Rights Watch, which argued that Yugoslavia could do more to provide the tribunal in The Hague with desired documents. Human Rights Watch saw the threat to continue the foreign aid freeze as a change-seeking policy, as do we, and was unhappy with the amount of change the United States considered sufficient to restart the aid. In this case, the mere threat of withholding aid was sufficient to get the recipient to alter policy.

---

[15] *New York Times*, March 20, 2002, p. A12.
[16] *New York Times*, April 2, 2002, p. A6, and April 12, 2002, p. A6.
[17] *New York Times*, May 22, 2002, p. A13.

TABLE 6.3
Relative Capabilities and Foreign Aid Donations

(Feasible Generalized Least Squares)	
Natural Log of Capabilities	1.680***
	(0.504)
Constant	4.647***
	(0.529)
R^2	0.349
Significance	0.0000
N	546

Dependent variable: natural log of foreign aid donations
Two-tailed significance levels reported (*** $p < .01$).
Standard errors in parentheses

The first hypothesis related to foreign aid that we want to test centers on the question of whether a state's allocation of foreign aid in the form of development assistance is affected by increases in state resources as our theory predicts. Specifically, we expect that states will allocate more resources to foreign aid as they grow stronger, and more powerful states will allocate more aid than weaker states. Second, as foreign aid is a change-seeking policy, we expect that the increases in aid allocation will grow at faster rates for more powerful countries. Recall that our theory says the change-seeking behavior grows at an increasing rate. This means that as state power increases, the rate at which aid allocation increases should itself go up. In other words, according to the theory, the income elasticity of aid allocation should be greater than one.

Hypothesis 6.4:   Allocations to foreign aid will increase at a more rapid rate than increases in resources.

Testing this first hypotheses is a simple matter. Our explanatory variable is state resources, and here we use Gross National Product (GNP). We take the natural log of this variable, as we want to see whether the slope becomes steeper at higher levels of power, which is indicated by a coefficient of greater than one (see Gujarati 1992). Our dependent variable is "total receipts net" of bilateral foreign aid donations, available from the OECD for the years 1966–95 (OECD 1997a). We test the hypothesis for twenty-one OECD states for the years 1966–91. The results of this analysis are presented in table 6.3.

The results show that the hypothesis is supported: the coefficient on our explanatory variable is greater than one, which means that with greater power, the allocation of foreign aid increases at an increasing rate. For example, if GNP increases by 3 percent, the allocations to foreign aid may increase by 4 percent in relatively smaller states; in larger states, a 3 percent increase in GNP may lead to a 5 percent increase in foreign aid. As foreign aid is a change-producing policy, this increasing rate is what the theory expects. More powerful states allocate more aid than less powerful states, both in absolute terms and as a proportion of their resource base. Our theory's expectations when applied to foreign aid allocations are supported.

Military Spending

In this section we analyze the effects of increased national capability on a state's military spending. This is a useful exercise for two reasons. First, it subjects our theory's expectations to a test in yet another area of foreign policy. Second, military expenditure is a widely analyzed aspect of foreign policy, and scholars have long focused on various causes of states' spending. Arms race specialists in particular have looked at the international determinants of a state's military budget.[18] Our focus in this section is on the general relationship our theory predicts between state power and military spending. While international factors certainly affect a state's decision about its military posture, we concentrate here only on the initial determinants of military spending, as identified by our model.

We regard defense spending as primarily maintenance-seeking activity. That is, defense allocations are more effective at protecting favored aspects of the status quo than they are at bringing about desired change. We recognize that the threat or use of military forces can be aimed at changing the behavior of other states and thereby increasing one's change, and of course we see conflict initiation as a change-seeking policy. That is, possession of sufficient military capability is a necessary condition for the initiation of military conflict. We presume, however, that the majority of aggregated military expenditures are devoted toward protecting what one already has. (In chapter 7, we break military spending into components, one of which [capital-intensive spending] we identify as being directed as change seeking.) Military capability is relatively better at keeping a situation intact than it is at altering it. There are a variety of reasons for this. For one, analysts generally argue that in battle the offense requires an advantage in capability of at least 3:1 to be successful (Levy 1984, 1987; Quester 1977; Jervis 1978, 1988; Walt 1989). That is, a given military capability is much better able to protect something than it is to bring about change. Consider, for example, a state, A, that is militarily equal to a rival, B. To be able to achieve victory, A must increase its military capability by 200 percent, a very difficult

---

[18] The work on arms races is voluminous, but we highlight some of the literature. The seminal work is Lewis Richardson's (1960a, 1960b). See Hess (1995) for a summary of Richardson's contributions, and Zinnes (1976) for a discussion of the specifics of his work. More recent work on the topic has been done by Hopmann and Smith (1977); Diehl (1983); Goertz and Diehl (1986); Siverson and Diehl (1989); Intriligator and Brito (1989); Hill (1992); Cashman (1993); and Sample (1997).

undertaking. Moreover, if the original situation has A's capability at about half of B's, to achieve victory A must now increase its military sixfold.

A second reason that military capability is better at achieving maintenance than change is that attempts to alter a situation are necessarily directional, while a state is able to protect a desired outcome from a variety of threats simultaneously. That is, to alter specific aspects of the status quo, a state must have a target. Change requires that another state, or a group of states, or a specific issue have resources directed toward them. Those same resources can be used, however, to protect some aspect of the status quo simultaneously from a variety of threats. A military unit can be used to attempt to alter North Korean security policy, but it can also be used, and more efficiently, to protect some valued outcome from North Korea as well as from Iraq as well as from Iran.

Third, a state pursuing change can do so more effectively than through allocating resources in military expenditures. A state is likely to derive much more change benefits from foreign aid, for example, than from an equivalent expenditure on defense. Imagine the policies that other states might be willing to adopt if the United States allocated the amount of its annual defense budget, about $300 billion, to foreign aid instead. That amount is more than the combined GDPs of Israel, Lebanon, Libya, North Korea, Syria, and Yugoslavia. North Korea might be willing to disarm for an amount like that. Finally, we regard the allocation of resources to the military to be change seeking only in the last resort. That is, a state would prefer to accomplish changes in the international arena through peaceful means, if possible; changes brought about by the use of force are politically, militarily, and economically expensive.[19]

One might ask, in this regard, about Nazi Germany's use of its military establishment to bring about change in the international situation. In that case, one might point out, the military was not an instrument of maintenance. Instead, Germany used the threat or reality of force to get its way and to alter the status quo. At Munich in 1938, for instance, the threat posed by the German army provided the main motive for the Western powers to make peace with Hitler. We agree, but we also note that Hitler's generals greatly feared military confrontation with the West, and Hitler's tactics relied more on his belief that the West lacked the will to risk war over the Sudetenland than on the ability of the Wehrmacht to achieve a military victory in war. The scale of the German demands on the international community was such that few instruments short of the threat or use of force would have accomplished its goals, as Germany found very little about the status quo to its liking. That is, extreme goals require extreme measures; foreign aid or the threat of economic sanctions

---

[19] In this, we agree with Bueno de Mesquita and Lalman (1992), who argue that states incur a cost in using force. In a similar vein, Organski (1968) maintains that the use of force is the most costly way for states to get what they want, after persuasion and reward, and that force is a tool states use only against others who are already enemies.

were unlikely to convince Britain or the Soviet Union that they should adopt Germany's preferred policies, for instance.[20]

Our test of our theory applied to this aspect of foreign policy rests on the rate at which changes in resources are translated into military expenditure—the income elasticity of military expenditure. Our theory says that weaker states have a relative advantage in the production of maintenance, and therefore these states should dedicate greater shares of any increased power to its pursuit, including expenditures on the military.[21]

Hypothesis 6.5:   There will be a negative relationship between the relative capability of a state and its relative income elasticity for military expenditure.

To investigate this, we look at a set of relatively similar countries: the eighteen industrialized members of the OECD for the years 1950–84. We want to avoid the confounding affects of development that would arise if we were to use a more economically diverse group of countries. To find the income elasticity, we use the equation:

$$\text{natural log (defense spending)} = \alpha + \beta \, (\text{natural log [GNP]})$$

where β represents the income elasticity of defense spending. We expect to find that more powerful states have lower income elasticity for military spending than do less powerful states. Before turning to the results of our analysis, we want to emphasize that this is a surprising and perhaps demanding test. We are used to thinking of military spending as something that is pursued most avidly by powerful states. While we do not dispute that the more powerful have greater military capabilities than the weak, we find our application of the model to military spending to have a surprising thing to say—the less powerful should turn increased resources into military capability at a greater rate than the more powerful. The results of the analysis are presented in table 6.4, which lists the states in order of their GNP.

The central question is whether the income elasticity is negatively related to GNP, as we hypothesize. Indeed, we find that the rank-order correlation between GNP and elasticity is strongly negative. For the countries we have analyzed, the measure of association—Spearman's rho—is −0.451, and this is significant at the 0.05 level. This tells us that, as we expected, the larger the country, the smaller its elasticity for defense spending. In other words, smaller

---

[20] And Germany did not, after all, realize its goals. As effective as it was, the Wehrmacht was insufficient not only for changing the status quo to Hitler's liking but for protecting the gains it realized in the early days of World War II. The change seeking pursued by Germany far exceeded its abilities to see its goals reached.

[21] This section of the chapter is drawn from Palmer (1991).

TABLE 6.4
Relative Capability and Income Elasticity of Defense Spending

	α	β (Elasticity)	Elasticity Rank-order	GNP Rank-order
United States	10.71	0.350	16	1
Japan	3.85	0.535	12	2
Germany	1.13	0.749	6	3
United Kingdom	11.97	0.196	17	4
France	5.81	0.494	13	5
Italy	2.77	0.625	10	6
Sweden	0.828	0.760	5	7
The Netherlands	5.65	0.470	14	8
Canada	15.76	−0.159	18	9
Switzerland	3.34	0.584	11	10
Norway	−2.505	0.943	3	11
Australia	1.715	0.662	8	12
Denmark	−2.074	0.895	4	13
Belgium	2.054	0.639	9	14
Finland	−6.75	1.173	2	15
New Zealand	0.747	0.697	7	16
Austria	−22.54	2.208	1	17
Ireland	3.75	0.434	15	18

Note: All β's are statistically significant at the .01 level, except that for Canada, which is significant at the .05 level.

$N = 35$ in the analyses for each state.

countries transfer additional wealth into military capability at a faster rate than do larger countries. The expectations of our theory when applied to this third area of foreign policy are realized.

Foreign Aid and Substitutability

We turn in this section to a different set of analyses focusing on the two-good theory's hypotheses on substitutability, particularly regarding foreign aid allocations. Substitutability is generally taken to mean that a change in allocation of resources given to one policy has implications for the resources dedicated to others. The two-good theory modifies this by emphasizing that policies can be directed toward producing not one but two goods, and that some policies are relatively better at producing one or the other good. It would be wrong, from the theory's perspective, to take substitutability to mean simply that if more resources are given to any policy A, resources given to all policies B must decline. Let us begin the application of the two-good theory to foreign policy substitutability.

We present simple tests of the two-good theory's implications for foreign policy substitutability. More specifically, we look to see whether, as the theory suggests, there are trade-offs between policies that are effective at producing the same goals, assuming that overall resources are unchanged. In initially testing the theory, we will be looking at whether a state's foreign aid allocations are affected by the adoption of another change-producing policy: conflict initiation. The theory says that we can generally expect policies such as these that produce the same good to be negatively related to each other, controlling for changes in resources. That is, when a state's resources are stable, we generally will see resources given over to one change-producing policy only when resources are taken from another change-seeking policy. (The exception is when a state's preferences change, such that it prefers to pursue change [or maintenance] more than previously. In that case, we would see more resources given over to all change-producing [or maintenance-producing] policies, and resources taken away from maintenance-producing [or change-producing] policies.) Our theory also specifies that a change-producing policy like foreign aid allocations should *not* be affected by the pursuit of policies that are better suited to producing maintenance. We will be using general military spending as an example of a maintenance-producing policy. Before moving to our analysis, though, let us summarize the formal arguments and conclusions presented in the previous chapter.

Our two-good theory says that states select policies to get a foreign policy portfolio that maximizes utility by reaching an optimal balance of change and maintenance. Some policies are better at producing change while others are generally more suited to the production of maintenance. Further, the theory assumes that all policies require the allocation of scarce resources. With these simple ideas in mind, we can predict how these different polices are substituted for one another and, therefore, what the phenomenon of substitutability should look like.

The theory says that in order to determine anticipated substitution effects, we must know what led to a particular change in resource allocation in the first place. This importance of the cause of the initial allocation change is frequently overlooked. Our theory says that there are three situations that can lead states to allocate more or fewer resources to particular policies, and that the predicted substitution effects vary with them. First, there can be a change in a state's resources. With greater (or fewer) resources, a state will be expected to increase (or decrease) its allocations to all policies. The precise increase (reduction) is determined by the relative marginal utility of each policy, but generally, in this case we would expect the changes in allocations for any two policies to be positively correlated: with increases in state resources, allocations to all policies should go up, and with decreases in state resources, all such allocations should decline. One additional and important implication of this—and one that is vital in the discussions that follow—is that to study substitution patterns, we *must control for changes in state resources*. Otherwise we may miss an important clue as to why allocations may have changed in the first place.

A second source of change in the allocation patterns across policies that can affect substitution effects is that state preferences may change. This could happen, for instance, if a new political leader's preferences for her state are notably different than those of her predecessor. If a state's new preferences favor the pursuit of one good over the other, we would expect to see the state allocate more resources to the policies that are better able to provide that good and move resources away from other policies. (Of course, this anticipation is based on the presumption that resources have remained relatively constant.) We are generally unable to observe changes in state preference, however, though we presented some examples of this in chapters 3 and 4; until we have some method other than *ex post* observation of determining which leaders have greater preferences for change or maintenance, we can only analyze the effects of change in preference in specific, well-defined situations. Thus, when we undertake our large-N analyses we are forced to assume (as do virtually *all* analyses of international relations) that state preferences are given and constant.

The third cause of some change in the allocation of resources across policies is that the efficiency of some policy in providing a good undergoes a change. Some policy that is relatively efficient at producing a good—say, change—may become even better. This could happen, for instance, if foreign aid is more desired by recipients, making them more willing to adopt changes in policy desired by donors. If there are no changes in preference and resources remain constant, we expect the state to be at its equilibrium and to have achieved its desired mix of change and maintenance. A more efficient policy that produces change does not lead the state to prefer change more than previously, however. The state can get the same amount of change by allocating more resources to the newly more efficient policy while putting fewer resources into the other change-producing polices. Therefore, we expect that the resources given over to policies that produce the same good should be negatively related to each other, controlling for changes in resources, as before. On the other hand, a more efficient policy that produces one good should have no effect on the resources given over to policies that produce the other good; we expect to see no substitution effect across policies aimed at the acquisition of different goods. These two statements serve as the hypotheses we want to test in this section:

Hypothesis 6.6:   The resources allocated to policies that produce the same good should be negatively related to each other, controlling for changes in state resources.

Hypothesis 6.7:   The resources allocated to policies that produce different goods should be unrelated to each other, controlling for changes in state resources.

TABLE 6.5
Foreign Aid and Substitutability, OECD Countries, 1966–1992

Variable	Coefficient	Probability Value
Number of disputes initiated	−130.42 (68.1)	0.056
Change in military expenditure	0.159 (0.131)	0.226
Change in GNP	0.183 (0.118)	0.122
Intercept	25.58 (43.9)	0.56

Dependent variable: Two-year change in foreign aid allocations
Log likelihood = −3069.39
Wald Chi-square = 6.42
Prob. Chi-square = 0.093
$N = 302$

Earlier in the chapter we introduced our ideas about some policies and the goods they are expected to produce. Here, we focus on three of those policies—foreign aid allocation, conflict initiation, and general military expenditures. As we have argued, the first two are primarily change-producing policies and the last is primarily maintenance producing. We test our hypotheses to see if, as we expect, the change-producing policies are negatively related to each other while there is no expected relationship between the maintenance- and change-producing policies, when we control for changes in resources. Resources are measured as GDP, and changes in those resources as changes in GDP. Specifically, to test the hypotheses we estimate the equation

$$\Delta \text{ Foreign Aid} = \alpha + \beta_1 \text{Disputes Initiated} + \beta_2 (\Delta \text{ Military Spending}) + \beta_3 (\Delta \text{GNP})$$

where changes in foreign aid, military spending, and GNP are taken over a two-year period. The units of analysis are country years. The years we use to estimate the equation are 1966–92; the countries are members of the OECD, as we want the sample of states analyzed to be relatively equivalent in terms of their political and economic natures. The equation was estimated using generalized least squares with panel corrected standard errors. The results are shown in table 6.5.

As we expected to see, the number of disputes a state initiates in a year is negatively related to how much foreign aid changes: the more conflict the country begins, the more foreign aid allocations decline. The number of disputes initiated and changes in foreign aid allocations appear to be substitutes for one another, as we suspected. They are each useful for bringing about desired changes in the status quo. We note, though, that the statistical significance of this coefficient is only marginal. Note as well that change in military spending is positively but not significantly related to changes in foreign aid allocation; our theory predicted that no relationship between these policies directed toward different goals should exist, as the two policies are generally directed toward producing different goods. Finally, changes in resources (GNP) are positively associated with foreign aid changes, but again, the effect is not statistically significant. In sum, the results are supportive of the theory's implications, but not overwhelmingly so.

One possible reason for our marginally significant results here may be that not all members of the OECD are as likely to employ force to meet their foreign policy goals, and so in some instances we may be analyzing states that lower (or raise) their foreign aid allocation without any militarized dispute having occurred; the substitution effects that we are looking for cannot, under those circumstances, take place. Over the period, the United States and Great Britain, for instance, initiated 56 percent of the conflicts that the entire group of eighteen countries did.[22] For these relatively powerful states, force to achieve desired foreign policy ends is more frequently used, as is foreign aid itself. Looking at the substitution patterns between conflict and foreign aid in these two countries, therefore, may be instructive; accordingly, we undertook the same analysis for these two countries separately, and the results are presented in table 6.6.

The results of these analyses support our expectations. In both the United States and Britain, the initiation of conflict is strongly, significantly, and negatively related to changes in foreign aid allocations, as our theory suggests. Those two policies are substitutes for one another and are seen by decision makers as achieving the same results. Recall that the two-good theory says that no particular relationship between military expenditures and foreign aid allocations need exist. And in Britain, changes in military expenditures are unrelated to foreign aid allocations, while in the United States this relationship is positive, though only marginally significant. Interestingly, changes in GNP appear unrelated to changes in foreign aid allocations.

It is important to take a moment to stress what we are not saying here, as our argument has sometimes been misstated. We do not assert that decision makers in Washington, D.C., for instance, debate whether to give aid to a country to alter their policies or to attack them militarily—though such discussions are certainly imaginable. States, we assert, use a variety of tools to try to make changes to their liking in parts of the world, and the choice of which tools to

[22] During the period we analyzed, Australia, Austria, Denmark, Finland, Japan, Luxembourg, New Zealand, and Sweden initiated no conflicts.

TABLE 6.6

Foreign Aid and Substitutability, United States and Great Britain, 1966–1992

Variable	United States		Great Britain	
	Coefficient	Prob. Value	Coefficient	Prob. Value
Number of Disputes Initiated	−567.34 (255.19)	0.026	−552.57 (227.83)	0.015
Change in Military Expenditure	0.598 (0.314)	0.057	0.347 (0.481)	0.471
Change in GNP	−0.183 (0.687)	0.790	−0.057 (0.471)	0.903
Intercept	332.67 (572.00)	0.561	158.13 (160.23)	0.324

Dependent variable: Two-year change in foreign aid allocations
Log-likelihood =   −160.45   −134.32
Wald Chi-square =   6.04   6.13
Prob. Chi-square =   .1098   .1055
N =   25   25

use is dictated by a number of factors, including the readiness of the target or targets to accommodate their policies in return for aid and the appropriateness and likely effectiveness of military conflict. In deciding how to allocate their resources, decision makers determine how able different policies will be to help achieve the desired goals. If foreign aid allocations are effective in getting desired changes, the use of force is not necessary. If, for whatever reasons, the application of military force is a good choice for realizing desired changes, fewer resources need be given over to foreign aid. The trade-off, to summarize, is not one that is necessarily made or contemplated in specific instances. It is the result of decisions about the anticipated effectiveness of policies choices, within the overall portfolio of policies.

To return to the topic, the simple statistical analyses presented here lend support to our theory's implications about foreign policy substitutability. Policies directed toward the production of the same good tend to be (but need not always be) substitutes, that is, resources given to one come at the expense of the other. Policies directed toward the other good, however, are usually unaffected by those resource decisions.

These tests are relatively simple and specific, however, and our theory purports to be general and thus applicable to a wide range of policies and situations. In the next chapter we examine a more difficult set of policy choices that national leaders face. Specifically, in looking at the effects of joining alliances, we will be investigating how a variety of policies are related and how the same action (joining an alliance) can have different, though predictable and presumably desired, effects on different states.

Summary

In this chapter we have done two things. First, we have applied our theory's simplest expectations—focusing on one policy area at a time—to three foreign policy behaviors. We have investigated whether changes in power and the available resources a state has affect allocations to change- or maintenance-seeking behavior as our theory predicts. The theory implies, for instance, that relatively strong and weak states have different advantages in the production of the two goods. Stronger states are better able to pursue change, while weaker states are relatively better at the production of maintenance. We investigated two change-seeking and two maintenance-seeking policies and found that the theory correctly predicted the relationship between state power and how resources were allocated to these policies. Stronger states are more likely to initiate conflict and to dedicate resources to foreign aid than are weaker states, while the weaker are more likely to reciprocate conflict and to allocate additional resources to military capability than are stronger states. These expectations are "simple" because they speak to the relationship between resources and change or maintenance. Our second set of tests was not so simple, because it addressed the issue of how the pursuit of one good through a policy affects other policies.

7

Substitutability and Alliances

IN THE PREVIOUS CHAPTER, we presented some simple statistical analyses of some of the hypotheses derived from the two-good theory. We focused on a number of foreign policy behaviors, such as dispute initiation, military expenditures, and foreign aid, as well as some simple substitutability relationships among them. The results are generally supportive of the theory, but they do not take us very far. We have seen that the simple relationships hypothesized do occur empirically, and we have seen that the theory can be applied in a number of policy areas. We have not yet shown that the theory is useful for guiding an in-depth investigation into any one policy area, however. This is our purpose in this chapter. We devote this entire chapter to an investigation of substitutability and alliances.

Why do states form alliances? In previous work this question has been answered through arguments that are based on the belief that states gain security through alliance membership. Large states are better able to protect highly valued international friends by extending security guarantees to them, and smaller states gain their allies' commitment to aid them if the need should arise. The function of alliances is to aggregate members' capabilities in order to increase their ability to protect things they value, or so the traditional argument goes. The argument that our theory produces is different. Our theory, of course, views alliances as one component of the state's foreign policy, and they serve as vehicles for the state to increase its change, its maintenance, or both. Indeed, our theory says that some members of a specific alliance may increase change while decreasing maintenance. That is, the alliance may have the effect of making some of its members less secure, though happier with the international arrangement, than they were without the alliance. Our theory also says that some states may sign an alliance to increase maintenance while others may join to increase change: the same alliance can provide different benefits to different members.

Our theory's perspective is at variance with more traditional approaches to foreign policy and international relations, such as realism, which see alliances as increasing security for their members and perhaps threatening other states in the process. According to those traditional approaches, alliances, particularly defense pacts, commit members to come to each other's assistance should they be attacked.[1] Small states enjoy the security provided by these pacts. Large states, again according to the traditional view, make alliances in an attempt to demonstrate their commitment to the smaller allies, dissuading potential enemies from attacking and thereby ensuring that valued partners are secure. While sharing the basic perspective, scholars directly associated with or following the assumptions of the realist approach have made different suggestions regarding the precise function of alliances. Some, for instance, argue that states form alliances to maintain a balance of power that immediately or indirectly leads to greater security and likelihood of survival for the state. (See, for instance, Kaplan 1957; Claude 1962; Rosecrance 1963; G. Snyder 1997.) Stephen Walt (1987) has pointed out that states may be moved to join an alliance to balance threat, a more immediate source of concern than adversaries' capabilities. Even those who develop more formal approaches often accept that alliances increase their members' security. Specifically, John Conybeare has looked at how states minimize their exposure to risk through the construction of their alliance portfolios (1992, 1994; see also Nelson 1991). Even some studies that focus on the effect of domestic political structure in alliance decisions suggest that domestic factors affect the choice of allies, though not the decision to seek allies in the first place, a decision that is seen to rest with security concerns (Barnett and Levy 1991; Siverson and Starr 1994; Gilligan and Hunt 1998).

Furthermore, the assumption that states join alliances to increase their security can be seen in work that looks at the effects of belonging to an alliance on the individual members. Much of this work begins with the longstanding premise that an alliance provides a collective good to its membership (Olson and Zeckhauser 1966; Conybeare and Sandler 1990; Murdoch and Sandler 1982; Oneal and Elrod 1989; Oneal 1990; Palmer 1990b; Sandler 1993). In this strand of research, the weaponry allies possess contributes to the deterrent or the defensive capability of the alliance; whether based on the threat of punishment that underlies deterrence or on the ability to protect territory from the enemy, the public good provided by the alliance is security.

---

[1] To be sure, not all alliances require that the signatories actually defend each other should they be attacked. Some "alliances," such as the United States–Japan security guarantee, call upon only one of the states to defend the other. Japan is not obligated to come to the defense of the United States, in the unlikely event the United States is attacked. Neutrality pacts only reflect a promise between the signatories not to attack one another. The von Ribbentrop-Molotov Pact between Germany and the Soviet Union, signed in August 1939, was nominally only an agreement that each state would not attack the other. (Secret parts of the treaty divided Poland between Germany and the USSR and reflected agreement about how war against Poland was to be conducted.) Ententes simply require that the states consult in times of high tension. The Triple Entente among Britain, France, and Russia prior to World War I is an example of such an arrangement. See Small and Singer (1969) for a presentation and discussion of this alliance typology. A.J.P. Taylor (1954), Inis Claude (1962), Stephen Walt (1987), John Vasquez (1993), and Glenn Snyder (1997) present instructive discussions of the historical and theoretical functions of alliances.

This large and disparate literature shares the realist belief that alliances serve simply to increase the security of their members. The two-good theory does not accept this general assumption, instead seeing alliances as potentially providing different benefits to different members. A major reason we focus so heavily on alliances in this chapter, therefore, is that investigating alliances is a fruitful and efficient way to show the differences between our theory and more standard approaches to international relations, such as realism, which forms the basis of so much of the work done on alliances.

Our two-good theory can explain much about alliance behavior that realism cannot. This is what one would expect from a theory such as ours that rejects some of the fundamental assumptions that undergird realism. While our assumptions are as general as realism's in that they are meant to apply universally (though unlike realism we allow for domestic circumstance and leaders' preferences to affect state behavior), they add the matter of state choice—states must determine how to allocate resources to achieve the desired balance of change and maintenance. That added central element of our theory—state choice—makes our theory more useful and more widely applicable. This is clearly illustrated by applying our theory to alliances and to the trade-offs that are implied in a state's decision to join or leave an alliance. Realism can speak to one side of the choice that leaders face and presents that choice starkly: does membership in the alliance increase or decrease the state's security. Our theory sees the decision as encapsulating a two-sided choice and permits a more nuanced consideration of the costs and benefits of alliance membership.

We give alliances the attention we do for three additional reasons. First, the theoretical work on alliances in international relations is vast, as is appropriate to a topic that so immediately affects a large number of states and has done so for centuries. Any theory of foreign policy that purports to be "general," as ours does, must be able to speak to a number of issues in international relations, and perhaps none more than the motivations states have for joining and remaining in alliances.

Second, it is absolutely clear that states enter into alliances with the expectation that other foreign policy behaviors will be affected. This is obviously the case if alliances are seen as a substitute for military expenditures. Even if we adopt the position that the only purpose of an alliance is to deter aggression and to provide for the common defense if deterrence fails (which we do not), the goal of entering into an alliance is to affect the use of another instrument of policy—the use of force. In fact, we accept the position advanced by Leeds and her colleagues (Leeds, Long, and Mitchell 2000) that states can enter into alliances for myriad purposes, but each involves a commitment by the signatories regarding other, specific behaviors. Thus, an important test for our theory, from both a scientific and a policy-prescriptive perspective, is whether it can explain and predict how alliance membership influences state behavior in other realms. Our theory provides both an understanding of why states add or subtract alliances from their overall foreign policy portfolio and what the alliances' effects are on other components of those portfolios.

Last, we devote so much attention to the study of alliances because of its contemporary relevance. The demise of the Soviet Union, for instance, has led some policymakers to argue that NATO should expand eastward and admit former members of the Warsaw Pact, perhaps even including Russia itself. What would be the effect of such an expansion? Would it, as is commonly argued, help ensure the survival of democracy in Eastern Europe? Would it (perhaps simultaneously) protect the new members from Russian intimidation? Our theory is able to provide some answers to these questions, not because it is deeply rooted in an understanding of NATO or the cold war but because its general nature should provide room for applications to a variety of circumstances, including ongoing ones. The relevance of our general theory, we think, should be illustrated not just through analyses of past events but also through the answering of more immediate and policy-relevant questions.

In this chapter we do three things. First, we present our theory's applicability to alliances. By now, the reader may be sufficiently informed about our theory that she may think little more is to be gleaned. One of the benefits of the two-good theory, however, is that some surprising things come to light through its use—and the general topic of alliances is one of the primary examples of this, in our view. So spending a little more time on theoretical development is useful. Second, we present empirical analyses testing some of the hypotheses that come out of our model. That empirical analysis is important because the hypotheses discriminate between the two-good theory and realism rather nicely. We show that the analyses support our model well. Last, we look at one international event in some detail—the Suez Canal Crisis of 1956. We do this because, at its base, our model says that alliances provide resources to states to pursue their own goals—they liberate states. Realism, on the other hand, sees alliances largely as international marriage contracts: alliances commit states to one another, perhaps even to the point where the signatories must do things that they would not otherwise choose to do. The Suez Canal Crisis contains several elements of what goes into alliances, and aspects of the crisis (particularly the American success in pressuring Britain and France into changing their behavior) seem, at first blush, inconsistent with our argument. But, as we hope to show, the very attempt by Britain and France to alter the situation in Egypt is almost impossible to imagine without the alliance with the United States. Specific elements of the crisis conform very closely to what our model would suggest.

What Do Alliances Do? Protect and Serve

In this section we refer to our theoretical argument to derive general hypotheses relating alliance membership to other foreign policy behaviors. Recall from our theoretical discussion of foreign policy substitutability in chapter 5 that our theory provides specific expectations regarding substitutability relationships, but these relationships are also complex. Previous empirical work on foreign policy substitutability was based on the expectation that the use of any two policies that are substitutable would be related inversely. Our theory suggests that the relationship between the uses of any two policies depends on two factors. First, it depends on whether the policies are intended to produce the same good or different goods. Second, it depends on whether resources were reallocated among policies because of a change in the state's capabilities, a change in the state's preferences over change and maintenance, or a change in the relative efficiency with which various policies produce respective goods. Here, we provide a more detailed theoretical development focusing specifically on alliances.

The first confounding factor we must face when dealing with alliances is that states can join an alliance to provide maintenance, to provide change, or to provide both. Furthermore, a single alliance can serve multiple purposes, providing a mechanism for each member to gain its more preferred good. In their detailed examination of the texts of alliance treaties, Leeds and her colleagues discovered that the actual agreements often require very different behaviors from various signatories (Leeds, Long, and Mitchell 2000). For example, one party might agree to come to the defense of its ally, if the latter is attacked, in exchange for the latter's agreeing to concessions in an entirely different realm, such as trade concessions. In essence, the first state is gaining change at the sacrifice of maintenance while the latter is gaining maintenance and sacrificing change. New Zealand's alliance with Great Britain provides a clear example of where the goals of allies can differ. Recall from chapter 4 that New Zealand gained protection from Britain in the late nineteenth and early twentieth centuries, while Britain gained almost exclusive access to New Zealand's trade and gained New Zealand's support for a variety of issues before the British Dominion's council.

As argued in earlier chapters, we assume that a state entering an alliance with a stronger partner is engaging predominantly in maintenance-seeking behavior while a state aligning with a weaker partner is engaging predominantly in change-seeking behavior.[2] That is, in allying with a stronger state, the weaker ally alters some aspect of its foreign, or domestic, policy in a direction favored by the stronger. In return, the stronger ally aids the weaker in maintaining some other aspect of the status quo, such as protecting its sovereignty against potential aggressors. Alliances that contain a mixture of states with different levels of power are called asymmetrical alliances. The two-good theory leads us to conclude that the states with different amounts of power are pursuing different goals through their membership. Thus, we expect the effect of alliance

---

[2] Much of the following discussion is taken from Morgan and Palmer (2003).

membership on other policies to differ across states, depending on whether they are strong or weak.

Next, to determine the effect of alliance membership on other policies, we must consider what must happen for two states that were previously unallied with each other to form an alliance. We assume that alliances, like all foreign policy behaviors, require resources that could be devoted to other instruments of policy. We further assume that states allocate their resources in the manner that provides them the most preferred mix of foreign policy goods possible. This implies that all *observed*[3] alliances are efficient.

This notion—that observed alliances are efficient—is critical to our argument and is thus worth a short digression. Essentially, we mean that no state will enter an alliance if it does not produce more change and/or maintenance than that state could produce by allocating those same resources to some other policy. If any state considering an alliance could produce a more preferred foreign policy without the alliance than with it, that state will not join the alliance. Thus, all alliances that actually form must produce more change and/or maintenance for all signatories than each could obtain without the alliance; that is, every alliance that actually forms is efficient. This point would seem rather uncontroversial, but it has implications that directly contradict standard ways of viewing alliances.

Traditionally, alliances are viewed as constraining state behavior.[4] Certainly, any state entering an alliance must give something up. It must devote resources to the alliance, and it makes commitments regarding its future behavior that it might come to regret. However, the state gains something by joining the alliance and, by our assumption regarding efficiency, those gains must be more than worth the costs for the state to enter the alliance. If an alliance enables a state to produce its desired foreign policy goods with fewer resources than it could otherwise, this actually frees resources for the pursuit of additional goods. In other words, observed alliances are liberating, not constraining. Certainly, many potential alliances would be, on balance, constraining for one or more members, but these alliances never form. We believe that the idea that observed alliances are liberating, rather than constraining, enables us to account for the effects of alliances far better than can traditional perspectives.

Now, why would two previously unaligned states opt to expend the resources necessary to become allies? Basically, for this to occur, something must have

---

[3] When we refer to an alliance as "observed" we mean one that has actually formed. We intend to distinguish these from all of the potential alliances that never form. In principle, any pair of states could be in an alliance at any time. We believe the fact that the vast majority of these potential alliances never form is an important aspect of understanding alliances. Our argument hinges on the notion that a potential alliance becomes an observed alliance *only if*, on balance, it benefits every signatory.

[4] We find it interesting, however, that most realists view alliances as constraining while also holding that alliance commitments are hollow promises.

happened to make at least one of the states willing to join an alliance that was previously viewed as undesirable.[5] It might be that the state has undergone an increase in capabilities, providing it more resources to devote to foreign policy. It might be that something has caused the alliance to become more efficient, relative to substitutable policies, at producing change and/or maintenance for the state. This could be that the potential partner is willing to make a better deal or for a host of technological or environmental factors (for example, improvements in communications technology). Or, it might be that one state has come to place a greater value on the good that it can obtain through the alliance. For example, if a state that would increase its maintenance through the alliance came under an increased threat, it would be willing to shift some resources from change-producing policies to the alliance.

We can now put all of these factors together to develop a fairly complex picture of the effect of alliances on other foreign policy behaviors. Figure 7.1 will serve to guide the discussion. Suppose that we observe a state's foreign policy portfolio at some moment in time. Its resources and the international environment determine a production possibility frontier (PPF), which we have labeled α, and its preferences over maintenance and change interact with this frontier to produce an equilibrium foreign policy portfolio, which we have labeled p. Further, suppose that this state has alliances with some set of countries and that this alliance portfolio provides it with levels of maintenance and change that would place it at point a in the space and that its other policies, such as defense spending and dispute behavior, move it from point a to point p.[6] What happens to other policies as a result of the formation of a new alliance?

The first thing to note is that our assumption that the new alliance is the most efficient available policy for the state in seeking its goals has an important implication for our argument—one result of the formation of a new alliance is that the state's PPF immediately moves outward. No state will form an inefficient alliance (causing the frontier to move inward). And if any policy using resources more efficiently than alternative existing policies becomes available, this produces the same effect as does gaining additional resources. The shift in the frontier can be small or large. We will assume that the amount by which the PPF is shifted outward is a function of the capabilities of the newly aligned

[5] It might be the case that both states' situations have changed, but that is not necessary. Since both must agree to ally before an agreement can be made, if A desires an alliance with B, but B does not want an alliance with A, A and B will not ally. In this case, it is necessary only for some aspect of B's situation to change for the alliance to form (assuming this change makes B willing to align with A).

[6] Note that while the example in figure 7.1 is quite specific, the conclusions we illustrate with it are fully general with respect to the state's preferences (which determine the location of p) and alliance portfolio (which determines a). That is, our conclusions are not dependent on the precise locations of a and p. Note also that a would be located at the origin in the case of a state with no alliances.

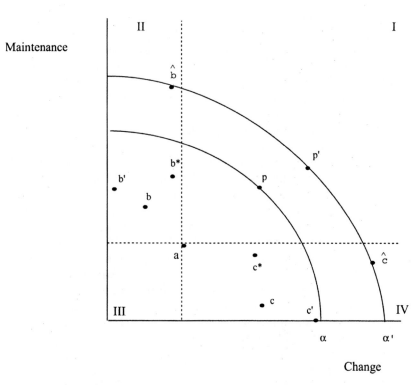

Figure 7.1. Alliances and Foreign Policy Substitution

state and the combined capabilities of its new alliance partners. Specifically, we believe that upon joining similar alliances, the frontier of a small state would be more affected than would that of a large state; a state's frontier will shift more when it aligns with a powerful state or states than when it aligns with less powerful states, all else being equal. In figure 7.1, we represent this effect with the frontier, α'. This shifted PPF leads us to expect that a new foreign policy portfolio formed will be at point p'. (The exact position of p' depends on the shape of the state's indifference contours.)

We want to reiterate the implications of this process on foreign policy substitutability. While substitutability has typically been viewed as suggesting that one policy can replace another—for example, a state seeking to increase its security can do so by forming an alliance or through increasing its defense spending—our formulation suggests that alliance formation should lead, in general, to more of all types of foreign policy behavior. To put it simply, we see alliances as providing states access to more resources, thereby allowing them to do more in their foreign policies, whether the new alliance is formed as a result of increasing capabilities or a greater desire for the alliance by the new partner.

If, for instance, we observe a state forming an alliance because its own resources have increased, we would see increases (or, at least, no decreases) in other types of behaviors. Likewise, if a state forms a new alliance because something in the environment has made that alliance more efficient (such as if the alliance partner only recently became more willing to join), the alliance is liberating, not constraining.

Returning to figure 7.1, recall that point a denotes the change and maintenance the state received from its previous alliance portfolio. When the state joins a new alliance, one of four general effects can take place: the new alliance can provide the state with additional maintenance and change, moving the point to the northeast; it can provide the state with less of both maintenance and change, moving the point to the southwest; it can increase the maintenance while decreasing the change the state derives from alliances, moving the point to the northwest; or it can increase the change while decreasing the maintenance the state derives from alliances, moving the point to the southeast. Note the dotted lines passing through point a. These lines cut the space into four quadrants associated with these four general effects. We can observe decisions by states to add to their alliance portfolios and identify how these changes affect the maintenance and change obtained from alliances. We can then derive hypotheses pertaining to how various alliances should affect other foreign policy behaviors.

First, consider shifts to the southwest, into quadrant III. According to the theory, shifts of this kind should not occur. States should be willing to decrease both their maintenance and change only when they are when required to, such as when they are seeing a decrease in their capabilities. States becoming weaker should be shedding (or, more likely, their partners are shedding them) not gaining alliances. Since states that are adding alliances should not be moving into quadrant III, we have no expectations regarding the effect such a move would have on other foreign policies. Indeed, in previous work we have shown that very few changes in alliance portfolios result in this southwesterly shift, that almost none of those that did involved a state that was gaining in power, and none of them involved a state adding alliances (Morgan and Palmer 1996).

Second, consider alliances that provide a state with additional maintenance and change, that is, shifts into quadrant I. These types of alliances would have the effect of moving the state fairly close to p′ without any other changes in foreign policy. Depending on whether the alliance alone shifted the state to the new frontier α′, and the precise mix of maintenance and change provided by the alliance, we could observe some changes in other foreign policies, though the general expectation is that any such change would be minor. If the alliance moved the state precisely to p′, we would expect no changes at all in other behaviors.

Next, consider alliances that increase maintenance and decrease change, that is, those that shift the state into quadrant II. We have clear expectations about the effect of such an alliance on a state's change-seeking behavior. These alliances have moved the state away from its most desired amount of change while increasing the ability of the state to pursue change. Not surprisingly, we expect all such states to increase their change seeking. In addition, we can empirically determine the angle of the shift in alliance portfolio (that is, the angle from the upward vertical line passing through point a and the line passing through a and the point representing the new levels of change and maintenance provided through alliances), and we expect that the increase in change-seeking policies should be directly related to this angle. This is because the greater the angle, the more the alliance has moved the state away from its most preferred point with regard to change. We cannot, however, determine how far the alliance has put the state from its PPF. If the alliance puts the state below p′ (at point b or b*), the state will increase its maintenance-seeking behaviors. If the alliance puts the state level with p′, the state will not change its maintenance seeking. If the alliance puts the state above p′ (at b̂), the state will decrease its maintenance-seeking behaviors. Thus, we have no firm expectations regarding the effect of such an alliance on maintenance policies.

Finally, we address the alliances that increase change and decrease maintenance, that is, those that shift the state into quadrant IV. Here, we have definite expectations regarding the effect of such an alliance on maintenance-seeking behavior. All such alliances have moved the state away from its most desired amount of maintenance and increased the ability of the state to pursue maintenance. Again, we can tell empirically when an alliance is a type IV alliance and we can determine the angle of the shift (now the angle between the downward vertical line through a and the line from a to the point representing the new levels of maintenance and change). All states joining such alliances should increase their maintenance-seeking behaviors, and we expect that the increase in maintenance-seeking policies should be inversely related to the angle of this shift. This is because the greater the angle, the less the alliance has moved the state away from its most preferred point with regard to maintenance. If the alliance puts the state to the left of p′ (at point c or c*), the state will increase its change-seeking behaviors. If the alliance puts the state level with p′, the state will not change its change-seeking behaviors. If the alliance puts the state to the right of p′ (at ĉ), the state will decrease its change-seeking behaviors. But note, as before, that we cannot determine how far the alliance has put the state from its original PPF, and thus we can have no firm expectations regarding the effect of type IV alliances on change-seeking policies.

Our discussion leads us to four general hypotheses regarding the changes in foreign policies that should be produced by states belonging to alliances or changing their alliance portfolios. First, in existing asymmetrical alliances—those consisting of powerful states and weaker states—the weaker states should pursue change more than would be expected in the absence of the alliance while more powerful states will pursue maintenance more than they would otherwise. Specifically, we expect that weaker allies should allocate more resources than we might expect to such policies as foreign aid and conflict initiation while more powerful allies should allocate less. Similarly, stronger allies should devote more resources to maintenance-seeking policies, such as defense spending, than we would otherwise expect while weaker allies should allocate less.

Second, we expect alliances that move states into quadrant II to produce an increase in change-seeking behavior and that this increase will be associated with the angle formed by the vertical line through a and the line through a and the point associated with the maintenance and change provided by the new alliance. Third and similarly, we expect alliances that place states in quadrant IV to produce an increase in maintenance-seeking behavior and we expect this increase to be associated with the angle formed by the downward vertical line through a and the line through a and the point associated with the maintenance and change provided by the new alliance.

Our last expectation is that, after forming a new alliance, states should generally increase both types of behavior, since the alliance has the effect of pushing the PPF out. We hypothesize that states forming alliances will increase all types of behavior (even when controlling for changes in the state's capabilities) and that the amount of this increase will be related to the capabilities of the new alliance partner(s) and the capability of the state. Similarly, when an alliance is terminated, all types of foreign policy behavior will decrease, and the amount of the decrease will be related to the capabilities of the lost allies.

In the next section we look at statistical analyses that show how alliance membership affects various aspects of a state's foreign policy portfolio.

Statistical Analyses: The Revealed Effects of Alliances

In this section we present our statistical investigations of the effects of alliances on other foreign policy behaviors. We expect that alliance membership will affect a wide variety of foreign policies and conceivably all other foreign policies. It would be beyond the scope of any work of this nature and beyond the tolerance of any reader to analyze the effects of alliances on any more than a few such policies. In this chapter we have chosen to analyze the effects of a state's altering its alliance portfolio on four foreign policy behaviors: foreign aid, dispute initiation, military spending, and the pursuit of a capital-intensive (or "change") military establishment.

We break this presentation into three parts. In the first, we focus on the effects of alliance *membership*. We focus specifically on the manner in which membership in an asymmetrical alliance affects foreign aid allocations. The second part is concerned with the effects of *joining* an alliance. In particular, we seek to determine whether the good (change or maintenance) produced by joining an alliance leads to a more active pursuit of the other good as reflected in defense expenditures and defense expenditures per military personnel. Finally, we see how *changes* in a state's alliance portfolio lead to changes in other foreign policies. In this part we focus on rates of conflict initiation as well as on our defense spending variables.

Asymmetrical Alliances and Foreign Aid

Our first task is to consider how alliance membership affects the use of other foreign policies. The two-good theory leads us to expect that this will depend on what is being produced by the alliance and what is being produced by the other policy in question. Return again to figure 7.1 and recall that we assume that in asymmetrical alliances, strong states gain change while weak states gain maintenance. A state gaining change from its alliance membership would move almost directly east in the figure. This would imply that we should expect it to increase other maintenance-seeking policies and reduce other change-seeking policies in order to move to its most preferred balance of change and maintenance. On the other hand, a state gaining maintenance from its alliance membership would move almost directly north in the figure, which leads us to expect this state to increase its change-seeking behaviors while reducing its other maintenance-seeking behaviors.[7] Thus, since we view foreign aid, at least in the form of development assistance, as change-seeking behavior, our empirical expectation is that weak states will devote more resources to foreign aid when allied than they otherwise would and that strong states will devote fewer resources to foreign aid when allied than they otherwise would.

Our first statistical analysis investigates the effect of membership in an asymmetrical alliance on foreign aid allocation of the member states. To determine this effect, we want to look at some states that are allied and some states that are not. We want, nonetheless, to restrict our analysis to countries that have the same level of economic development, as there are probably strong effects of development on the foreign aid allocation process. As in the previous chapter, we chose to restrict our analysis to countries that are members of the OECD for the years 1966–95. Some of the OECD states during this period are members of an asymmetrical alliance, NATO, some are not, and some became members during the period. According to the model, participation in an asymmetrical alliance provides maintenance to its weaker members (such as Norway and the Netherlands in NATO, as well as New Zealand and Australia during their years of participation in ANZUS), leading them to seek a balance in their foreign policy portfolio that can be realized through an increase in their change-seeking policies. This implies that NATO participation will have a systematic positive effect on the development assistance donations of these less

---

[7] These expectations were derived mathematically in chapter 5.

powerful states, relative to similar non-aligned states. The other, more powerful alliance members (for example, the United States and Great Britain), however, efficiently gain change through the alliance, and they will seek their most preferred foreign policy portfolio by allocating fewer resources to foreign aid than they might be expected to in the absence of the alliance. This means that weaker allied OECD members should spend more on foreign aid than similar non-allied states, while stronger OECD allied states should donate less than might otherwise be expected.

To test this, we employ a log-linear model, taking the natural logarithms of foreign aid and GNP, our dependent and primary independent variables, respectively. (The data sources are described in appendix A.) In this log-log model, the slope coefficient measures the income elasticity of foreign aid.[8] As the error terms are correlated, we lagged the dependent variable.[9] Further, we included dummy variables for each of the countries[10] in our analysis (with the exception of Luxembourg), as the data indicated that unit effects exist here (Greene 1997, 615–18), though we present the results in the table here without all the dummy variables included. (The complete table is presented in the appendix.) We utilized ordinary least squares to estimate the equation with panel-specific autocorrelation and generated panel corrected standard errors (Beck and Katz 1995; Greene 1995). Excluding those country dummy control variables, the statistical model is:

$$\text{Natural Log of Aid} = a + b(\text{Natural Log of Capabilities}) + c(\text{ALLIED}) \\ + d(\text{ALLIED} \times \text{Natural Log of Capabilities}). \quad (1)$$

Our theory leads us to expect that the coefficient on ALLIED will be positive (indicating that smaller allied states spend more on foreign aid than smaller non-allied states) and that d, the coefficient on the interaction term,

---

[8] For a detailed discussion of log-log models, see Gujarati (1992). There is a more extended discussion of the precise expectations that are being tested with this particular log-log model in Palmer, Wohlander, and Morgan (2002). Briefly, as we see foreign aid as primarily a change-seeking policy, we expect its income elasticity to be greater than 1. In other words, as a state's resources increase by some percentage, we expect the amount allocated to foreign aid to increase by more than that percentage.

[9] Lagging the dependent variable is a technique that has its critics (see, for instance, Achen 2000). We conducted the analysis including and excluding the lagged term, and the results were substantively similar.

[10] The OECD countries we analyzed that were allied throughout the period are: Australia, Belgium, Canada, Denmark, France, Germany, Italy, Japan, Luxembourg, the Netherlands, Norway, United Kingdom, and the United States. Austria, Finland, Sweden, and Switzerland are non-allied during the whole time. Spain and Portugal join NATO in 1982, while New Zealand leaves its asymmetrical alliance in 1985.

TABLE 7.1
Alliances and Foreign Aid Donations, 1966–1992

Ordinary Least Squares with Panel Corrected Standard Errors	
Log of GNP	4.79***
	(0.376)
Allied?	22.79***
(1 = yes; 0 = no)	(4.04)
(Log Capabilities)	−2.25***
(Allied)	(0.449)
Lag Log (Aid)	0.273***
	(0.032)
Constant	2.241***
	(0.749)
R^2	0.9292
Significance	0.0000
Wald Chi-square (24)	16956.91
N	566

Dependent Variable: Natural log of foreign aid
One-tailed significance levels reported (*** $p < .01$).
Standard errors in parentheses.
Dummy variables for the countries have been excluded from the table. All were statistically significant at the .01 level.

will be negative. Essentially, the two-good theory predicts that the line describing the relationship between resources and foreign aid allocation for the NATO members has a higher intercept and is flatter than the line for the non-allied states. The results of this analysis are presented in table 7.1. The analysis supports the hypotheses derived from the two-good theory: smaller allied states tend to allocate more resources to foreign aid than their non-allied counterparts, while larger allied states spend less that one would expect to see. Figure 7.2 depicts the form of the relationship found in the statistical analysis between a state's resources and its foreign aid allocation, both for allied and non-allied states.

The two-good model's expectations are borne out here, and alliances apparently give different benefits to their members. Quite predictably, then, the members respond to alliance by altering their other policies—states that receive maintenance through alliance membership pursue more change, and states that receive change use other change-providing instruments less than might otherwise be expected. Instead of analyzing how membership in alliances affects policies, we now turn to see how *new* alliance membership affects how states behave.

Foreign Aid

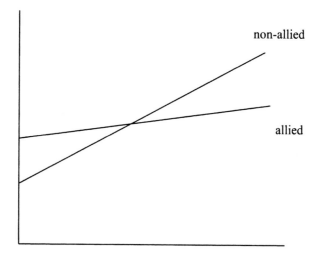

Resources

Figure 7.2. Resources, Alliances, and Foreign Aid

The Gained Good and the Response

The next set of analyses that we present concerns the effects of joining particular types of alliances, those that provide either change or maintenance to the
new allies. While some new allies gain both change and maintenance, some of
our past work shows that by far most gain only one good while giving up the
other (Morgan and Palmer 1996). In this section, we look at the effect of new
membership in alliances that require states to make trade-offs.

First, consider states that gain maintenance through their new alliance at the
cost of change (that is, those states in quadrant II in figure 7.1). Upon joining
the alliance, these new allied states have foreign policy portfolios that are more
maintenance heavy, putting them northwest of their original equilibrium in
the figure and initially away from the most desired equilibrium point, given
their resources. The two-good theory predicts that these states should respond to their new situation by increasing the change they pursue unilaterally,
even if that comes at the cost of maintenance. On the other hand, some states
join alliances that increase their change at the cost of maintenance. The reactions of states in this situation are different. Specifically, these states have
moved southeast of the original equilibrium point in figure 7.1, meaning that
their foreign policy portfolio now has more change and less maintenance than
previously, and they have not achieved the most desired mix of change and
maintenance, given their relative capabilities; the theory predicts that these
states will act so as to increase their maintenance.

To test this, we use the standardized values of change and maintenance that states get from their new alliances to measure the angle created by the movement from the old to the new foreign policy portfolio. For states that gained maintenance at the expense of change, we can determine how far "west" of the equilibrium point the state moved upon entering its new alliance. To do this, we measure the degrees from straight "north" a state moved, and refer to this variable as "Degrees." A movement of 90 degrees would represent, for instance, a loss of change with no gain of maintenance—a move directly "west"; 0 degrees represents a move straight "north" with no loss of change, only a gain in maintenance. (The precise manner in which this variable was created is described in the appendix.) Our expectation for states that have moved into quadrant II is that the more change that is given up to achieve the alliance-supplied maintenance—in other words, the more westward the state moves—the larger the value on "Degrees" and, we believe, the greater the probability that the state will subsequently engage in change-seeking behavior. For states that increase change while decreasing maintenance, that is, those states that move into quadrant IV, "Degrees" measures how far from directly "south"—loss of maintenance with no gain in change—a state has moved. A movement of 45 degrees, for these states, would mean a standardized loss of maintenance matched by a standardized gain in change; 90 degrees represents a gain in change with no loss of maintenance. The theory's expectation for these states is that as "Degrees" increases—that is, the movement becomes more "eastward"—the probability that the state will engage in maintenance-seeking behavior decreases.

"Degrees" cannot tell us how much maintenance and/or change was given up, only the direction in which the state moved, and so our measures cannot predict how much maintenance or change will be regained unilaterally. We can only make the expectations probabilistic, and our dependent variables are therefore dichotomous. The dependent variable for quadrant II countries is created by determining whether a state, in the year immediately after it joined an alliance, increased its change-seeking behavior or not. To determine this, we measure one aspect of a state's foreign policy behavior, what we call "change military."

A state's military establishment is used largely, though not exclusively, for maintenance seeking, but large military establishments, particularly those with large naval capabilities, may be directed toward affecting politics on a more regional or even global level (Modelski and Thompson 1988; Thompson 1988). Investment in the creation or upkeep of military capabilities that can be projected great distances are, generally speaking, capital intensive. Thus, the more capital intensive a state's military, the greater the change-seeking capacity of the military establishment is designed to be. A reasonable indicator of this is a state's military expenditure per personnel. The higher this ratio, the more capital intensive is the military. We modified this indicator slightly, however, as there is an extremely high correlation between time and defense expenditures per personnel; inflation and greater expenditure on capital cause this ratio to grow over time. To avoid the resulting confounding effects, we have chosen to base the indicator on the COW system shares (Singer, Bremer, and Stuckey 1972, 26). Our operationalization of "change military" is defined as a state's system share of the annual military expenditure divided by its system share of military personnel. A dummy variable measuring whether there were increases in "change military" or not serves as our dependent variable and indicates a military establishment's becoming more oriented toward the projection of military power and increases in change seeking.

We expect newly allied states that move into quadrant IV to increase their maintenance-seeking behavior. As our indicator of maintenance seeking, we have chosen general military spending. As we discussed in the previous chapter, military forces can certainly be used to change the behavior of other states and thereby increase one's change. We presume, however, that the great majority of military expenditures are devoted toward protecting what one already has, including the state's sovereignty and continued existence. Additionally, seeking greater change can be more efficiently accomplished by allocating resources to things other than the military. A state is likely to derive much more benefit from foreign aid or from contributions to the International Monetary Fund, for example, than from an equivalent expenditure on defense.[11] Thus, increases in defense spending represent increased maintenance-seeking behavior and decreases represent a reduction in maintenance-seeking behavior. Defense spending data are supplied by the COW Project. For states in quadrant IV, maintenance-seeking behavior is revealed if the state increased its defense spending the year after joining the alliance.[12]

The units analyzed here are nation-years. As we are interested only in the immediate effect of new membership, we restrict the analysis to the year after the nation joined a new alliance.

[11] The U.S. annual military budget (approximately $300 billion) is about three times the combined GNPs of Cuba (about $18 billion), North Korea ($22 billion), and Iraq ($60 billion), according to CIA estimates. Should the United States decide to allocate that $300 billion to foreign aid, major changes in the foreign and domestic policies of U.S. adversaries might be elicited. Of course, such extreme change-seeking behavior would probably leave unprotected some American interests, moving the United States away from its most preferred mix of change and maintenance, and we are not suggesting the United States do that. Our point—which we also raised in chapter 6—is simply that resources given to foreign aid are more likely to bring about desired changes in the behavior of other states than the same resources given to military spending.

[12] We also include two control variables in the analyses. "Time" is created by subtracting 1815 from the year under analysis and is included because there are secular increases in defense expenditure that require the control. "Dollar" is a dummy variable included because the COW data set measures expenditures in British pounds prior to 1920, U.S. dollars thereafter; the variable is coded 1 for years after 1920, 0 for prior years. We have no theoretical expectations regarding either of the variables and do not report the coefficients on those two variables.

TABLE 7.2
New Alliances, Trade-Offs, and Change Seeking

Variable	Coefficient	Probability
Degrees	0.013	0.02*
	(0.006)	
Intercept	0.027	0.93
	(0.326)	

Dependent Variable: Increase in defense spending/personnel (1 = Yes, 0 = No)
$n = 318$
Log-likelihood: −414.77
Restricted model: −420.50
Chi-square: 5.73
Significance = .14
* One-tailed significance test

The results are presented in tables 7.2 and 7.3. As table 7.2 shows and as the model predicts, as "Degrees" increases the probability that the state engages in a change-increasing policy increases: states that have given up more change relative to the maintenance received from their new alliance are subsequently more likely to increase their change seeking. Specifically, the results indicate that a state whose new alliance portfolio moved it 10 degrees into quadrant II has a .53 probability of increasing this type of change-seeking behavior after joining the alliance, while a state that has moved 75 degrees into the quadrant has a .72 probability of seeking more change through increases in the force-projection capabilities of its military. The model's expectations are supported.

Table 7.3 presents the results for the very few (twelve) states that lost maintenance but gained change through their new alliance. As one can see, the coefficient on "Degrees" is not statistically significant, but the number of cases in this quadrant is extremely low, making any measure statistical significance of doubtful value. Note, nonetheless, that the coefficient on "Degrees" is in the direction predicted by the model. States are more likely to increase their military spending as the relative amounts of maintenance lost in their new alliances increase.

The results of the analysis indicate that, as the two-good model suggested would happen, when states join alliances that supply them with one good at the expense of the other, those states respond by increasing the effort they put into reacquiring the lost good. Previously, we showed that existing membership in an alliance has predictable effects on a state's behavior, specifically that small states were more change oriented than would otherwise be expected and large states were less so. We now move to investigate how alliance membership affects other policies—that is, how foreign policy substitutability and alliance membership affect the components of a state's foreign policy portfolio.

TABLE 7.3
New Alliances, Trade-Offs, and Maintenance Seeking

Variable	Coefficient	Probability
Degrees	−0.086	0.16*
	(0.084)	
Intercept	−0.174	0.93
	(1.92)	

Dependent Variable: Increase in defense spending (1 = Yes, 0 = No)
$n = 12$
Log-likelihood: −12.88
Restricted model: −16.30
Chi-square: 3.42
Significance = .33
* One-tailed significance test

Alliances and Substitutability

In this section we present the results of statistical analysis designed to see how changing a state's alliance portfolio affects its other foreign policies. Specifically, we will be testing whether our notion that the state's PPF is pushed outward by entering a new alliance and that the amount by which it is extended affects how much other policies are changed. In other words, the two-good theory says that alliance membership has the effect of increasing the resources available to a state and so allied states do more and are more active in foreign policies than they had been prior to their membership. Further, the theory tells us that the more the alliance contributes to the state's resources, the more active we expect that state to become. That is, the more powerful the new alliance, the more we expect the state to pursue both change and maintenance. This fundamental idea—that alliances liberate states to pursue their interests more vigorously—is directly contradictory to the assumption on which much prior work has been based, specifically that alliances constrain behavior. Seeing whether alliances have the effect of liberating or constraining subsequent behavior is an excellent way to discriminate between the predictions of the two-good theory and approaches more closely tied to realism.

We will be looking at how new alliance membership affects three policies, two of which we discussed in the previous section—"change military" and general military expenditure. "Change military," recall, is a relatively capital-intensive military that can be used to project force great distances and therefore be able to achieve desired changes in the international status quo, while general military expenditure is more effective at achieving maintenance. The third policy we will investigate is conflict initiation. Conflicts are initiated primarily by actors seeking to alter the status quo. Certainly some conflicts are maintenance oriented, or preemptive in nature. But we believe that by and large, conflict initiation is a change-seeking activity. For this indicator, we use the data set on MIDs for 1816–1992 (Jones, Bremer, and Singer 1996).

In undertaking this, we analyze all years for the members of the international system from 1816 to 1992, as defined by the COW Project; the unit of analysis is the nation-year. For "change military" and for general military spending, the cases are restricted to instances where a state gained power through its alliance portfolio. That is, we analyze situations where the state joined an alliance or gained an ally within an existing alliance. Our analysis of dispute behavior is different, however. Because dispute initiation is a relatively rare event, we do not restrict the analysis of that behavior to years where a state added an ally but include all nation-years. To capture the effect of adding to the alliance portfolio, we include a dummy variable for the years where the state gained allies, either through joining a new alliance or adding new members to an existing alliance. For the analysis of militarized disputes, the independent variables (which we discuss presently) that measure the effects of new alliances have values of zero in years where no new alliance was joined, so that the analysis measures the effects of changes in the state's alliance portfolios.

Let us summarize the independent variables used in the analysis. First, our primary hypothesis is that the power gained through an alliance should increase both types of behavior, and the greater this power, the more the new policies will be pursued. To see whether this is so, the first independent variable we use is the power a new alliance provides a given state. (We have discounted this measure by a diffusion factor and weighted it according to the number of other members of the alliance. The precise technique we used is fully described in the appendix.) Second, our theory leads us to believe that the level of a state's power will affect the mixture of policies it will pursue and thus also influence the precise effect of changes in power (whether through alliances or internal growth) on those policies, so we include a variable that measures the state's existing total power, prior to the formation of an alliance, as a control variable. This variable is the sum of the state's power and its *existing* allies' power, discounted and weighted appropriately. Third, we expect that changes in a state's own capabilities will affect its foreign policies—our theory says that as states increase (decrease) in power, they should pursue both change and maintenance more (less) than previously. Therefore, we include the change in the state's own power as one of the independent variables. Last, we expect the effect of *changes* in power to be contingent on the *level* of power, and so we include a variable capturing the interaction between these two. The theory suggests that, holding preferences constant, an increase in power will have a relatively greater effect on change-seeking policies for strong states and a relatively greater effect on maintenance-seeking policies for weak states. The variable captures the interaction between a state's total level of power before an alliance change and the total change in that state's power from both new alliances and internal growth; it is created by taking the sum of change in power and new alliance power and multiplying this by the state's existing total power.

The results of the statistical analyses of the three policies are presented in detail in the appendix. Table 7.4 shows the predicted effects drawn from results of the analysis of joining alliances on the three policies we analyzed. We present the predicted effects of joining alliances for four types of states—weak, average, strong, and very strong—for four allied types—no alliance, an alliance of average power, a strong alliance, and a very strong alliance.[13] To derive the predictions, we held change in state power constant at zero. The second column of table 7.4 shows the predicted probability that a state will initiate a dispute under the various conditions. The third column contains the predicted percentage increase in "change military"; and the final column is the predicted percentage increase in defense spending.[14]

The probability that a state will initiate conflict increases upon joining an alliance, as we thought it would. Consistent with the model, it appears that additions to a state's alliance portfolio allow it to pursue changes in the status quo. The alliance, rather than constraining the state, liberates it and allows the state to pursue foreign policy goals by initiating conflict. As this important implication of the model is supported by the analysis but may nonetheless be contrary to many readers' beliefs, we provide an example of the predictions of the analysis. In August 1939, Nazi Germany and the Soviet Union signed a nonaggression pact with each other. According to the statistical analysis, that alliance had the effect of increasing the probability that Germany would initiate a dispute from already high value of .505 to .841; the alliance raised the probability the USSR would initiate a dispute from .433 to .505. In other words, in 1939, after the signing of the von Rippentrop-Molotov Pact, there was less than an 8 percent chance that neither Germany nor the Soviet Union would initiate a dispute.

The finding that alliances increase the probability of conflict is consistent with some previous empirical work that has investigated the relationship (for example, Ostrom and Hoole 1978; Senese 1997a; Morgan and Palmer 2000). It

---

[13] Average, strong, and very strong values for both alliance capability and state power are determined by the mean, the mean plus one standard deviation, and the mean plus two standard deviations, respectively, of the power values. "Weak" states have COW Combined Index of National Capabilities values of 1.00; "average" states have values of 2.27; "strong" 7.04; and "very strong" states 11.81. The weighted values for the "average," "strong," and "very strong" alliances are 0.286, 1.03, and 1.77, respectively.

[14] "Change military," to remind the reader, is the ratio of COW system shares of military spending to COW system shares of military personnel; the percentage increase in this indicator is therefore difficult to interpret directly and is only weakly correlated (empirically and conceptually) with general military spending, which is the unaltered amount spent. We want to point out, though, that the average annual change in the "change military" indicator is zero, while the average annual increase in military spending in the states we analyzed is about 6 percent, with inflation.

TABLE 7.4
Predicted Effects of Additions to a State's Alliance Portfolio

Alliance Status	Predicted Probability of Dispute Initiation	Predicted Percentage Increase in "Change" Military	Predicted Annual Increase in Military Spending
	Weak State		
Non-allied	0.112	——	——
Joined alliance of average power	0.171	2.0%	13.4%
Joined a "strong" alliance	0.159	7.1%	14.0%
Joined a "very strong" alliance	0.148	12.2%	14.6%
	Average State		
Non-allied	0.126	——	——
Joined alliance of average power	0.191	1.7%	12.9%
Joined a "strong" alliance	0.178	6.4%	13.5%
Joined a "very strong" alliance	0.167	11.1%	14.1%
	Strong State		
Non-allied	0.191	——	——
Joined alliance of average power	0.280	1.1%	11.2%
Joined a "strong" alliance	0.268	4.0%	11.6%
Joined a "very strong" alliance	0.258	6.9%	11.9%
	Very Strong State		
Non-allied	0.278	——	——
Joined alliance of average power	0.391	0.4%	9.4%
Joined a "strong" alliance	0.383	1.5%	9.5%
Joined a "very strong" alliance	0.374	2.6%	9.6%

is important to stress that some empirical work has found that states that are allied *with each other* are less likely to have low levels of conflict between them (Bremer 1992; Maoz and Russett 1993), though the relationship between the existence of a mutual alliance and war is more complicated (Bueno de Mesquita 1981; Bremer 1993). In conjunction with our results, it appears that joining an alliance increases the probability a state will initiate a dispute against countries with whom it is not allied.

Returning to the table, we note that, surprisingly for us, joining stronger alliances does not lead to higher rates of conflict initiation. The effect of the power of the new alliance is not terribly strong (joining a "very strong" alliance leads to a probability of conflict initiation that is only .017 lower than joining an "average" alliance), but it is contrary to what we expected to see. We see that the effect of joining a new alliance itself is greater than the power of that new alliance. This does not invalidate our theory by any means, but it does suggest that at least for conflict initiation, states may not expect to draw directly upon their allies' capabilities.

Turning to increases in "change military" table 7.4 shows a similar pattern. The alliance's contribution to a state's capabilities can have dramatic effects: for all types of states, the more powerful the new alliance, the more capital intensive and change directed the state's military establishment becomes. Further, smaller states tend to move their military establishments in a change-oriented direction to a greater extent than do larger states, though all types of states respond to the new alliance by adopting more change-seeking allocation policies, which is consistent with the model.

All types of states also adopt more maintenance-seeking policies, as indicated by the relatively large increases in general military spending shown in the final column. Frequently (as we noted in the previous chapter), alliance formation and increases in a state's military capability are taken to be substitutes for one another—a state can become more secure undertaking one policy or the other, but it need not do both. We find, as we expected, that joining an alliance generally leads to *higher*, not lower, levels of military effort. Note that the greater impact on military spending is seen in smaller states. This is surprising. Apparently the alliance has a greater effect on the spending patterns of smaller states than more powerful ones, while the more overt behavior of conflict initiation is affected more in larger states.

Alliances, as we expected, increase both change- and maintenance-seeking behaviors. The statistical evidence indicates that joining an alliance significantly increases the likelihood that a state will initiate a dispute—that is, that it will attempt to alter the status quo through the use of military force. Further, new alliance membership increases the extent to which a state's military is oriented toward achieving change: it becomes significantly more capital intensive, and the more powerful the new alliance, the greater that orientation, particularly for small states. For smaller states, the alliance provides protection (our maintenance) and allows them to pursue change more actively. Last, the new alliance is associated with higher general military spending, consistent with our notions but contrary to standard treatments of foreign policy substitutability.

The effect of these results, taken as a whole, is to lend support to the two-good theory. More precisely, the implications of the theory for foreign policy substitutability, and specifically for the effects on change and maintenance seeking of altering an alliance portfolio, have largely been borne out. States that gain maintenance from their new alliance partners respond by increasing their change-seeking behavior, while states that gain change allocate more resources to their maintenance-seeking policies, as we expected.

This differentiated response to alliance membership has some interesting implications. For one, it explains the "exploitation of the great by the weak" that is the hallmark of the collective goods analyses of alliances (see Olson and Zeckhauser 1966). The collective goods perspective has it that the powerful members of an alliance provide the collective good of security to the weaker members. Because this security cannot be withheld from any member of the alliance, the weaker members are able to free ride and make only limited contributions to the alliance's military preparedness. Our explanation for the observed different levels of military spending for the powerful and the weaker differs. According to the two-good theory, the powerful allies gain the capacity to induce change from the asymmetrical alliance and respond to that by increasing allocations to policies that provide maintenance, such as increasing their military capabilities; the weaker states gain maintenance from alliance membership and allocate greater resources to policies that are better able to provide change, such as foreign aid. The two-good theory's explanation is based on the simple assumption that states may have more than one goal in their foreign policy behavior, and states engaging in some particular behavior—such as joining an alliance—may have more than one motivation. This simple assumption, we believe, is a powerful one and takes us a long way.

We move presently to apply the two-good theory's implications to a specific historical case—the Suez Canal Crisis of 1956. This is a particularly good case to study, as there are divergent interpretations of the role alliances play in it, and those interpretations highlight the distinction between the two-good theory and more traditional understandings of alliances. Specifically, the crisis is often used to illustrate how alliances can constrain the behavior of their members.[15] Our theory, on the other hand, sees alliances as providing their members the wherewithal to pursue their goals more efficiently: alliances are liberating. These two views of alliances are readily juxtaposed and compared in the Suez Crisis.

---

[15] The classic statement along these lines is by Neustadt (1970). See also Osgood (1968).

The Suez Canal Crisis

There are many reasons to study the Suez Canal Crisis of 1956 and a wide range of lessons to be learned from doing so. The crisis involved such international issues as the appropriateness of military force in meeting political difficulties, escalation of the Arab-Israeli conflict, the role of the superpowers in a regional conflict, an attempt by Western states to retain an imperialist past, the perceived need by those same Western states to protect their access to oil, the role of international law and the United Nations, the legality and recognition afforded nationalization of property, the difficulty of successfully managing intra-alliance relations, and the role of domestic politics in affecting foreign policy. We will not be able in this chapter to explore all aspects of this crisis.[16] Instead, our focus is dictated by our theory. We will be looking at the effect of international alliances in the behavior of the states—particularly Britain— involved in the crisis. The main issue we want to address is whether the British alliance with the United States through NATO served to provide Britain with the wherewithal to undertake an action it would not have been able to in the absence of that alliance (as our theory might suggest), or whether the alliance provided a mechanism that allowed the United States to constrain Britain (and France and Israel).

That the alliance with the United States constrained Britain and its two collaborators is a commonly drawn conclusion and one with which we do not quarrel. For several reasons, the United States was clearly unhappy with the joint invasion of Egypt by Britain, France, and Israel and acted decisively to have the military forces of the three countries withdrawn. The alliance, or the network of relations that had been established between the United States and its European partners, allowed the United States to put pressure on Britain and France. But the picture of a major power using an alliance to rein in its wayward partners is an incomplete rendering of NATO's effects in this case. While presenting the major aspects of the crisis, we want to focus on Britain's decision and its ability to undertake the intervention. Specifically, we will demonstrate that, in accord with the two-good theory, the alliance with the United States provided Britain with the means to pursue its own interests in two ways. First, the alliance with the United States provided additional resources to Britain and France. Specifically, the American presence in and commitment to the defense of Western Europe contained in NATO allowed the U.K. and France to move military resources that would have been required elsewhere. Related, and by no means trivial, the British and French invasion forces were made up in no small part of U.S.-supplied equipment, and that equipment would have been difficult if not impossible to replace. Second, NATO allowed

---

[16] The best general treatments we have found of the crisis are Thomas (1966), Love (1969), Carlton (1988), Kyle (1991), Lucas (1991), Freiberger (1992), and Richardson (1996).

the British to pursue policies designed to alter the status quo to a greater extent than previously by providing two forms of protection. For one, the American-led alliance protected one vital aspect of the international status quo—a Western Europe safe from Soviet domination—freeing the U.K. and France to pursue changes in other aspects of the status quo. Additionally, during the crisis itself Britain and France relied on the United States to deter Soviet intervention in the Middle East, and without that protection no invasion could or would have been contemplated.

We will begin by presenting an outline of the crisis and its background and then move to a discussion of the options as Britain saw them.

Background of the Crisis

The Suez Canal Crisis was precipitated, in Western eyes, when President Gamal Nasser of Egypt nationalized the Suez Canal on July 26, 1956. This action had two practical effects: Egypt would be responsible for providing the pilots who would navigate ships through the canal, and the profits from the canal would no longer go directly to the Suez Canal Company. (British interests held about three-eighths of the stock in the company [Love 1969; Richardson 1996].) To understand why Nasser's act would lead in three months' time to an invasion of his country by Israeli, French, and British forces, we need to understand the context more fully.

The Suez Canal was completed in 1869 by a mostly French-owned consortium. Britain's interest in the canal had been slow to develop (due largely to the anti-imperialist leanings of Lord Palmerston), but once it was complete Britain quickly recognized its stake in it, as "seventy percent of the ships that used the Canal in succeeding years flew the Union Jack" (Love 1969, 168). By 1875, Prime Minister Benjamin Disraeli had managed to purchase 44 percent of the shares in the Suez Maritime Company, and the following year Egypt granted "dual control" to France and Britain. After strong and sometimes violent nationalist reaction to this inside Egypt, Britain invaded and occupied the country beginning in 1882, protecting the canal and exercising control over it. That control was to last another seventy-two years. In 1888 the Constantinople Convention assured that the canal "would always be open 'in time of war as in time of peace, to every vessel of commerce or of war without distinction of flag'" (cited in Bowie 1974, 4). In 1904 Britain and France agreed that French interests in Morocco would not be countered by Britain, while the U.K. received a free hand in Egypt from France (Love 1969, 171).

At least theoretically, British occupation from 1882 through 1914 was done by Turkish consent. With the outbreak World War I in 1914, Britain declared Egypt a protectorate, and later granted it independence in 1922. And in a treaty signed in 1936, Egypt agreed to allow up to 10,000 British soldiers to be stationed "in the vicinity of the Canal . . . together with the necessary ancillary personnel for administrative and technical duties" (in Hurewitz 1989, 19–20). Last, in October 1954 Britain agreed to withdraw troops "from the Canal Zone in return for the right to re-enter in the event of an attack on the Arab states or Turkey" (Louis 1989, 43) by a state "*other than Israel*" (Bowie 1974, 5; emphasis added). Subsequently, by June 1956 only 1,200 British civilians remained to administer the canal, which was still to be operated by the Suez Maritime Company until at least 1968, when its concession was scheduled to expire.

The political situation in the 1950s between Egypt and the West was complicated by the interplay between rising nationalism within Egypt and Nasser's attempts to consolidate his power domestically and bolster Egypt's role within the Arab world.[17] For our purposes, however, we need only relate the international circumstances and events.

Western animosity toward Egypt in general and toward Gamal Nasser in particular can be traced to four main issues, though there is an underlying theme of the assertion of political independence to all of them. First, Nasser had been engaged in an anti-Western and specifically anti-British rhetorical campaign for some time, both to bolster his domestic political situation and to assert his leadership within the Arab world.[18] This was also a vital part of Nasser's participation in the Nonaligned Movement, indicated as well in May 1956 by Egypt's diplomatic recognition of the People's Republic of China. (Nasser was the "first head of state to recognize" China [Richardson 1996, 13].) Second, the British had made an effort beginning in the early 1950s to counter what it saw as a growing Soviet presence in the Middle East by supporting the formation of the Baghdad Pact, a collective security arrangement like NATO under British leadership. Turkey and Iraq supported the idea, but Egypt was opposed, and to counter the momentum toward the pact it negotiated bilateral defense agreements with Syria, Saudi Arabia, and Yemen (Bowie 1974, 11); without "Egyptian support . . . many smaller countries, including even Jordan, were inclined to waver" (Carlton 1988, 10). While the Baghdad Pact was formed, with both British and American involvement, it never realized its potential role as a stabilizer of the region, as the British had hoped. The U.K. attributed this diplomatic failure directly to Nasser. Third, after lengthy and fruitless negotiations with the United States, in September 1955 Egypt reached an agreement with the Soviet Union that provided Egypt with approximately $200 million of weaponry from Czechoslovakia in return for shipments of Egyptian cotton.[19] The United States in particular was genuinely alarmed by

---

[17] For good presentations of Nasser's domestic concerns, see Heikal's treatments (1972, 1986).

[18] Carlton (1988) also stresses Egyptian historical animosity toward the British, stretching back to the occupation of 1882.

[19] This was approximately ten times the amount the Americans had been willing to give to Egypt. The United States was concerned about not beginning an arms race in the Middle East and with maintaining a relative parity between the Israelis and Egyptians.

this agreement, which signaled a heightened involvement by the Soviet Union in Middle Eastern affairs: Secretary of State John Foster Dulles called it "the most serious development since Korea, if not since World War II" (Finer 1964, 28; cited in George and Smoke 1974, 317). After this event, the West generally saw Nasser as more pro-Soviet than truly nonaligned and was dubious of his intentions. Fourth, of course, was Egypt's continuing support of fedayeen guerillas operating against Israel in the Gaza Strip and the Sinai.[20] While one should be careful not to exaggerate the pro-Israeli sentiment, particularly among the British (though the French had been active for years in providing Israel with advanced weapons, particularly planes), the Western states were concerned that the fedayeen attacks were politically and militarily destabilizing, creating "among the Israelis a deep sense of siege and imminent war" (Bar-On 1989, 147).

The immediate events leading to the Suez Canal Crisis center on the financing of the Aswan High Dam. The dam had been envisioned as a way to harness the waters of the Nile, providing a more stable supply of water as well as electrical power, while eliminating the river's periodic floods. The size of the project was mammoth, costing an estimated $1.3 billion (equivalent to about $8.4 billion in 2001 dollars), requiring an estimated twelve to fifteen years for completion. Perhaps in part due to Nasser's arms agreement with the USSR, perhaps as an attempt to cool his anti-Western speeches, perhaps to establish economic leverage over him, or perhaps simply on humanitarian grounds, in December 1955 the United States and Great Britain offered to help fund the project, in conjunction with the International Bank for Reconstruction and Development (World Bank). There was immediate opposition to the offer, however. The aid offer to Egypt was controversial inside the United States, as some argued that its lesson was that foreign leaders critical of American policy were treated better than American friends. The Israeli lobby also was opposed, as were some financial analysts who felt that Egypt would be unable to finance its share of the project, particularly in the face of the recent arms deal with the Soviet Union. Further, the offer to Egypt was not followed by a more moderate tone coming out of Cairo; nor was a hoped-for agreement with Israel seen as likely (Burns 1985; Richardson 1996).[21] And, of course, foreign aid is seldom popular in Congress.

Negotiations over the fiscal safeguards went on for months, with Nasser in

---

[20] Egypt and Israel did, however, hold quiet (and at times unofficial) talks in the early to mid-1950s aimed at stabilizing their relations. It is not clear how much room for optimism there was for these talks. See Shamir (1989) and Eban (1977).

[21] The British were also unhappy about the perceived role Nasser played in Jordan's dismissal of Glubb Parsha, the British commander of the Arab Legion, who was given twenty-four hours to leave the country. While the British placed blame on Nasser, it appears that the Glubb was fired for reasons having to do with his personal relationship with King Hussein. The dismissal was a serious blow to British prestige, and Prime Minister Anthony Eden was hard put to design an adequate response. See Churchill (1959), Nutting (1967), and Carlton (1981).

particular unhappy with the proposed arrangements (Bowie 1974, 11). Finally, however, on July 19, 1956, the Egyptian ambassador to the United States met with Secretary Dulles to accept the American arrangement and, stunningly, "Dulles took the opportunity to rescind the offer" (Richardson 1996, 14). Britain and the World Bank withdrew their offers the next day.

Nasser's response was quick in coming. On July 26, he announced the nationalization of the Suez Canal Company, saying that profits from it would be put toward the building of the Aswan Dam.

British and French Reactions

The nationalization led the British immediately to consider its possible responses. The evening the nationalization was announced, British prime minister Anthony Eden held a meeting with "several members of his Cabinet, three of the four Chiefs of Staff . . . the French Ambassador . . . and the American Chargé d'Affaires, Andrew Foster, whose chief, [Withrop] Aldrich happened to be on leave" (Carlton 1981, 407). The discussion focused on reversing the Egyptian action, by force if necessary, and the chiefs were asked to prepare an assessment of the military options available. (Foster reported the discussion to Washington, and thus the United States was aware of the British consideration of an immediate recourse to force.) The next day the chiefs reported that any "assault on Egypt would take weeks to prepare" (Carlton 1981, 407), and Eden decided to use the time to create a unified front with the Americans.

The French were similarly alarmed by Nasser's action and supported taking military action to reverse it for three reasons. First, French financial interest in the canal was almost as great as that of the British, as the majority of the stockholders in the canal company were French. Second, France relied on the canal for transportation for about two-thirds of its crude oil needs, about the same fraction as Britain's. And third, France "believed that their problems in Algeria could not be resolved as long as Nasser continued to assist the Algerian rebels" (Richardson 1996, 14). France, then, supported not just a reversal of the nationalization but also removal of Nasser, by force if necessary.[22]

---

[22] These two goals—the reversal of the nationalization and the removal of Nasser—were clearly distinct, though their relative priority was never fully established by the political leadership. Rather, as the tactical planning for the invasion of Egypt developed, it became clear that a landing at Port Said (at the mouth of the canal) would probably meet with much less resistance than one at Alexandria, which led more directly to Cairo. Removal of Nasser was thought to require a military advance on the capital, a difficult if not impossible goal under the circumstances, particularly with the recent Soviet/Czech arms agreement. Therefore, Port Said was chosen as the landing site, answering in practice the question of the purpose of the invasion. Further, the Israeli attack on Egypt provided the pretext for the allied invasion (protection of the canal), giving more definition to the operational goal. Because the issue of the canal was the one, in practice, that held center stage and is the one that most clearly was addressed by the United States, in our account we focus on the reactions to nationalization.

We do not have space to go into the particulars of the events between the nationalization of the canal and the beginning of the Israeli attack and the subsequent British and French invasion of the canal in October 1956. Instead, we want to focus on the British decision to resist the nationalization by force, a decision that was roundly condemned internationally and domestically, and led to a shameful conclusion to Anthony Eden's political career. We have established that the Suez Canal mattered to the British and that they saw Nasser as a political pariah. The choice of the use of force to alter the status quo—either to remove Nasser or to gain direct control of the canal—was not an obvious one to make. We want to show that Britain and France's alliance with the United States through NATO allowed them to challenge the status quo directly. The alliance served this purpose in two ways. First, the alliance allowed Britain to draw on American resources so that it might be able to pursue its own ends elsewhere. Second, the alliance provided maintenance (or deterrence) to all NATO members. This deterrence took two forms. First, NATO deterred the Soviet Union from invading Western Europe (or so it was thought). Second, during the planning of the Suez invasion, it was assumed that the United States would deter the Soviets from intervening militarily in the Middle East.[23] We address these points now.

NATO came into being in 1949. Its fundamental points were to stress the need for coordinated military planning and to assure an American commitment to defend its Western European allies should they be attacked. This commitment to defend became the cornerstone for NATO deterrence strategy, as it was thought that the Soviet Union would not attack Western Europe and risk major war with the United States.

As the United States was providing deterrence (or, in our theory's terms, maintenance) to its allies, our theory would expect them to respond to this by cutting back their own pursuit of maintenance and to pursue more change. We would expect to see, among other things, lower military spending by the smaller countries and larger spending by the more powerful countries after the formation of the alliance. Yet, as table 7.5 shows, the military spending of the United States, Britain, and France all increased after NATO's formation. One explanation for this is that all three countries were responsible for the deterrence that NATO provided. Indeed, the military doctrine of the alliance held that position. A second explanation for the large military spending is the Korean War (1950–53), which saw substantial action by the forces of all three

---

[23] As it worked out, the invasion of Suez took place one day before the Russians invaded Hungary, so that the Soviets had other concerns during the crisis. (Despite this, the Soviets did threaten military intervention.) The British and French planners working from late July through late October could not know this, however, but expected the United States to keep the Russians at bay. In other words, the expectation that the American deterrent would prove effective mattered in a very real and direct sense.

TABLE 7.5
Military Spending as a Percentage of GNP, 1949–1956

	1949	1950	1951	1952	1953	1954	1955	1956
United States	5.7	5.4	10.9	14.9	14.7	12.7	11.0	10.6
United Kingdom	7.0	7.2	8.9	11.1	11.2	9.9	9.2	8.8
France	6.4	6.5	8.4	10.3	11.0	8.7	7.6	9.2

Source: NATO Facts and Figures (Brussels: NATO Information Service, 1971), 256–57.

countries. But note that even after the Korean War, military spending remains high, higher even than before the alliance was formed. The answer cannot lie entirely in the effects of the cold war. In the earliest days of the cold war, in the aftermath of the Communist coup in Czechoslovakia and during the Berlin blockade, military spending was not as high as in the mid-1950s. This later period saw a lessening of tension between the United States and the Soviet Union and between West and East more generally (Gaddis 1982; Goldstein and Freeman 1990). The main reason for the high levels of military spending by the British and French, aside from providing security to the NATO allies, lies in their activities in other areas.

From the end of World War II through the mid-1950s, Britain and France had each been involved in a series of relatively minor but nonetheless bloody and difficult conflicts. Britain, for instance, fought against a rebellion in the East Indies from 1945 to 1946, where they incurred about 1,000 fatalities (Small and Singer 1982), successfully against the Mau-Mau in Kenya from 1952 to 1956, where perhaps 13,000 combatants died (Olson and Shadle 1996), and in Malaya from 1948 through 1960, where as many as 9,000 insurgents and "security forces" were killed (Lomperis 1996). Combined with Korea, these engagements meant that Britain was involved in violent military actions almost continually throughout the entire period of 1945–60. The French, meantime, had been fighting a terribly expensive and destructive war in Indochina from 1946 until the French surrender in 1954. That war had gradually escalated so that by 1954, French, allied, or Foreign Legion forces fighting in Indochina totaled 236,000 (against about 300,000 Vietminh troops). The war's toll was extensive: by the end of the war French military dead from the conflict totaled about 33,000 with another 42,000 African or Indochinese allied dead (Clodfelter 1995, 23–27). In addition, of course, Britain and France each contributed to the allied effort in the Korean War, where the British eventually suffered 670 battle fatalities and the French 290. Clearly, the military establishments of both countries were active in furthering the individual interests of their states and were able to project force globally, as well as to contribute to the operation of NATO. The large military expenditures reflect the decisions to pursue independent national goals while enjoying the benefits of NATO membership.[24]

Despite the large investment in the military that Britain made in the 1950s, the invasion of the Suez Canal could not have taken place without American resources in a very direct sense. Louise Richardson, in her excellent treatment of the crisis, is able to draw on recently released communications among the principal British decision makers. Minister of Defense Sir Walter Monckton was concerned about British reliance on American equipment, particularly as supplied under the Mutual Defense Assistance Program (MDAP). Richardson's summary of that reliance is worth quoting at length:

> The Royal Navy was using 62 aircraft, 46 Seahawks, 2 Avengers, 9 Skyraiders, and 5 Whirlwind Helicopters supplied under the MDAP. Every one of these aircraft, and another 95 that Britain had bought, were fitted with radio or radar equipment supplied under MDAP for which there were no British substitutes. Similarly, there were no available substitutes for the American electronic equipment with which most of the British ships were fitted. The dependence was not confined to the navy. The army's list included 24 self-propelled guns, radio relay and wireless equipment, specialized vehicles, infantry antitank weapons, and radar equipment. The RAF had . . . 1,500 1,000-pound bombs supplied under MDAP. Many of the RAF's aircraft . . . were supplied under other American defense assistance programs. . . . *Clearly, Britain could not launch an assault [against Egypt] without the use of American equipment.* (Richardson 1996, 61; emphasis added)

Equipment supplied under MDAP was intended solely for use within NATO. If Britain intended or planned to use that equipment in non-NATO activities, it was required first to get U.S. approval. In the case of Suez, the British were concerned that the United States might deny them that permission, if requested. The British therefore decided, according to the minutes of a cabinet meeting on August 20, "that it would be better to say nothing to the Americans for the present" (quoted in Richardson 1996, 60). Clearly the British worried that the possibility that the Americans would deny them authorization would force them into a very unpleasant situation. If the United States were to deny authorization, the British could choose to defy their close ally, risking serious political and economic responses, including public denunciation as well as being cut off from future military assistance. Alternately, of course, the British might have decided to cancel the entire operation (which, in retrospect, may

---

[24] It is difficult to discern how many British and French troops were given directly over to NATO. It appears, though, that NATO did not receive British front-line troops, at least in the 1950s. There are reports that in 1956 the state of the British army in Western Europe necessitated "equipment being borrowed from other armies stationed in Germany so that a passable show could be made on combined maneuvers" (Fullick and Powell 1979, 34).

have been wise), requiring them to accept the dictates of Cairo and Washington. Either course of action was to be avoided, and hence the British decision to keep Washington in the dark about its plans.

The reliance on American-supplied equipment had a worrisome effect on Prime Minister Eden. As a defender of the British Empire, as a believer in Britain's (and his) role as protector of the Commonwealth, accepting the American role in determining Britain's actions was difficult for him. After the decision to keep the United States uninformed about the plans for invading Egypt, a frustrated Eden wondered to Monckton in a memo of August 26, "Have we . . . got ourselves into the position that we cannot send British units to Kenya or to Singapore without first seeking American consent? . . . Is it tolerable that our right—indeed our duty—to maintain law and order in our own Colonial possessions should be open to question and indeed to veto by the United States?" (quoted in Richardson 1996, 60) Eden's unhappiness with the British reliance on American materiel is understandable. Of course, Eden's complaint overlooks the fact that in the post–World War II period, without American assistance, Britain would not have been in a position to contemplate taking action at all.

Our point, of course, is that the alliance with the United States provided the United Kingdom the wherewithal to take the action it desired in Suez and to protect its interests elsewhere. The two-good theory tells us that alliances serve to make the members more able to pursue their own goals; alliances provide latitude and the capabilities for states to do things they might not otherwise be able to do. British reliance on American equipment during the Suez Canal Crisis makes this point very well. Without the capability it derived directly from its alliance with the United States, a British military response to the nationalization of the Suez Canal of the scale envisioned was unthinkable.

Besides providing direct military capability, the alliance with the United States also provided Britain with two forms of protection, each of which served to allow the British to calculate that their deployment of force to the Mediterranean was affordable. Without those forms of protection, it is unlikely that the British would have concluded that direct military intervention in Suez was worth the risk of confrontation with the Soviet Union, the major Egyptian sponsor.

First, the U.S. involvement in NATO provided deterrence to the Western allies. Whatever concerns they may have had regarding Soviet intentions in Western Europe, the allies could rely on the fact that the Soviets could not attack Europe militarily without incurring the greatest possible danger. At the time, American nuclear superiority was unquestioned. The Eisenhower-Dulles doctrine of massive retaliation, announced in 1954, said that the United States would respond to actions against the interests of the free world "if necessary with nuclear weapons and against any suitable targets—not just those in the immediate combat zone" (Freedman 1982, 85). In other words, the United States was prepared to initiate the use of nuclear weapons anywhere it deemed appropriate. When the USSR lacked the ability to retaliate with nuclear weapons, the American threat had a measure of credibility, and its allies felt safe from Soviet attack.

The U.S.-supplied deterrence affected the British in two ways. First, it meant that an attack against a Soviet client like Egypt was not likely to provoke a Soviet move against Europe. The USSR simply could not take the chance of initiating a nuclear war that could very well lead to its own devastation. Second, American nuclear superiority exercised through NATO meant that British conventional (and even nuclear) contributions to NATO were not central to maintaining the alliance's deterrence, at least in the short run. The U.K. could remove at least some of its military presence from Europe to use in its attack on Egypt without endangering the continent.[25]

The second form of protection provided by the Americans to their allies was more immediate. During the planning of the invasion, the British expected the United States to keep the Russians from intervening in the Mediterranean theater of operations. This might not require active American support (Eden was well aware that Eisenhower might be unsympathetic to the effort), but surely the United States would not let the Russians intervene and bring harm to its allies. As Eden put it to Robert Murphy, the U.S. undersecretary of state for political affairs, "we do hope you will take care of the Bear" (cited in Richardson 1996, 39). Without this inherent confidence that the Russians would not challenge the American naval presence in the Mediterranean, the planning for the invasion would have been vastly more complicated.[26] It is not going too far to say that without the assumed support of the Americans, the British would have been unwilling to launch the invasion of the Suez Canal at all. The risk of confrontation with the Russians was simply too great.

The point of our short investigation of the Suez Canal Crisis has been to show how the effect of alliances may be much different than is generally expected. Alliances, to reiterate our basic point, serve to liberate member states to pursue their desired policies more directly. The Suez Crisis is sometimes used as an example where one ally, the United States, constrained the behavior of another, Great Britain. Our story shows that the alliance allowed Britain to do something it would not have been able to do without the alliance.

---

[25] It is impossible to determine from the public record what British troops were redeployed from Europe for the invasion of Egypt. It is clear, though, that at least some troops from Europe were used (Fullick and Powell 1979). In any event, that the British could afford to deploy their best troops for duty outside the European theater is undeniably attributable to their reliance on the American deterrent.

[26] We remind the reader that the British could not have known that when the invasion eventually happened (late October), the Russians would be badly distracted by the situation in Hungary.

Conclusion

In this chapter we have focused on how alliance membership can be expected to alter other elements of a state's foreign policy portfolio. Two primary conclusions can be drawn. First, alliances do affect the use of other instruments of foreign policy, but the precise nature of this effect depends on the state's goal in joining the alliance initially. The theory's expectations are counterintuitive. If—as is the case for most small countries—the state gained maintenance through the alliance, we expect to see it respond by pursuing more change. If the state gains change (as most powerful states do), we expect it to pursue more maintenance. In other words, we expect weaker states to attempt to alter aspects of the status quo more after joining alliances with more powerful states, while the more powerful will act to protect components of the status quo.

The second implication of the theory has to do with the general effect of alliance membership. The theory says that since alliance membership represents the most efficient foreign policy available at the time to accomplish a state's goals, it has the effect of increasing the state's capabilities. In other words, states can do more after having joined an alliance than previously. This implication is counter to much of what we have been told about alliances—that they bind signatories to do things they may not want to do, that they are ways for the signatories to constrain one another's behavior, and so forth. Instead, the two-good theory says that alliances are liberating: they allow states to do more and to pursue their interests more actively. In support of this, we saw that the effect of new alliance membership on states is that they became more active; they engage in more interstate conflict, increase their military spending, and—if weaker—allocate more resources to foreign aid.

We investigated the British response to the Suez Canal Crisis of 1956 to see how its alliance with the United States may have affected its behavior. Its relationship with the United States is often credited with requiring Britain to back down after its military intervention; clearly the United States was unhappy with the British action and its threats to remove support for the pound led to the British withdrawal. This is consistent with the traditional assumption regarding alliances and their effects: they serve to constrain members' behavior. It is also consistent with the two-good theory, which holds that the United States would have gained change, in the form of an ability to influence British policy, from the alliance. We also considered the British plans for the invasion of the canal, however, and showed that the alliance with the Americans was critical to providing Britain with the means to carry out the invasion. A strong case can be made that, without the alliance, the invasion of the canal would not have happened. This suggests that the alliance gave the British the ability to do more in pursuit of their own interests than they otherwise could have done. This is entirely consistent with the two-good theory's expectations but is completely at odds with traditional perspectives. We believe that the two-good theory provides a much more complete explanation of the effects of alliances than do other theories.

We have shown that the two-good theory has some interesting and surprising implications and that they are supported by the historical record. In other words, the theory provides a useful way to approach the analysis of international relations. In the next chapter we conclude our remarks, asking in particular how the two-good theory measures up to the primary alternative approaches.

8

Conclusion

What We Have Learned

WE BEGAN this book with a list of events representing a range of foreign policy decisions made by the United States around the turn of the twenty-first century. Shortly after presenting the list, we promised that we would present a general theory of foreign policy that can provide an integrated explanation for all of the events and show that the decisions leading to them were interconnected. The pages since have, we hope, convinced the reader of the value of our approach. We have presented the theory, used it to explain a variety of events, including some on our initial list, and we have demonstrated that it has some empirical support from large-N statistical analyses. We believe our approach provides an extremely useful means for thinking about foreign policy as well as an extremely fruitful theory upon which to base future research. We will conclude with a brief discussion of our views on the most promising avenues for future research, but first we summarize what we have accomplished and tie up a few loose ends.

The essence of the two-good theory is this: international relations is a struggle between and among states to establish or protect desired outcomes. States want different things and vary in their ability to get those things. More powerful states can bring about the changes they want better than weaker states can. We believe two facets of our theory constitute its main contribution. First, it encompasses the recognition that foreign policy is best understood and explained as a portfolio of actions. Second, it allows for the fact that foreign policy is aimed at producing more than one good. Together, these features allow us to use the theory to explain a wide variety of foreign policy events and to show how seemingly disparate events can be interconnected and interdependent. Consider the list with which we began:

- During much of the 1990s the United States supported expanding NATO by admitting states that had previously been members of the Warsaw Pact. This support was essential to the success of the negotiations that resulted in Poland, the Czech Republic, and Hungary joining NATO on March 12, 1999.
- On April 2, 1996, Secretary of Defense William Perry reported that Libya was constructing an underground chemical weapons facility and warned that the United States would use force, if necessary, to halt construction rather than allow the plant to operate. Libya halted work on the facility immediately, and after diplomatic intercession by Hosni Mubarak of Egypt, Libya agreed not to resume construction.

- On April 30, 2001, the United States announced a major arms deal with Taiwan. The United States agreed to sell Taiwan four Kidd class destroyers, twelve P3 Orion antisubmarine planes, and eight diesel submarines.
- In the spring of 2001, the United States reversed its long-held opposition to allowing the People's Republic of China to join the WTO. On November 10, 2001, the WTO welcomed China as a member.
- On January 5, 2002, the United States announced that it would not bail Argentina out of its financial crisis; the United States said it wanted to avoid being a "financial firefighter." Argentine President Eduardo Duhalde placed blame for Argentina's situation on the American economic model, pushed by Washington, which stressed deregulation and decentralization. On January 15, President Bush warned Argentina not to use its difficulties as an excuse to back down from its free-market reforms. On January 31, the United States cut foreign aid to Argentina because, in the words of Treasury Secretary Paul O'Neill, "it just didn't reform."
- On January 14, 2002, the United States and the Philippines prepared for joint military operations against Abu Sayyaf, an extremist Muslim group with links to Al Qaeda. A plan was agreed to by the two countries whereby 650 U.S. military personnel were to be sent to the Philippines within weeks.
- On April 11, 2003, the U.S. government announced that it had reached a settlement with the New York Yankees, in which the baseball team would pay a penalty of $75,000 for violating U.S. economic sanctions against Cuba by negotiating a contract with a Cuban baseball player.

At first blush, it appears that these actions are unrelated and that each would require its own idiosyncratic explanation. This is, in fact, the approach that most previous efforts at explaining foreign policy would take. From the perspective of our theory, however, these actions are connected parts of the overall foreign policy portfolio of the United States during the immediate post–cold war era and are best understood as such.

With the collapse of the Soviet Union, the United Stated experienced a rapid and extreme increase in its relative capabilities. In terms of our model, the production possibility frontier moved outward, by a substantial amount. Our theory leads us to expect that in such circumstances, the United States would increase all its foreign policy activities significantly. Moreover, since the United States is a very powerful country, we would expect that much of this increase would be devoted to change-seeking activities. That is, we would expect that a large country, such as the United States, experiencing a significant increase in relative capabilities, would be very likely to seek alliances with smaller powers, initiate militarized disputes, devote more of its defense expenditures to force projection capabilities, and use its economic power to induce other countries to alter their behavior. Obviously, most of the actions on our list are examples of change-seeking behavior that were part of an overall effort by the United

States to make the world more to its liking. Nearly all were clearly designed to encourage, or induce, other states to bring their political or economic activities more in line with American preferences. Our theory does not say that such a state would seek change exclusively, however. We do expect it to use some of its resources to maintain aspects of the status quo that it likes. Hence, we continue to see some policies, like the arms sale to Taiwan, aimed at preventing changes that others might seek.

Our theory points out another, perhaps more significant source of interconnectedness among policies. Every foreign policy action requires a commitment of some portion of a state's finite resources. Each unit of resources (even if it is only the few minutes of a border guard's time it takes to examine a passport) devoted to one policy action is one fewer unit of resources that can be devoted to any other activity. Each state must determine how best to allocate the finite resources available for foreign policy. This involves deciding, first, how to balance the pursuit of change with the pursuit of maintenance and, second, which portfolio of available policy actions will be most efficient at producing the desired mix of change and maintenance. Our theory leads us to expect that the resources devoted to any specific policy will vary with the availability of resources, the relative preferences for change versus maintenance, *and* the relative efficiency with which policies produce the desired goods. The clear implication is that one cannot explain fully any foreign policy action without understanding the trade-offs involved in allocating resources among all policies. Consider the least significant item on our list—the penalty assessed the New York Yankees for recruiting baseball players from Cuba. Potential violations of U.S. sanctions law are investigated by bureaucrats in the Treasury Department's Office of Foreign Assets Control. This office also negotiates penalties with violators of the law.[1] This office currently has a budget of about $22 million per year. This is a small amount in the context of the overall U.S. foreign policy budget; but it is $22 million that could be devoted to other policy actions.

Thus, our theory leads us to view the policies on our list as being interconnected in the sense that each is a component of a portfolio of policies designed to produce the desired mix of change and maintenance and in the sense that resources devoted to one must come at the expense of resources devoted to others. We believe that this is the most important feature of our theory—it forces us to consider the trade-offs among policies and to recognize that you cannot provide an explanation for one type of policy action without also

---

[1] These things could end up in the courts. The size of the penalty paid by the Yankees is probably a good indicator of why they wouldn't. One can imagine that pursuing such a matter would easily cost the Yankees far more than $75,000 in legal fees. In this regard, it is worth noting that the penalty assessed the Yankees is among the highest meted out to companies (or individuals) for violations of sanctions laws.

accounting for other actions. We are offering a general theory, applicable to all states at all times and capable of advancing our understanding of a wide range of phenomena.

There are, of course, disadvantages to such a general theory. Some might argue that we are better served by searching for "islands of theory," each of which can provide a better, more detailed explanation for a narrower range of events. Many books have focused specifically on the Marshall Plan, for example, and a reader might believe that one of these provides a better explanation for that significant event than have we. Other scholars have focused extensively on providing explanations for militarized disputes, and some of these might account for more of the variance in dispute initiation than does our theory. Still others have provided explanations for decisions regarding trade policy, or alliance behavior, or military expenditures, and so on.

We are convinced that there is greater value in a general theory that accounts for all of these things. To our knowledge, none of the explanations for the Marshall Plan can also provide an explanation for the 1996 threat to use force against Libya, none of the explanations for dispute initiation can explain the reversal of U.S. policy toward admitting China to the WTO, and none of the explanations for trade policy can offer an account of why New Zealand was willing to see the end of ANZUS. Our theory might cause us to lose some of the details, but it provides a common and parsimonious explanation for all that we observe. Moreover, we have only begun the development of this theory. With further theoretical and empirical work, the explanations it provides for specific events and for particular types of events might prove superior even to specific "islands of theory."

Another objection to our theory might be that it is too complicated. A reader fond of one of the more general approaches to the study of international relations might believe that their favorite approach offers a similarly general framework, capable of providing explanations for a wide range of events, and that it does so with a simpler construction. We believe such claims of simplicity on the part of other perspectives are often more apparent than real. Consider for a moment the leading contender, neorealism. At first blush, neorealism would seem to be much simpler than what we have offered. It suggests states are primarily interested in only one good, security, and it relies on the simple assumption that greater power leads to a greater ability to provide security rather than on the specific assumption that the ability to produce change increases at an increasing rate with capabilities while the ability to produce maintenance increases at a decreasing rate with capabilities. We believe such claims are mistaken on at least two points.

First, we believe our theory provides a better basis for explanation. The first item on our initial list of events involves the first in a recent series of expansions in the NATO alliance. This is a particularly interesting example precisely because this goes completely against what traditional views of international relations and foreign policy would have led us to expect. In fact, in the immediate aftermath of the collapse of the Soviet Union, many observers believed that NATO was obsolete and would soon go the way of the Warsaw Pact. Neorealists viewed NATO as providing for the security of all its members and believed that with the elimination of the security threat posed by the Soviet Union, those members would cease enjoying any benefits from the alliance. As we have noted, our theory views the collapse of the Soviet Union as leading to a substantial increase in the relative capabilities of the United States (among others). We expect such an occurrence to be followed by a significant increase in the change-seeking behavior of the United States, which would include forming alliances with weaker states. In short, our theory provides an explanation for an event that was surprising to many. Furthermore, our theory can allow us to predict such events, as proven by the fact that our forecast (published in Morgan and Palmer 1999) that China would soon form alliances with smaller powers has come to pass.

Second, we believe the claim that neorealism is simpler than our theory is more apparent than real. We hold that neorealism is underspecified in two critical ways and that when that shortcoming is corrected, it is nearly as complex as what we offer. As we have stressed throughout this volume, we must accept that foreign policy is intended to produce more than one good. Without this, we cannot address the trade-offs that are made in policy decisions, and, therefore, our understanding of those decisions will be incomplete. Some neorealists acknowledge that states can have goals other than security, but they do not explicitly incorporate this into their explanation of events. We have adopted the simplest assumption possible that allows us to consider trade-offs; that is, that states pursue two goods. Suppose, however, that one does not buy our argument on this point. We believe neorealism is still underspecified precisely because it does not incorporate a specific assumption regarding the functional form of the relationship between power and the ability to provide security. Without such a specification, precise hypotheses, explanations, and predictions cannot be formulated. As we have shown elsewhere (Morgan and Palmer 2000), one can construct a single-good version of our theory. This looks very much like a fully specified version of neorealism. For this reason, we believe that our theory is a) largely consistent with neorealism and b) as simple as a sufficiently specified version of neorealism.

A final point in favor of our theory is that it has a great deal of policy relevance. We mean this in two ways. First, the theory provides a basis for policy prescriptions. Our analysis of China, for example, indicates that China is presently a particularly maintenance-seeking country. For U.S. policymakers, that suggests that China presents little threat in the near future though it would react strongly to efforts to change the status quo in ways it does not like (such as a declaration of Taiwanese independence). As it grows, however, China will become more change seeking, even without altering its preferences.

All this implies that efforts to contain Chinese growth might lead to the very conflicts they would be intended to forestall. The policy prescription the United States should draw from this theory is to adopt policies toward China that do not threaten Chinese positions on issues they consider highly salient and to work to channel Chinese change seeking in directions that are acceptable to the United States. The policies mentioned at the beginning of this chapter (arms sales to Taiwan and bringing China into the WTO) do exactly that. By increasing the costs of unifying Taiwan by force and reducing the costs of developing economically, these policies affect the relative efficiency of change-seeking policies for China and, hopefully, induce them to seek acceptable changes peacefully.

Second, the theory has much to say about how we evaluate foreign policy. Typically, we evaluate policies simply on the basis of whether or not they achieve their objectives. For example, the U.S. policy of maintaining economic sanctions on Cuba is deemed by many to be a failure simply because it has not been able, for over forty years, to accomplish its objective of bringing down Castro's government. Our theory suggests that we need to adopt a much broader perspective when evaluating policies. That is, we need to consider each policy action in terms of what it contributes to a state's overall policy portfolio. A policy deemed a failure on its own terms might look quite different when considered as a part of a larger strategy, and an apparently successful policy might be found wanting when we are forced to consider what the resources devoted to it could have otherwise produced.

Where Do We Go from Here?

We believe that this work constitutes a significant advance by providing a more complete, more coherent, and logically consistent framework from which to address the analysis of foreign policy. The weight of the empirical evidence is supportive of our argument, and we have used it to provide compelling explanations for a broad range of specific behaviors. Naturally, we make no claim that the work presented in this book contains all the answers. We have not solved all the puzzles facing students of international relations and foreign policy. Moreover, the fact that some of our empirical results are relatively weak suggests that some of the answers we do provide are not completely satisfying. One of the major strengths of our theory is that it can be extended in a number of ways that can increase its explanatory power without introducing inconsistencies or ambiguities. We conclude this book with a brief discussion of where we think future work should go.

The most obvious suggestion is that more empirical work should be done. The theory leads to an almost limitless supply of hypotheses relating how changes in capabilities, preferences, and the relative efficiency of policies affect changes in policy portfolios. We have demonstrated that the model can guide an explanation for changes in U.S. and Chinese foreign policy as they have increased their capabilities, and we have shown that the empirical evidence supports our general hypotheses relating changes in capabilities to changes in the frequency with which some specific policy instruments are employed. An almost limitless list of similar empirical studies could be offered, but one strength of our theory is that it suggests novel questions, the empirical verification of which would constitute strong evidence for the value of the theory. For example, let us assume that some forms of political systems are more efficient at extracting and using resources from society than are others. Our theory suggests that a change from a less efficient political system to a more efficient one would serve to increase the capabilities of the state, thereby leading to an increase in foreign policy activities. The specific form of this increase would depend on the existing capability level of the state, however, with smaller states seeing a greater increase in maintenance-seeking policies and larger states seeing a greater increase in change-seeking policies. This theory could thus guide an empirical investigation into the foreign policy effects of regime transitions which, if the hypotheses were borne out, would have significant implications. First and foremost, we might conclude that transitions to democracy would not produce uniform effects and that the effects of such a transition might be undesirable in some cases.

Empirical tests of our hypotheses regarding the effect of preference changes could also prove useful and interesting. Most studies of foreign policy either assume that preferences are fixed (which is appropriate when the time horizon of the study is short) or that changes in preferences are indicated by changes in policy (which leads to tautology if the change in policy is explained by the change in preferences). If we can associate preference change with specific observable events, we can develop testable hypotheses relating these events with changes in foreign policy behavior. Such events might be internal to a state, such as a leadership change, or external to a state, such as a change in an adversary that affects the state's evaluation of the status quo. Nothing in our theory tells us how to associate such events with preferences, but empirical analyses potentially could do so. Such work would greatly improve the predictive capacity of our theory.

Finally, additional empirical work investigating the effect of changes in the relative efficiency of various policy options would be especially useful. Many old questions could be cast in a new light, which would open the possibility of substantially increasing our understanding of international relations and foreign policy. For example, scholars have sought to determine how the balance of offensive versus defensive military capabilities affects the occurrence of war. This can be seen as a question regarding the relative efficiency of change- versus maintenance-seeking instruments of policy. Our theory would lead to precise hypotheses regarding how changes in the offensive versus defensive balance would affect the use of various instruments of policy, including the use of military force, and tests of these hypotheses would serve to validate our theory as well as to inform an existing debate. Moreover, work in this area could improve our understanding of fairly recent phenomena. A great deal of recent work has sought to determine the effects of increased globalization. Increasing economic interdependence should make economic instruments of foreign policy more efficient, relative to other possible policies. Thus, our theory would lead to fairly specific expectations regarding, for example, how increased economic globalization would affect the frequency with which states use economic means of coercion. Tests of these hypotheses could prove quite useful for current theoretical and policy debates.

While additional empirical work can be most useful, particularly in demonstrating the broad applicability of our theory, the greatest benefit can accrue through additional theoretical developments. We believe that the most useful aspect of empirical analyses comes from finding out where the theory is wrong. We have been willing to present results that contradict the theory's expectations precisely because these are the findings from which we learn the most. Certainly, were our empirical results consistently against our theoretical hypotheses, we would have to conclude that our theory is wrong. The results are sufficiently supportive to convince us that we are on the right track, however. It is worth considering how to modify the theory to improve its explanatory and predictive ability.

The simplest extensions would be to alter, slightly, the existing theoretical structure. We have assumed specific functional forms throughout (for example, Cobb-Douglas utility functions) that were selected explicitly for their simplicity. It would be a straightforward exercise to experiment with different functional forms. The most obvious such extension addresses our assumption that each foreign policy action contributes to the production of only one foreign policy good. We have noted throughout that assuming, for example, that dispute initiation provides only change and military expenditures provide only maintenance are questionable assumptions (which is painfully obvious when the two are stated together). The formal version of the theory is sufficiently general to allow for any given activity to contribute to both goods. Allowing for this is conceptually and empirically much more complicated but the improvements might be well worth the cost.

Another extension would be to allow for the consideration of domestic politics. In the context of this theory, domestic politics would come into play through the determination of a state's preferences regarding the most desired balance of change and maintenance. We offered some insight into how we think this would be incorporated in our discussion of post–World War II U.S. foreign policy. Basically, we believe that domestic political institutions have a significant effect on how individual preferences are aggregated into state preferences. Better understanding these processes could account for changes in foreign policy that our theory cannot now explain.

We believe the greatest shortcoming in the current version of our theory is that it does not take into account strategic interaction. The states in our model make decisions regarding how to allocate their foreign policy resources without consideration for the effect these decisions will have on other states' decisions. Clearly, foreign policy decisions are not made in a vacuum. Decision makers take into account how others will react to their decisions and many decisions are *re*actions to the behavior of others. Our theory is founded on the notion that this is the case; after all, there would not be a need to seek maintenance if not for the change-seeking behavior of others. Moreover, a key determinant of the relative efficiency of various policies would be how others would react to each. Although we have not modeled this explicitly, the theory is intended to accommodate extensions that would allow strategic interaction to be incorporated. We believe it is best to build theory by starting from the simplest possible construction and then allowing the empirical evidence to dictate which complications and elaborations are likely to be most fruitful. The theory presented in this book provides, to our way of thinking, a very good foundation on which to build. It provides a useful reconceptualization for analyzing foreign policy, it leads to novel and interesting empirical hypotheses—many of which are supported by the evidence—and it can be generalized and complicated in ways the evidence suggests will be productive. In short, this is only a good place to pause; this is not the end.

Appendix

THIS APPENDIX presents the data sources, index construction, and details of the statistical analyses undertaken in chapter 7. We begin with a presentation of the analysis of alliances and foreign aid.

Foreign Aid Analysis

The dependent variable used in the analysis is foreign aid, operationalized using the "total receipts net"[1] of bilateral foreign aid donations, available from the OECD for the years 1966–95 (OECD 1997a), and is measured in constant 1986 dollars. The explanatory variable in this model, resources, is measured using GNP measured in constant 1986 U.S. dollars.

The results of the analysis presented in the text are a summary of a larger equation that includes dummy variables for all the countries in the analysis except for Luxembourg, the excluded category. The larger results are presented in table A.1.

The "Gained Good" and Substitutability

In this part of the appendix, we describe that data used to test the directional effects of alliances discussed in chapter 7. Specifically, we operationalize our independent and dependent variables, and describe how we create the main indicators we constructed: the amount of power a state gains from its alliance portfolio, or from any additional allies, or the amount of power it loses with any subtractions from its alliance portfolio; and the amounts of change and maintenance derived from membership in a new alliance or through any change in the alliance portfolio.

We use the Correlates of War Composite Index of National Capabilities (CINC) (Singer, Bremer, and Stuckey 1972) to measure a state's relative capability. This measure also serves as the basis for our measurement of how much power a new alliance adds to a state's capability. This index is available from 1816 through 1992. To serve as our dependent variables, we have chosen two

---

[1] The "total receipts net" includes Official Development Assistance (ODA), Official Aid (OA), and other official bilateral transactions which are not concessional or which, even though they have concessional elements, are primarily trade facilitating in character and changes in bilateral long-term assets of the private nonmonetary and monetary sectors.

TABLE A.1
Alliances and Foreign Aid Donations

(Ordinary Least Squares with Panel Corrected Standard Errors)			
Log of GNP	4.79***	Belgium	4.86***
	(0.376)		(0.267)
ALLIED	22.79***	Denmark	4.14***
	(4.04)***		(0.232)
ALLIED* (Log GNP)	−2.25***	Australia	5.99***
	(0.449)		(0.591)
Lag of Log of Aid	0.273***	Spain	4.84***
	(0.032)		(0.517)
United States	5.80***	Austria	6.17***
	(0.319)		(0.577)
Japan	9.03***	Switzerland	4.80***
	(0.731)		(0.593)
United Kingdom	5.84***	Norway	3.90***
	(0.387)		(0.234)
Germany	6.46***	Finland	5.13***
	(0.318)		(0.582)
France	7.86***	Portugal	3.32***
	(0.551)		(0.509)
Italy	5.35***	New Zealand	4.72***
	(0.298)		(0.623)
Sweden	5.98***	Netherlands	5.14***
	(0.587)		(0.265)
Canada	4.71***	Ireland	5.80***
	(0.252)		(0.599)
		Constant	−46.23***
			(3.41)
		R^2	0.9292
		Significance	0.0000
		Wald Chi-square (24)	16956.91
		N	566

Dependent variable: Natural log of foreign aid donations
Two-tailed significance levels reported (*** $p < .01$).
Standard errors in parentheses.
* (Omitted category is Luxembourg)

indices of policies that are designed to increase change.[2] The first is conflict initiation. Conflicts are initiated primarily by actors seeking to alter the status quo. While some conflicts are maintenance oriented, or preemptive in nature, we believe that by and large, conflict initiation is a change-seeking activity. In earlier work (Morgan and Palmer 1997) we used dispute initiation as an indicator of change seeking and found the variable to be consistent with the model's expectations. For this indicator, we use the data set on MIDs for

1816–1992 (Jones, Bremer, and Singer 1996). The second indicator is percentage change in what we call "change military." While the military is used largely, though not exclusively, for maintenance seeking (see below), large military establishments, particularly those with large naval capabilities and the ability to project force long distances, may be more directed toward affecting politics on a regional or even global level (Modelski and Thompson 1988; Thompson 1988). Large-scale investments in military capabilities that can be projected great distances are, generally speaking, capital intensive. Thus, the greater the military expenditure per personnel, the greater the change-seeking capacity of the military establishment. We have modified this indicator slightly. There is an extremely high correlation between time and defense expenditures per personnel; inflation and greater expenditure on capital cause this ratio to grow over time. To avoid confounding effects, we have chosen to base the indicator on the COW system shares (Singer, Bremer, and Stuckey 1972, 26). Our operationalization of "change military" is defined as a state's system share of the annual military expenditure divided by its system share of military personnel. Increases in "change military" indicate a military establishment more oriented toward the projection of military power, and decreases indicate the opposite. We also measure changes in this variable over the four years.

We have chosen defense spending as our indicator of maintenance-seeking behavior. We acknowledge that military forces can be used to change the behavior of other states and thereby increase one's change. We presume, however, that the majority of defense expenditures are devoted toward protecting what one already has. Additionally, if a state seeks greater change, we believe that resources can be better spent than on defense. A state is likely to derive much more benefit from foreign aid or from contributions to the International Monetary Fund, for example, than from an equivalent expenditure on defense. Thus, increases in defense spending represent maintenance-seeking behavior and decreases represent a movement away from maintenance-seeking behavior. Percent changes in defense spending, the first dependent variable, are measured over a four-year period. This allows sufficient time for the state to adapt itself to the new foreign policy environment. Defense spending data are supplied by the Correlates of War Project.

The cases we analyze are nation-years for members of the international system for 1816–1992, as defined by the Correlates of War Project. The cases are restricted to instances where a state changed its alliance portfolio. That is, we analyze situations where the state joined an alliance, where a new member

---

[2] Any policy may, in a given situation, be exclusively change or maintenance seeking, but since substitution effects allow capabilities to be used for different purposes, to generalize from any policy in a situation to all similar acts inevitably introduces error into our measurement. Building a fortification, for instance, might be a clear maintenance-seeking action, unless that fortification is built on another country's territory. The inherent and unavoidable error in our measure means that our results may not be terribly strong, but it does not introduce bias in our tests.

joined an existing alliance, when it quit an alliance, or when an existing partner left.

Our analysis of dispute initiation differs from the other analyses. Dispute initiation is a relatively rare event, and this rarity requires an adjustment. We do not restrict the analysis to years where a state joined an alliance but include all nation-years. We include a dummy variable to measure the effect of a state's having gained allies, either through joining a new alliance or having new members join an existing alliance. The three independent variables that measure the effects of new alliances have values of zero in years where no new alliance was joined, so that the analysis measures the effects of changes in the state's alliance portfolios.

We turn now to a description of the index construction necessary to test the hypotheses. First, we discuss how we create indices of the change and maintenance a state derives from its alliance portfolio. To do this, we follow the assumption that in an asymmetrical alliance the stronger state is gaining change through the alliance while the weaker is gaining maintenance. That requires that we measure whether a state is more or less powerful than the mean member of the alliance: if a state's power is greater than the alliance mean, we view it as getting change; if the state has less power than the alliance mean, it is gaining maintenance.[3] For example, in an asymmetrical alliance, the weaker member is agreeing to do some things the strong desires (perhaps offering land for military bases or agreeing to vote the "right" way in the United Nations), while the strong is offering protection of the weak's interests, presumably on issues that are highly salient to the weak. Further, we assume that the amount of change or maintenance produced by an alliance is related to the degree of power asymmetry between the members. Therefore, following Palmer and Souchet (1994) and Palmer and David (1999), we use the standard deviation in capabilities of the allied states to measure the symmetry of an alliance. The larger the standard deviation, the more asymmetrical the alliance and the more the two goods are being produced through the alliance, other things being equal.

We also take into account the number of states in an alliance, since more change and maintenance are produced in a larger alliance than in a smaller alliance, ceteris paribus.

To measure the change a state produces from its entire alliance portfolio, we sum the change over the alliances to which the state belongs:

$$\sum_{i=1}^{n} SD_i \times N_i \times CHANGE_{ij}$$

[3] We could have operationalized this variable as the difference between a state's power and the alliance's mean, making the variable continuous instead of dichotomous. We believe this alternative operationalization relies too heavily on a state's power, creating an undesired correlation between the indicator and state power that is theoretically unmerited.

where SD_i is the standard deviation of the capabilities of the states in alliance i; N_i is the number of states in alliance i; and $CHANGE_{ij}$ is coded $+1$ if state j's capability is greater than the mean of the members of alliance i (that is, it is gaining change), -1 if less (it is giving up change).

We operationalize the maintenance a state produces through its alliances as the sum of the capabilities of a state's allies.[4] This operationalization allows states to draw on the capabilities of their allies when protecting the status quo. The measurement does not imply that the allies become actively involved in disputes but that the state is able to refer to its allies' political and potential military support.

The units we use to measure maintenance and change are not directly comparable. To determine the "angle" that a new alliance moves a state from its original foreign policy equilibrium, we need to be able to put these into similar units to determine whether a state is obtaining (or losing) more maintenance or change through its alliance membership. The technique selected uses all allied states for the period being analyzed. We observed the mean values and the standard deviations for our measures of change and the maintenance among these allied states and created z-scores using those parameters. This method allows us to determine into which quadrant a change in a state's alliance portfolio moves it, that is, whether the state should be placed in quadrant I, II, III, or IV.

Our hypotheses tested in the section "Alliances and Substitutability" in chapter 7 explore how states alter their policies in response to the power they derive from their allies' capabilities, and so we need a method to measure that power. The theory suggests that states will adopt unilateral policies in response to newly formed alliances and that those policies will be determined in part by the capabilities of their allies. Our first decision, then, is to sum the power of a state's allies. We believe, second, that as the number of states in an alliance increases, the more the additional power of each ally is diffused. This rate of diffusion could occur in proportion to the number of states in an alliance, that is, the marginal power derived from each ally is proportional to $1/N$, where N is the number of allies. We think, however, that an "economies of scale" exists within an alliance and that the mutual commitment involved in them lowers this rate of diffusion slightly. We have chosen $1.5/N$ to represent this diffusion rate.[5]

---

[4] This operationalization means that all states gain maintenance through all their alliances. Theoretically, this is not entirely consistent with our model. But below we discuss two alterations that make this basic measure more appropriate: we standardize the amount of maintenance a state derives from its alliances, and we weight this measure by the relative capabilities of the state being analyzed and of its allies.

[5] To us, 1.5 seems intuitively reasonable but is, admittedly, an arbitrary number. It is not, however, any more arbitrary than 1, or 2, or, in this situation, 3.1416. We ran the statistical analysis when the number was changed to 1, and the results were not substantially altered. While arbitrary, 1.5, does not seem to be biased.

The power derived from a state's allies in a particular alliance, AllCapi, is:

$$\sum_{i=1}^{n} \frac{1.5}{N(\text{Power}_i)}$$

where Power_i is the power of each ally within an alliance.

Last, to create the measure of total power for each state, we need to weight each alliance's marginal power contribution relative to a state's own capabilities. That is, a state's total power is the sum of its own power and its allies' capabilities, once discounted by the appropriate diffusion

$$\text{Total Power} = \text{State Capability} + B \,(\text{Allies' Capabilities})$$

where B is a weighting parameter. Working from our model, we wanted this parameter to meet several criteria: (1) to vary by state and by alliance; (2) to be less than unity in all cases; (3) to be greater for more powerful alliances, smaller for less powerful alliances; and (4) to be smaller for more powerful states, larger for less powerful states. Given these considerations, we defined the weighting parameter to be

$$B = (\text{AllCap}_i + \text{Cap}_i)/(\text{Cap}_i + 100) - 0.005\,(\text{Cap}_i)$$

where AllCapi is the diffusion-discounted capability of i's allies, and Cap_i is country i's own capability. Note that the units we use to measure the alliance's capabilities are not directly comparable to the state's own capability. Having established the weighting factor B, we then determine the state's total power by adding its allies' capabilities (properly discounted) to its own unilateral capabilities.

Statistical Analyses

Here we present the results of the analysis done in chapter 7 to determine the effects of new alliance membership on each of the three policies. The construction of the independent variables is discussed above, and the dependent variables are presented in the text. The first policy we analyzed was the initiation on militarized interstate disputes. As the dependent variable in this case is dichotomous, we utilized logit analysis. The results of that analysis are presented in table A.2.

TABLE A.2
Alliances and Change: I

Variable	Coefficient	S.E.	Probability
Existing Power	0.103	0.005	0.001
Change in Power	−0.043	0.030	0.151
Alliance Power	−0.124	0.045	0.006
Interaction Power	0.007	0.003	0.028
Alliance Dummy	0.520	0.121	0.001
INTERCEPT	−2.171	0.037	0.001

Dependent Variable: Initiation of militarized interstate dispute
1 = Yes; 0 = No; (Logit)
$n = 9229$
Log-likelihood: −7054.87
Restricted model: −7533.38
Chi-square: 478.5
Significance = .00

As the table shows, the variable "Alliance Dummy" has a very powerful and positive effect; as the model predicts, states that join alliances are much more likely to initiate disputes, ceteris paribus. The effect of this variable is shown in the text. "Alliance Power," contrary to our expectations, has a negative effect on the probability of initiation; stronger alliances, apparently, lead to their members' initiating conflict less than do weaker alliances. The effect of this is not powerful, however, as is again shown in the text. "Interaction Power" has the predicted positive coefficient. And the coefficient on "Existing Power" is positive: as the model predicts, stronger states are more likely to initiate disputes than weaker states.

Table A.3 shows the effect of alliance membership on "change military." As

TABLE A.3
Alliances and Change: II

Variable	Coefficient	S.E.	Probability
Existing Power	−0.005	0.004	0.159
Change in Power	−0.062	0.030	0.042
Alliance Power	0.074	0.018	0.000
Interaction Power	−0.005	0.001	0.000
INTERCEPT	0.009	0.031	0.777

Dependent Variable: Percentage change in COW system Shares of military spending/military personnel (ordinary least squares)
$n = 834$; adjusted $R^2 = .103$; SSE = 474.95; DW = 2.03

TABLE A.4
Alliances and Maintenance

Variable	Coefficient	S.E.	Probability
Existing Power	−0.019	0.007	0.007
Change in Power	0.016	0.046	0.733
Alliance Power	0.054	0.024	0.027
Interaction Power	−0.004	0.002	0.039
INTERCEPT	0.656	0.058	0.001

Dependent Variable: Percentage change in military spending (generalized least squares)

the model predicts, the contributions of the new alliance positively effect the changes in "change military." The coefficient on the interactive variable is negative, contrary to the model's expectations. When controlling for these factors and for a state's capabilities, change in power is negatively related to changes in "change military." Ordinary least squares (OLS) was used in this equation, as there apparently is virtually no autocorrelation. We also ran the analysis utilizing panel corrected standard errors (Beck and Katz 1995). When we did so, there was change in any of the coefficients only at the fourth decimal place.

Last, table A.4 presents the results of the analysis of percentage change in defense spending. As there was some autocorrelation present in this analysis when we used OLS, we present the results of the analysis done using generalized least squares.[6] As was true for "change military" and as the model predicted, the size of the new alliance's contribution is positively related to change in defense spending. Unlike some past research, our analysis shows that joining alliances *increases* defense spending, other things being equal. The interactive variable is, as expected, negatively related to the change in spending—the level of state power reduces the impact of alliance formation on the change in defense spending.

[6] Additionally, the significance level of two coefficients changes materially when using panel corrected standard errors. The statistical significance of "Alliance Power" becomes .054, which is still significant, particularly when using a one-tailed significance test. The significance of "Interaction Power" is .081 after the correction.

Bibliography

Abrams, Robert. 1980. *Foundations of Political Analysis.* New York: Columbia University Press.

Achen, Christopher H. 2000. "Why Lagged Dependent Variables Can Suppress the Explanatory Power of Other Independent Variables." Paper presented at the annual meeting of the political methodology section of the American Political Science Association, Los Angeles, 20–22 July.

Albinski, Henry S. 1988. "The ANZUS Crisis: U.S. Policy Implications and Responses." In *ANZUS in Crisis*, ed. Jacob Bercovitch, 83–103. London: Macmillan.

Almond, Gabriel. 1960. *The American People and Foreign Policy.* New York: Praeger.

Altfeld, Michael F. 1984. "The Decision to Ally: A Theory and Test." *Western Political Quarterly* 37:523–44.

Ambrose, Stephen. 1993. *Rise to Globalism.* 7th ed. New York: Penguin Books.

Andrews, Christopher. 1995. *For the President's Eyes Only: Secret Intelligence and the Amercian Presidency from Washington to Bush.* New York: Harper Perennial.

Arase, David. 1995. *Buying Power: The Political Economy of Japan's Foreign Aid.* Boulder, CO: Lynne Rienner.

Bailey, Thomas. 1964. *A Diplomatic History of the American People.* New York: Appleton-Century-Crofts.

Bar-On, Mordechai. 1989. "David Ben-Gurion and the Sevres Collusion." In *Suez 1956: The Crisis and Its Consequences*, ed. William Roger Louis and Roger Owen, 145–60. Oxford: Clarendon.

Barnett, Michael, and Jack Levy. 1991. "Domestic Sources of Alliances and Alignments: The Case of Egypt, 1962–1973." *International Organization* 45:369–95.

Beck, Nathaniel, and Jonathan N. Katz. 1995. "What to Do (and Not to Do) with Time-Series Cross-Section Data." *American Political Science Review* 89:634–47.

Bennett, D. Scott. 1997. "Testing Alternative Models of Alliance Duration." *American Journal of Political Science* 41:846–78.

Bennett, D. Scott, and Allan C. Stam. 2000. "Research Design and Estimator Choices in the Analysis of Interstate Dyads: When Decisions Matter." *Journal of Conflict Resolution* 44:653–85.

———. 2004. *The Behavioral Origins of War: Cumulation and Limits to Knowledge in Understanding International Conflict.* Ann Arbor: University of Michigan Press.

Bernardo, C. Joseph, and Eugene H. Bacon. 1955. *American Military Policy.* Harrisburg, PA: Military Service Publishing.

Blainey, Geoffrey. 1973. *The Causes of War.* New York: Free Press.

Blanton, Shannon L. 1994. "The Impact of Human Rights on U.S. Foreign Assistance to Latin America." *International Interactions* 19:339–58.

Blechman, Barry, and Stephen Kaplan. 1978. *Force without War.* Washington, DC: Brookings.

Borowski, Harry R. 1982. *A Hollow Threat: Strategic Air Power and Containment before Korea.* Westport, CT: Greenwood.

Bowie, Robert R. 1974. *Suez 1956: The International Crisis and the Role of Law*. New York: Oxford University Press.

Boyer, Mark A. 1993. *International Cooperation and Public Goods: Opportunities for the Western Alliance*. Baltimore: Johns Hopkins University Press.

Brands, H. W. 1993. *The Devil We Knew: Americans and the Cold War*. New York: Oxford University Press.

Bremer, Stuart A. 1980. "National Capabilities and War Proneness." In *The Correlates of War II: Testing Some Realpolitik Models*, ed. J. David Singer, 57–82. New York: Free Press.

———. 1992. "Dangerous Dyads: Interstate War, 1816–1965." *Journal of Conflict Resolution* 36:309–41.

———. 1993. "Democracy and Militarized Interstate Conflict, 1816–1965." *International Interactions* 18:231–49.

Brodie, Bernard, ed. 1946. *The Absolute Weapon*. New York: Harcourt Brace.

Brodie, Bernard. 1959. *Strategy in the Missile Age*. Princeton: Princeton University Press.

Brown, Seyom. 1974. *New Forces in World Politics*. Washington, DC: Brookings.

Bueno de Mesquita, Bruce. 1981. *The War Trap*. New Haven: Yale University Press.

———. 1985. "Toward a Scientific Understanding of International Conflict: A Personal View." *International Studies Quarterly* 29:121–36.

———. 2000. *Principals of International Politics*. Washington, DC: Congressional Quarterly Press.

Bueno de Mesquita, Bruce, and David Lalman. 1992. *War and Reason*. New Haven: Yale University Press.

Bueno de Mesquita, Bruce, James D. Morrow, and Ethan R. Zorick. 1992. "Capabilities, Perception, and Escalation." *American Political Science Review* 91:5–27.

Bueno de Mesquita, Bruce, James D. Morrow, Randolph M. Siverson, and Alastair Smith. 1999. "An Institutional Explanation of the Democratic Peace." *American Political Science Review* 93:791–807.

Burns, William J. 1985. *Economic Aid and American Policy toward Egypt, 1955–1981*. Albany: State University of New York Press.

Buzan, Barry. 1983. *People, States, and Fear*. Chapel Hill: University of North Carolina Press.

Camilleri, Joseph A. 1987. *The Australia, New Zealand, U.S. Alliance*. Boulder, CO: Westview Press.

Campbell, John Franklin. 1971. *The Foreign Affairs Fudge Factory*. New York: Basic Books.

Caraley, Demetrios. 1966. *The Politics of Military Unification*. New York: Columbia University Press.

Carleton, David, and Michael Stohl. 1987. "The Role of Human Rights in U.S. Foreign Assistance Policy." *American Journal of Political Science* 31:1002–18.

Carlson, Lisa J. 1995. "A Theory of Escalation and International Conflict." *Journal of Conflict Resolution* 39:511–34.

Carlton, David. 1981. *Anthony Eden: A Biography*. London: Allen Lane.

———. 1988. *Britain and the Suez Crisis*. New York: Basil Blackwell.

Carr, E. H. 1946. *The Twenty Years' Crisis*. New York: Harper.

———. 1953. *The Bolshevik Revolution*. Vol. 3. New York: Macmillan.

Cashman, Greg. 1993. *What Causes War?* San Francisco: Jossey-Bass.

Caspary, William. 1970. "The 'Mood Theory': A Study of Public Opinion and Foreign Policy." *American Political Science Review* 64:536–47.

Chan, Steve. 1984. "Mirror, Mirror on the Wall. . . . Are the Freer Countries More Pacific?" *Journal of Conflict Resolution* 28:617–48.

Christensen, Thomas J., and Jack Snyder. 1997. "Progressive Research on Degenerative Alliances." *American Political Science Review* 91:919–22.

Churchill, Randolph S. 1959. *The Rise and Fall of Sir Anthony Eden.* New York: G. P. Putnam's Sons.

Cingranelli, David L., and Thomas E. Pasquarello. 1985. "Human Rights Processes and the U.S. Distribution of Foreign Aid to Latin American Countries." *American Journal of Political Science* 29:539–63.

Cioffi-Revilla, Claudio, and Brian Lai. 2001. "Chinese Warfare and Politics in the Ancient East Asian International System, 7200 B.C. to 722 B.C." *International Interactions* 24:1–23.

Claude, Inis. 1962. *Power and International Relations.* New York: Random House.

Clodfelter, Michael. 1992. *Warfare and Armed Conflicts: A Statistical Reference.* Vol. 2. London: McFarland.

———. 1995. *Vietnam in Military Statistics: A History of the Indochina Wars, 1772–1991.* Jefferson, NC: McFarland.

Cohen, Stephen. 1980. *Bukharin and the Bolshevik Revolution.* Oxford: Oxford University Press.

———. 1985. *Sovieticus.* New York: W. W. Norton.

Cohen, Warren. 1993. *Cambridge History of American Foreign Relations.* Vol. 4: *American in the Age of Soviet Power, 1945–1991.* Cambridge: Cambridge University Press.

Conybeare, John. 1992. "A Portfolio Diversification Model of Alliances." *Journal of Conflict Resolution* 36:53–85.

———. 1994. "Arms versus Alliances: The Capital Structure of Military Enterprise." *Journal of Conflict Resolution* 38:215–35.

Conybeare, John, and Todd Sandler. 1990. "The Triple Entente and the Triple Alliance, 1880–1914: A Collective Goods Approach." *American Political Science Review* 84:1197–1206.

Cordesman, Anthony H. 1998. *Trends in U.S. Defense Spending, Procurement, and Readiness.* Washington, DC: Center for Strategic and International Studies.

De Conde, Alexander. 1963. *A History of American Foreign Policy.* New York: Charles Scribner's Sons.

De Long, J. Bradford, and Barry Eichengreen. 1991. *The Marshall Plan: History's Most Successful Structural Adjustment Program.* Working Paper No. 3899. Cambridge, MA: National Bureau of Economic Research.

de Soysa, Indra, John R. Oneal, and Yong-Hee Park. 1997. "Testing Power Transition Theory Using Alternative Measures of National Capabilities." *Journal of Conflict Resolution* 41:171–84.

Denemark, Robert A. 1999. "World System History: From Traditional International Politics to the Study of Global Relations." *International Studies Review* 1:43–76.

Destler, I. M., Leslie Gelb, and Anthony Lake. 1984. *Our Own Worst Enemy: The Unmaking of American Foreign Policy.* New York: Simon and Schuster.

Deutsch, Karl W. 1966. *The Nerves of Government*. New York: Free Press.

Diehl, Paul F. 1983. "Arms Races and Escalation: A Closer Look." *International Studies Quarterly* 27:205–12.

———. 1992. "What Are They Fighting For? The Importance of Issues in International Conflict Research." *Journal of Peace Research* 29:333–44.

———. 1994. "Substitutes or Complements? The Effects of Alliances on Military Spending in Major Power Rivalries." *International Interactions* 19:159–76.

Dixon, William J. 1993. "Democracy and the Management of International Conflict." *Journal of Conflict Resolution* 37:42–68.

———. 1994. "Democracy and the Peaceful Resolution of International Conflict." *American Political Science Review* 88:1–17.

Dougherty, James E., and Robert L. Pfaltzgraff. 1997. *Contending Theories of International Relations*. 4th ed. New York: Longman.

Downs, Anthony. 1957. *An Economic Theory of Democracy*. New York: Harper and Row.

Doyle, Michael. 1986. "Liberalism and World Politics." *American Political Science Review* 80:1151–71.

Dupuy, T. N. 1989. "Combat Data and the 3:1 Rule." *International Security* 14: 195–201.

Eban, Abba. 1977. *Abba Eban: An Autobiography*. New York: Random House.

Elman, Miriam Fendius. 1997. *Paths to Peace: Is Democracy the Answer?* (Cambridge, MA: MIT Press).

Elman, Colin, and Miriam Fendius Elman. 2002. "How Not to Be Lakatos Intolerant: Appraising Progress in IR Research." *International Studies Quarterly* 46:231–62.

Enelow, James M., and Melvin J. Hinich. 1981. "A New Approach to Voter Uncertainty in the Downsian Spatial Model." *American Journal of Political Science* 25: 484–93.

———. 1984. *The Spatial Theory of Voting*. Cambridge: Cambridge University Press.

Epstein, Joshua M. 1989. "The 3:1 Rule, the Adaptive Dynamic Model, and the Future of Security Studies." *International Security* 13:90–127.

Farber, Henry, and Joanne Gowa. 1995. "Polities and Peace." *International Security* 20:123–46.

———. 1997. "Common Interests or Common Polities? Reinterpreting the Democratic Peace." *Journal of Politics* 59:393–417.

Fearon, James D. 1994. "Domestic Political Audiences and the Escalation of International Disputes." *American Political Science Review* 88:577–92.

Finer, Herman. 1964. *Dulles Over Suez*. Chicago: Quadrangle Books.

Freedman, Lawrence. 1982. *The Evolution of Nuclear Strategy*. New York: St. Martin's.

Freiberger, Steven Z. 1992. *Dawn Over Suez*. Chicago: Ivan R. Dee.

Friedberg, Aaron. 1980. "A History of U.S. Strategic 'Doctrine'—1945 to 1980." *Journal of Strategic Studies* 3:37–71.

Fullick, Roy, and Geoffrey Powell. 1979. *Suez: The Double War*. London: Hamish Hamilton.

Gaddis, John Lewis. 1982. *Strategies of Containment*. New York: Oxford Univeristy Press.

———. 1987. *The Long Peace*. New York: Oxford University Press

———. 1997. *We Now Know: Rethinking Cold War History*. New York: Oxford University Press.

Gardner, Lloyd C. 1988. *Approaching Vietnam*. New York: W. W. Norton.

Gartzke, Erik. 1998. "Kant We All Just Get Along? Opportunity, Willingness, and the Origins of the Democratic Peace." *American Journal of Political Science* 42:1–27.

Gates, Scott, Torbjorn Knutsen, and Jonathon Moses. 1996. "Democracy and Peace: A More Skeptical View." *Journal of Peace Research* 33:1–10.

Gati, Charles, ed. 1974. *Caging the Bear*. Indianapolis: Bobbs-Merrill.

Gelb, Leslie H., with Richard K. Betts. 1979. *The Irony of Vietnam: The System Worked*. Washington, DC: Brookings.

Geller, Daniel S. 2000. "Material Capabilities: Power and International Conflict." In *What Do We Know about War?* ed. John A. Vasquez, 259–80. Boulder, CO: Rowman and Littlefield.

George, Alexander L., and Richard Smoke. 1974. *Deterrence in American Foreign Policy*. New York: Columbia University Press.

Ghosn, Faten, Glenn Palmer, and Stuart A. Bremer. 2004. "The MID3 Data Set, 1993–2001: Procedures, Coding Rules, and Description." *Conflict Management and Peace Science* 21(2):133–54.

Gibler, Doug M. 1997. "Control the Issues, Control the Conflict: The Effects of Alliances That Settle Territorial Issues in Interstate Rivalries." *International Interactions* 22:341–68.

Gilligan, Michael J., and W. Ben Hunt. 1998. "The Domestic and International Sources of Foreign Policy: Alliance Formation in the Middle East, 1948–78." In *Strategic Politicians, Foreign Policy, and Institutions*, ed. Randolph Siverson, 143–68. Ann Arbor: University of Michigan Press.

Gilpin, Robert. 1981. *War and Change in World Politics*. Cambridge: Cambridge University Press.

———. 2001. *Global Political Economy*. Princeton: Princeton University Press.

Gleditsch, Nils Petter, and Havard Hegre. 1997. "Peace and Democracy: Three Levels of Analysis." *Journal of Conflict Resolution* 41(2):283–310.

Goemans, H. E. 2000. *War and Punishment: The Causes of War Termination and the First World War*. Princeton: Princeton University Press.

Goertz, Gary, and Paul F. Diehl. 1986. "Measuring Military Allocations: A Comparison of Different Approaches." *Journal of Conflict Resolution* 30:553–81.

Goldstein, Joshua S., and John R. Freeman. 1990. *Three-Way Street: Strategic Reciprocity World Politics*. Chicago: University of Chicago Press.

Gowa, Joanne. 1994. *Allies, Adversaries, and International Trade*. Princeton: Princeton University Press.

———. 1999. *Ballots and Bullets: The Elusive Democratic Peace*. Princeton: Princeton University Press.

Greene, William H. 1995. *LIMDEP Version 7.0 User's Manual*. Plainview, NY: Econometric Software.

———. 1997. *Econometric Analysis*. 3rd ed. Upper Saddle River, N.J.· Prentice-Hall.

Grieco, Joseph M. 1988. "Anarchy and the Limits of Cooperation: A Realist Critique of the Newest Liberal Institutionalism." *International Organization* 42:485–507.

———. 1995. "The Maastricht Treaty, Economic and Monetary Union and the Neo-Realist Research Program." *Review of International Studies* 21:21–40.

Gujarati, Damodar. 1992. *Essentials of Econometrics*. New York: McGraw-Hill.

Gulick, Edward V. 1955. *Europe's Classical Balance of Power*. New York: Norton.

Haas, Ernest B. 1964. *Beyond the Nation-State.* Stanford: Stanford University Press.

Harding, Harry. 1981. "China and the Third World: From Revolution to Containment." In *The China Factor*, ed. Richard H. Solomon, 257–95. New York: Prentice-Hall.

Harkavy, Robert E. 1982. *Great Power Competition for Overseas Bases: The Geopolitics of Access Diplomacy.* New York: Pergamon.

Heikal, Mohamed H. 1972. *Nasser: The Cairo Documents.* London: New English Library.

———. 1986. *Cutting the Lion's Tail: Suez through Egyptian Eyes.* London: Andre Deutsch.

Henderson, Errol A., Jr. 2002. *Democracy and War: The End of an Illusion?* Boulder, CO: Lynne Rienner.

Hensel, Paul R. 1996. "Charting a Course to Conflict: Territorial Issues and Militarized Interstate Disputes, 1816–1992." *Conflict Management and Peace Science* 15:43–73.

———. 2001. "Contentious Issues and World Politics: The Management of Territorial Claims in the Americas, 1816–1992." *International Studies Quarterly* 45:81–110.

Herring, George C. 1979. *America's Longest War.* New York: Knopf.

Herz, John H. 1951. *Political Realism and Political Idealism.* Chicago: University of Chicago Press.

Hess, G. D. 1995. "An Introduction to Lewis Fry Richardson and His Mathematical Theory of War and Peace." *Conflict Management and Peace Science* 14:77–113.

Hill, Walter W., Jr. 1992. "Deterministic Quasi-Periodic Behavior of an Arms Race Model." *Conflict Management and Peace Science* 12:79–98.

Hinich, Melvin J., John O. Ledyard, and Peter C. Ordeshook. 1973. "A Theory of Electoral Equilibrium: A Spatial Analysis Based on the Theory of Games." *Journal of Politics* 35:154–93.

Hoadley, Steve. 1994. "New Zealand's Regional Security Policies." In *The ANZUS States and Their Region*, ed. Richard W. Baker, 29–48. Westport, CT: Praeger.

Hogan, Michael J. 1991. "European Integration and German Reintegration: Marshall Planners and the Search for Recovery and Security in Western Europe." In *The Marshall Plan and Germany*, ed. Charles Maier and Gunter Bischof, 115–70. New York: Berg.

Hohan, Michael F. 1987. *The Marshall Plan: America, Britain, and the Reconstruction of Western Europe, 1947–1952.* Cambridge: Cambridge University Press.

Holborn, Hajo. 1982. *A History of Modern Germany.* Princeton: Princeton University Press.

Holsti, Ole, and James Rosenau. 1979. "Vietnam, Consensus and the Belief Systems of American Leaders." *World Politics* 32:1–56.

———. 1984. *American Leadership in World Affairs.* Boston: Allen and Unwin.

Hook, Steven W. 1995. *National Interest and Foreign Aid.* Boulder, CO: Lynne Rienner.

Hopmann, P. Terrence, and Theresa C. Smith. 1977. "An Application of a Richardson Process Model: Soviet-American Interactions in the Test Ban Negotiations, 1962–1963." *Journal of Conflict Resolution* 21:701–26.

Hough, Jerry F., and Merle Fainsod. 1979. *How the Soviet Union Is Governed.* Cambridge, MA: Harvard University Press.

Huntington, Samuel P. 1961. *The Common Defense: Strategic Programs in National Politics.* New York: Columbia University Press.

Hurewitz, J. C. 1989. "The Historical Context." In *Suez 1956: The Crisis and Its Consequences*, ed. William Roger Louis and Roger Owen, 19–30. Oxford: Clarendon Press.

Inoguchi, Takashi. 1999. "Peering into the Future by Looking Back: The Westphalian, Philadelphian and Anti-Utopian Paradigms." *International Studies Review* 1:173–92.

Intriligator, Michael D., and Dagobert L. Brito. 1989. "Richardsonian Arms Race Models." In *Handbook of War Studies*, ed. Manus I. Midlarsky, 219–36. Ann Arbor: University of Michigan Press.

Jackson, Keith, and Jim Lamare. 1988. "Politics, Public Opinion and International Crisis: The ANZUS Issue in New Zealand Politics." In *ANZUS in Crisis*, ed. Bruce Bercovitch, 160–90. London: Macmillan Press.

James, Patrick. 1993. "Neorealism as a Research Enterprise: Toward Elaborated Structural Realism." *International Political Science Review* 14:123–48.

———. 1995. "Structural Realism and the Causes of War." *Mershon International Studies Review* 39:181–208.

Jervis, Robert. 1978. "Cooperation under the Security Dilemma." *World Politics* 30:167–214.

———. 1984. *The Illogic of American Nuclear Strategy*. Ithaca: Cornell University Press.

———. 1988. "Realism, Game Theory, and Cooperation." *World Politics* 40:317–49.

———. 1989. *The Meaning of the Nuclear Revolution*. Ithaca: Cornell University Press.

Jettleson, Bruce. 1992. "The Pretty Prudent Public: Post Post-Vietnam American Opinion on the Use of Military Force." *International Studies Quarterly* 36:49–74.

Johnson, Loch K. 1991. *America as a World Power*. New York: McGraw-Hill.

Jones, Daniel, Stuart A. Bremer, and J. David Singer. 1996. "Militarized Interstate Disputes, 1816–1992: Rationale, Coding Rules, and Empirical Patterns." *Conflict Management and Peace Science* 15:163–213.

Kahn, Herman. 1960. *On Thermonuclear War*. Princeton: Princeton University Press.

———. 1965. *On Escalation*. New York: Praeger.

Kaplan, Morton. 1957. *System and Process in International Politics*. New York: John Wiley and Sons.

Karnow, Stanley. 1983. *Vietnam: A History*. New York: Viking.

Kasten Nelson, Anna. 1987. "John Foster Dulles and the Bipartisan Congress." *Political Science Quarterly* 102:43–64.

Kegley, Charles W., and Steven W. Hook. 1991. "U.S. Foreign Aid and UN Voting: Did Reagan's Linkage Strategy Buy Deference or Defiance?" *International Studies Quarterly* 35:295–312.

Kegley, Charles W., and Eugene R. Wittkopf. 1991. *American Foreign Policy: Pattern and Process*. 4th ed. New York: St. Martin's.

Kennan, George F. 1954. *Realities of American Foreign Policy*. Princeton: Princeton University Press.

———. 1957. *American Diplomacy, 1900–1950*. New York: Mentor Books.

Kennedy, Paul. 1987. *The Rise and Fall of Great Powers*. New York: Random House.

Keohane, Robert O. 1984. *After Hegemony*. Princeton: Princeton University Press.

———, ed. 1986a. *Neorealism and Its Critics*. New York: Columbia University Press.

———. 1986b. "Realism, Neorealism, and the Study of World Politics." In *Neorealism and Its Critics*, 1–26. New York: Columbia University Press.

Keohane, Robert O., and Joseph S. Nye. 1989. *Power and Interdependence*. 2nd ed. Glenview, NY: Scott, Foresman.

Kim, Woosang, and James D. Morrow. 1992. "When Do Power Shifts Lead to War?" *American Journal of Political Science* 36:896–922.

Kipping, Matthias, and Ove Bjarnar, eds. 1998. *The Americanization of European Business: The Marshall Plan and the Transfer of U.S. Management Models.* New York: Routledge.

Kissinger, Henry A. 1957. *A World Restored—Europe after Napoleon: The Politics of Conservatism in a Revolutionary Age.* New York: Grosset and Dunlap.

———. 1994. *Diplomacy.* New York: Simon and Schuster.

Klingberg, Frank. 1983. *Cyclical Trends in American Foreign Policy Moods.* New York: University Press of America.

Kocs, Stephen A. 1994. "Explaining the Strategic Behavior of States: International Law as System Structure." *International Studies Quarterly* 38:535–56.

Kolodziej, Edward A. 1966. *The Uncomon Defense and Congress, 1945–1963.* Columbus: Ohio State University Press.

Krasner, Stephen D. 1978. *Defending the National Interests.* Princeton: Princeton University Press.

———. 1985. "Toward Understanding in International Relations." *International Studies Quarterly* 29:137–44.

Kreps, David M. 1988. *Notes on the Theory of Choice.* Boulder, CO: Westview Press.

Kugler, Jacek, and Douglas Lemke, eds. 1996. *Parity and War.* Ann Arbor: University of Michigan Press.

Kyle, Keith. 1991. *Suez.* London: Weidenfeld and Nicolson.

Lakatos, Imre. 1978. *The Methodology of Scientific Research Programmes.* Vol 1. London: Cambridge University Press.

Lake, David. 1999. *Entangling Relations: American Foreign Policy in Its Century.* Princeton: Princeton University Press.

Laking, G. R. 1988. "The Public Pursuit of Peace: What Can a Small Country Do?" In *International Conflict Resolution,* ed. Ramesh Thakur, 43–59. Boulder, CO: Westview Press.

Lamborn, Alan C. 1997. "Theory and Politics in World Politics." *International Studies Quarterly* 41:187–214.

Landais-Stamp, Paul, and Paul Rogers. 1989. *Rocking the Boat.* Oxford: Berg.

Latham, Robert. 2001. "Cooperation and Community in Europe: What the Marshall Plan Proposed, NATO Disposed." In *The Marshall Plan: Fifty Years After,* ed. Martin Schain, 61–90. New York: Palgrave.

Lebovic, James H. 1988. "National Interests and U.S. Foreign Aid: The Carter and Reagan Years." *Journal of Peace Research* 25:115–35.

Leeds, Brett Ashley, Andrew G. Long, and Sara McLaughlin Mitchell. 2000. "Reevaluating Alliance Reliability: Specific Threats, Specific Promises." *Journal of Conflict Resolution* 44:686–99.

Leffler, Melvyn. 1992. *A Preponderance of Power.* Stanford: Stanford University Press.

Lemke, Douglas. 2002. *Regions of War and Peace.* Cambridge: Cambridge University Press.

Lemke, Douglas, and William Reed. 1996. "Regime Type and Status Quo Evaluations: Power Transition Theory and the Democratic Peace." *International Interactions* 22:143–64.

Leng, Russell. 1993. *Interstate Crisis Behavior, 1816–1980: Realism versus Reciprocity.* New York: Cambridge University Press.

Levy, Jack. 1984. "The Offensive/Defensive Balance of Military Technology: A Theoretical and Historical Analysis." *International Studies Quarterly* 28:219–38.

———. 1987. "Declining Power and the Preventive Motivation for War." *World Politics* 40:82–107.

———. 1989. "The Causes of War: A Review of Theories and Evidence." In *Behavior, Society, and Nuclear War*, ed. Philip E. Tetlock, Jo L. Husbands, Robert Jervis, Paul C. Stern, and Charles Tilly: 209–33. NewYork: Oxford University Press.

Lomperis, Timothy J. 1996. *From People's War to People's Rule.* Chapel Hill: University of North Carolina Press.

Louis, William Roger. 1989. "The Tragedy of the Anglo-Egyptian Settlement of 1954." In *Suez 1956: The Crisis and Its Consequences*, ed. William Roger Louis and Roger Owen, 43–71. Oxford: Clarendon.

Love, Kenneth. 1969. *Suez: The Twice-Fought War.* New York: McGraw-Hill.

Lucas, W. Scott. 1991. *Divided We Stand: Britain, the U.S. and the Suez Canal.* London: Hodder and Stoughton.

Lundestad, Geir. 1990. *The American "Empire."* Oxford: Oxford University Press.

Mack Smith, Denis. 1968. *The Making of Italy: 1796–1970.* New York: Harper.

Maggiotto, Michael, and Eugene Wittkopf. 1981. "American Public Attitudes toward Foreign Policy." *International Studies Quarterly* 25:601–31.

Mandelbaum, Michael. 1981. *The Nuclear Revolution.* New York: Cambridge University Press.

Mansbach, Richard W., and John A. Vasquez. 1981. *In Search of Theory: Toward a New Paradigm for Global Politics.* New York: Columbia University Press.

Mansfield, Edward D. 1994. *Power, Trade and War.* Princeton: Princeton University Press.

Maoz, Zeev. 1983. "Resolve, Capabilities, and the Outcomes of Interstate Disputes." *Journal of Conflict Resolution* 26:195–230.

———. 1995. "The Onset and Initiation of Disputes." In *The Process of War*, ed. Stuart A. Bremer and Thomas R. Cusak, 35–62. Amsterdam: Gordon and Breach.

Maoz, Zeev, and Nasrin Abdolali. 1989. "Regime Types and International Conflict, 1816–1976." *Journal of Conflict Resolution* 33:3–36.

Maoz, Zeev, and Bruce Russett. 1993. "Normative and Structural Causes of Democratic Peace, 1946–1986." *American Political Science Review* 87:624–38.

Mas-Colell, Andreu, Michael D. Whinston, and Jerry R. Green. 1995. *Microeconomic Theory.* New York: Oxford University Press.

McCauley, Martin. 1995. *The Origins of the Cold War, 1941–1948.* 2nd ed. New York: Longman.

McCormick, James M., and Neil Mitchell. 1988. "Is U.S. Aid Really Linked to Human Rights in Latin America?" *American Journal of Political Science* 32:231–39.

McCormick, James M., and Eugene Wittkopf. 1990. "Bipartisanship, Partisanship, and Ideology in Congressional-Executive Foreign Policy Relations, 1947–1988." *Journal of Politics* 52:1077–1100.

McGlade, Jacqueline. 2001. "A Single Path for European Recovery? American Business Debates and Conflicts over the Marshall Plan." In *Marshall Plan: Fifty Years After*, ed. Martin Schain, 185–204. New York: Palgrave.

McKinlay, R., and R. D. Little. 1977. "A Foreign Policy Model of U.S. Bilateral Aid Allocation." *World Politics* 30:58–86.

———. 1979. "The U.S. Aid Relationship: A Test of the Recipient Need and Donor Interest Models." *Political Studies* 27:236–50.

McMillan, Stuart. 1987. *Neither Confirm Nor Deny.* New York: Praeger.

Mearsheimer, John J. 1983. *Conventional Deterrence.* Ithaca: Cornell University Press.

———. 1989. "Assessing the Conventional Balance: The 3:1 Rule and Its Critics." *International Security* 13:54–89.

———. 1990. "Back to the Future: Instability in Europe after the Cold War." *International Security* 15:5–56.

———. 2001. *The Tragedy of Great Power Politics.* New York: W. W. Norton.

Meernick, James, Eric Krueger, and Steven Poe. 1998. "Testing Models of United States
Foreign Policy: Foreign Aid during and after the Cold War." *Journal of Politics*
60:63–85.

Melanson, Richard. 1991. *Reconstructing Consensus.* New York: St. Martin's Press.

Millis, Walter. 1958. *Arms and the State: Civil-Military Elements in National Policy.* New
York: Twentieth Century Fund.

Mitchell, Sara, and Brandon Prins. 1999. "Beyond Territorial Contiguity: An Examination of the Issues Underlying Democratic Interstate Disputes." *International Studies
Quarterly* 43:169–83.

Mitrany, David. 1943. *A Working Peace System.* London: Royal Institute of International
Affairs.

Modelski, George. 1987. *Long Cycles in World Politics.* Seattle: University of Washington
Press.

Modelski, George, and William Thompson. 1988. *Sea Power and Global Politics since
1494.* Seattle: University of Washington Press.

Morgan, T. Clifton. 1984. "A Spatial Model of Crisis Bargaining." *International Studies
Quarterly* 28:407–26.

———. 1994. *Untying the Knot of War.* Ann Arbor: University of Michigan Press.

Morgan, T. Clifton, and Sally Campbell. 1991. "Domestic Structure, Decisional Constraints
and War: So Why Kant Democracies Fight?" *Journal of Conflict Resolution* 35:187–212.

Morgan, T. Clifton, and Glenn Palmer. 1995. "Alliance Formation and Membership:
The Pursuit of Happiness and Security." Paper presented at the annual meeting of the
Peace Science Society, Columbus, OH.

———. 1996. "For Love or Money: Alliances and Domestic Politics." Paper delivered at
the Annual Meeting of the International Studies Association, San Diego.

———. 1997. "A Two-Good Theory of Foreign Policy: An Application to Dispute Initiation and Reciprocation." *International Interactions* 22:225–44.

———. 1998. "Room to Move: Security, Proaction, and Institutions in Foreign-Policy
Decisionmaking." In *Strategic Politicians, Institutions, and Foreign Policy,* ed. Randolph Siverson, 193–220. Ann Arbor: University of Michigan Press.

———. 1999. "Chinese Foreign Policy in the Twenty-First Century: Insights from the
'Two-Good' Theory." *Issues and Studies* 35:35–60.

———. 2000. "A Model of Foreign Policy Substitutability: Selecting the Right Tools for
the Job(s)." *Journal of Conflict Resolution* 44:11–32.

———. 2003. "To Protect and to Serve: Alliances and Foreign-Policy Portfolios." *Journal of Conflict Resolution* 47:180–203.

Morgenthau, Hans. 1951. *In Defense of the National Interest*. New York: Knopf.

———. 1952. "Another 'Great Debate': The National Interest of the United States." *American Political Science Review* 46:961–88.

———. 1965a. *Politics among Nations*. 3rd ed. New York: Knopf.

———. 1965b. *Vietnam and the United States*. Washington, DC: Public Affairs Press.

Morrow, James D. 1986. "A Spatial Model of International Conflict." *American Political Science Review* 80:1131–50.

———. 1987. "On the Theoretical Basis of a Measure of National Risk Attitudes." *International Studies Quarterly* 31:423–38.

———. 1991. "Alliances and Asymmetry: An Alternative to the Capability Aggregation Model of Alliances." *American Journal of Political Science* 35:904–33.

———. 1993. "Arms versus Allies: Trade-offs in the Search for Security." *International Organization* 47:207–33.

———. 1994. "Alliances, Credibility, and Peacetime Costs." *Journal of Conflict Resolution* 38:270–97.

Most, Benjamin, and Harvey Starr. 1984. "International Relations Theory, Foreign Policy Substitutability, and 'Nice' Laws." *World Politics* 36:383–406.

———. 1987. *Inquiry, Logic, and International Politics*. Columbia: University of South Carolina Press.

Mousseau, Michael. 2000. "Market Prosperity, Democratic Consolidation, and Democratic Peace." *Journal of Conflict Resolution* 44:472–507.

Murdoch, James C., and Todd Sandler. 1982. "A Theoretical and Empirical Analysis of NATO." *Journal of Conflict Resolution* 26:237–63.

Murphy, Robert. 1964. *Diplomat among Warriors*. Garden City, NY: Doubleday.

Myers, David. 1988. *George Kennan and the Dilemmas of U.S. Foreign Policy*. New York: Oxford University Press.

Nelson, Daniel N. 1991. "Power at What Price? The High Cost of Security in the Warsaw Pact Organization." In *The Political Economy of Defense*, ed. Andrew Ross, 41–66. New York: Greenwood.

Neustadt, Richard E. 1970. *Alliance Politics*. New York: Columbia University Press.

Neustadt, Richard E., and Ernest R. May. 1986. *Thinking in Time: The Uses of History for Decision Makers*. New York: Free Press.

Newnham, Randall E. 1998. "Sovereignty for Sale? The Purchase of Diplomatic Recognition by West Germany, Taiwan and South Korea." Paper presented at the Annual Meeting of the International Studies Association, Minneapolis.

Niou, Emerson, Peter Ordeshook, and Gregory Rose. 1989. *The Balance of Power*. New York: Cambridge University Press.

Nutting, Anthony. 1967. *No End of a Lesson: The Story of Suez*. New York: Clarkson N. Potter.

Nye, Joseph S. 1971. *Peace in Parts: Integration and Conflict in Regional Organizations*. Boston: Little, Brown.

O'Hanlon, Michael E. 2001. *Defense Policy Choices for the Bush Administration, 2001–2005*. Washington, DC: Brookings.

Olson, James S., and Robert Shadle. 1996. *Historical Dictionary of the British Empire*. Westport, CT: Greenwood.

Olson, Mancur, and Richard Zeckhauser. 1966. "An Economic Theory of Alliances." *Review of Economics and Statistics* 48:266–79.

Oneal, John. 1990. "Burden Sharing in NATO and the Theory of Collective Action." *International Organization* 44:379–402.

Oneal, John, and Mark A. Elrod. 1989. "NATO Burden Sharing and the Forces of Change." *International Studies Quarterly* 33:435–56.

Oneal, John, and Bruce Russett. 1999. "The Kantian Peace: The Pacific Benefits of Democracy, Interdependence, and International Organizations, 1885–1992." *World Politics* 52:1–37.

Organization for Economic Cooperation and Development (OECD). 1997a. Geographical Distribution of Financial Flows to Aid Recipients. Compact Disc. Paris: OECD Publications.

———. 1997b. Development Assistance Committee. http://www.oecd.org/dac.

Organski, A.F.K. 1968. *World Politics.* 2nd ed. New York: Knopf.

Organski, A.F.K., and Jacek Kugler. 1980. *The War Ledger.* Chicago: University of Chicago Press.

Osgood, Robert. 1968. *Alliances and American Foreign Policy.* Baltimore: Johns Hopkins University Press.

Osiander, Andreas. 1998. "Rereading Early Twentieth-Century IR Theory: Idealism Revisited." *International Studies Quarterly* 42:409–32.

Ostrom, Charles W., and Francis W. Hoole. 1978. "Alliances and War Revisited." *International Studies Quarterly* 22:215–36.

Palmer, Glenn. 1990a. "Alliance Politics and Issue Areas: Determinants of Defense Spending." *American Journal of Political Science,* 34:190–211.

———. 1990b. "Corralling the Free Rider: Deterrence and the Western Alliance." *International Studies Quarterly* 34:147–64.

———. 1991. "Deterrence, Defense Spending and Elasticity: Alliance Contributions to the Public Good." *International Interactions* 17:157–69.

Palmer, Glenn, and Archana Bhandari. 2000. "The Investigation of Substitutability in Foreign Policy." *Journal of Conflict Resolution* 44:1–10.

Palmer, Glenn, and J. Sky David. 1999. "Multiple Goals or Deterrence: A Test of Two Models in Nuclear and Nonnuclear Alliances." *Journal of Conflict Resolution* 43: 748–70.

Palmer, Glenn, and Andrew Souchet. 1994. "Security, Autonomy, and Defense Burdens: The Effects of Alliance Membership in the 19th and 20th Centuries." *Defense and Peace Economics* 5:189–204.

Palmer, Glenn, Patrick M. Regan, and Tamar R. London. 2004. "What's Stopping You? The Sources of Political Constraints on International Conflict Behavior in Parliamentary Democracies." *International Interactions* 30:1–24.

Palmer, Glenn, Scott B. Wohlander, and T. Clifton Morgan. 2002. "Give or Take: Foreign Aid and Foreign Policy Substitutability." *Journal of Peace Research* 39:5–26.

Partell, Peter J. 1997. "Escalation at the Outset: An Analysis of Targets' Responses in Militarized Interstate Disputes." *International Interactions* 23:1–27.

Partell, Peter J., and Glenn Palmer. 1999. "Audience Costs and Interstate Crises: An Empirical Assessment of Fearon's Model of Dispute Outcomes." *International Studies Quarterly* 43:389–405.

Patterson, James T. 1996. *Great Expectations: The United States, 1945–1975.* Oxford: Oxford University Press.

Pipes, Richard. 1954. *The Formation of the Soviet Union.* Cambridge: Cambridge University Press.

Poe, Steven C. 1992. "Human Rights and Economic Aid Allocation under Ronald Reagan and Jimmy Carter." *American Journal of Political Science* 36:147–67.

Poe, Steven C., and James Meernik. 1995. "U.S. Military Aid in the 1980s: A Global Analysis." *Journal of Peace Research* 32:399–411.

Poe, Steven C., and Rangsima Sirirangsi. 1993. "Human Rights and U.S. Economic Aid to Africa." *International Interactions* 18:309–22.

Posen, Barry R. 1984. *The Sources of Military Doctrine.* Ithaca: Cornell University Press.

Powell, Robert. 1999. *In the Shadow of Power.* Princeton: Princeton University Press.

Prados, John. 1991. *Keepers of the Keys: A History of the National Security Council from Truman to Bush.* New York: William Morrow.

Prins, Brandon, and Christopher Sprecher. 1999. "Institutional Constraints, Political Opposition, and Interstate Dispute Escalation: Evidence from Parliamentary Systems, 1946–1989." *Journal of Peace Research* 36:271–88.

Pruessen, Ronald. 1982. *John Foster Dulles: The Road to Power.* New York: Free Press.

Przeworski, Adam, and Fernandfo Limongi. 1997. "Modernization: Theories and Facts." *World Politics* 49:155–83.

Pugh, Michael C. 1989. *The ANZUS Crisis, Nuclear Visiting and Deterrence.* Cambridge: Cambridge University Press.

Quandt, William B. 1977. *Decade of Decisions.* Berkeley: University of California Press.

Quester, George. 1977. *Offense and Defense in the International System.* New York: John Wiley.

Ranelagh, John. 1992. *CIA: A History.* London: BBC Books.

Rasler, Karen, and William R. Thompson. 1983. "Global Wars, Public Debts, and the Long Cycle." *World Politics* 35:489–516.

Ray, James Lee. 1995. *Democracy and International Conflict: An Evaluation of the Democratic Peace Proposition.* Columbia: University of South Carolina Press.

Reed, William. 2000. "A Unified Statistical Model of Conflict Onset and Escalation." *American Journal of Political Science* 44:84–93.

Regan, Patrick M. 1994. "War Toys, War Movies and the Militarization of the United States, 1900–85." *Journal of Peace Research* 31:45–58.

———. 1995. "US Economic Aid and Political Repression: An Empirical Evaluation of U.S. Foreign Policy." *Political Research Quarterly* 48:613–28.

Richardson, Lewis F. 1960a. *Statistics of Deadly Quarrels.* Pittsburgh: Boxwood Press.

———. 1960b. *Arms and Insecurity.* Pittsburgh: Boxwood Press.

Richardson, Louise. 1996. *When Allies Differ.* New York: St. Martin's.

Rosecrance, Richard N. 1963. *Action and Reaction in World Politics.* Boston: Little, Brown.

Roskin, Michael. 1974. "From Pearl Harbor to Vietnam: Shifting Generational Paradigms and Foreign Policy." *Political Science Quarterly* 89:563–88.

Rourke, John. 1983. *Congress and the Presidency in U.S. Foreign Policy Making.* Boulder, CO: Westview Press.

Rousseau, David L., Christopher Gelpi, Dan Reiter, and Paul K. Huth. 1996. "Assessing the Dyadic Nature of the Democratic Peace, 1918–88." *American Political Science Review* 90:512–33.

Russett, Bruce M., John R. Oneal, and Michaelene Cox. 2000. "Clash of Civilizations, or Realism and Liberalism Déjà Vu? Some Evidence." *Journal of Peace Research* 37:583–608.

Sample, Susan. 1997. "Arms Races and Dispute Escalation: Resolving the Debate?" *Journal of Peace Research* 34:7–22.

Sandler, Todd. 1993. "The Economic Theory of Alliances: A Survey." *Journal of Conflict Resolution* 37:446–83.

Schelling, Thomas. 1960. *The Strategy of Conflict.* Cambridge, MA: Harvard University Press.

Schilling, Warner R., Paul Y. Hammond, and Glenn H. Snyder. 1962. *Strategy, Politics, and Defense Budgets.* New York: Columbia University Press.

Schmitter, Philippe. 1970. "A Revised Theory of Regional Integration." *International Organization* 24:836–68.

Schraeder, Peter J., Steven W. Hook, and Bruce Taylor. 1998. "Clarifying the Foreign Aid Puzzle: A Comparison of American, Japanese, French, and Swedish Aid Flows." *World Politics* 50:294–323.

Schroeder, Paul W. 1994. *The Transformation of European Politics, 1763–1848.* Oxford: Oxford University Press.

Schultz, Kenneth A. 1999. "Do Democratic Institutions Constrain or Inform? Contrasting Two Institutional Perspectives on Democracy and War." *International Organization* 53:233–66.

Schulzinger, Robert D. 1984. *American Diplomacy in the Twentieth Century.* New York: Oxford University Press.

Schuman, Frederick L. 1948. *International Politics.* New York: McGraw-Hill.

Schweller, Randall L. 1994. "Bandwagoning for Profit: Bringing the Revisionist State Back in." *International Security* 19:72–107.

———. 1998. *Deadly Imbalances.* New York: Columbia University Press.

Schweller, Randall L., and David Priess. 1997. "A Tale of Two Realisms: Expanding the Institutions Debate." *Mershon International Studies Review* 41:1–32.

Senese, Paul D. 1996. "Geographic Proximity and Issue Salience: Their Effects on the Escalation of Militarized Interstate Conflict." *Conflict Management and Peace Science* 15:133–62.

———. 1997a. "International Sources of Dispute Challenges and Reciprocation." *Journal of Conflict Resolution* 41:407–27.

———. 1997b. "Between Dispute and War: The Effect of Joint Democracy on Interstate Conflict Escalation." *Journal of Politics* 59:1–27.

Senese, Paul D., and John A. Vasquez. Forthcoming. "Alliances, Territorial Disputes, and the Probability of War: Testing for Interactions." In *Toward an Understanding of War,* ed. Paul F. Diehl. Ann Arbor: University of Michigan Press.

Shamir, Shimon. 1989. "The Collapse of Project Alpha." In *Suez 1956: The Crisis and Its Consequences,* ed. Wm. Roger Louis and Roger Owen, 73–100. Oxford: Clarendon.

Shulman, Marshall. 1965. *Stalin's Foreign Policy Reappraised.* New York: Atheneum.

Signorino, Curtis. 1999. "Strategic Interaction and the Statistical Analysis of International Conflict." *American Political Science Review* 93:279–98.

Simowitz, Roslyn, and Barry L. Price. 1990. "The Expected Utility Theory of Conflict: Measuring Theoretical Progress." *American Political Science Review* 84:439–60.

Singer, J. David, Stuart Bremer, and John Stuckey. 1972. "Capability Distribution, Uncertainty and Major Power War, 1820–1965." In *Peace, War and Numbers,* ed. Bruce Russett, 19–48. Beverly Hills, CA: Sage.

Siverson, Randolph M., and Paul F. Diehl. 1989. "Arms Races, the Conflict Spiral, and the Onset of War." In *Handbook of War Studies,* ed. Manus I. Midlarsky, 195–218. Ann Arbor: University of Michigan Press.

Siverson, Randolph M., and Harvey Starr. 1994. "Regime Change and the Restructuring of Alliances." *American Journal of Political Science* 38:145–61.

Small, Melvin, and J. David Singer. 1969. "Formal Alliances, 1816–1965: An Extension of the Basic Data." *Journal of Peace Research* 3:257–82.

———. 1976. "The War Proneness of Democratic Regimes, 1816–1965." *Jerusalem Journal of International Relations* 1:50–69.

———. 1982. *A Resort to Arms: International and Civil Wars, 1816–1980*. Beverly Hills, CA: Sage.

Smith, Alastair. 1999. "Testing Theories of Strategic Choice: The Example of Crisis Escalation." *American Journal of Political Science* 43:1254–83.

Smith, Michael J. 1986. *Realist Thought from Weber to Kissinger*. Baton Rouge: Louisiana State University Press.

Snyder, Glenn H. 1961. *Deterrence and Defense*. Princeton: Princeton University Press.

———. 1984. "The Security Dilemma in Alliance Politics." *World Politics* 36:461–96.

———. 1997. *Alliance Politics*. Ithaca: Cornell University Press.

Snyder, Glenn, and Paul Diesing. 1977. *Conflict among Nations*. Princeton: Princeton University Press.

Snyder, Jack. 1991. *Myths of Empire*. Ithaca: Cornell University Press.

Sorokin, Gerald L. 1994. "Alliance Formation and General Deterrence: A Game-Theoretic Model and the Case of Israel." *Journal of Conflict Resolution* 38:298–325.

Spanier, John. 1991. *American Foreign Policy since World War II*. 12th ed. Washington, DC: Congressional Quarterly Press.

Starr, Harvey. 2000. "Substitutability in Foreign Policy: Theoretically Central, Empirically Elusive." *Journal of Conflict Resolution* 44:128–38.

Stein, Arthur A. 1990. *Why Nations Cooperate*. Ithaca: Cornell University Press.

Taft, Robert A. 1951. *A Foreign Policy for Americans*. Garden City, NY: Doubleday.

Tammen, Ronald L., Jacek Kugler, Douglas Lemke, Allan C. Stam III, Carole Alsharabti, Mark Andrew Abdollahian, Brian Efrid, and A.F.K. Organski. 2000. *Power Transitions*. New York: Chatham House.

Taubman, William. 1982. *Stalin's American Policy*. New York: W. W. Norton.

Taylor, A.J.P. 1954. *The Struggle for the Mastery of Europe*. Oxford: Oxford University Press.

———. 1961. *The Origins of the Second World War*. Greenwich, CT: Fawcett.

Thomas, Hugh. 1966. *The Suez Affair*. London: Weidenfeld and Nicolson.

Thompson, William. 1988. *On Global War*. Columbia: University of South Carolina Press.

Thucydides. 1954. *History of the Peloponnesian War*. Trans. Rex Warner. New York: Penguin.

Travis, Rick, and Nikolaos Zahariadis. 1992. "Aid for Arms: The Impact of Superpower Economic Assistance on Military Spending in Sub-Saharan Africa." *International Interactions* 17:233–43.

Tyrkova-Williams, Ariadna. 1919. *From Liberty to Brest-Litovsk*. London: Macmillan.

Ulam, Adam. 1974. *Expansion and Coexistence*. 2nd ed. New York: Praeger.

———. 1983. *Dangerous Relations*. New York: Oxford University Press.

Van Evera, Stephen. 1999. *Causes of War*. Ithaca: Cornell University Press.

Vasquez, John A. 1983. *The Power of Power Politics*. Cambridge: Cambridge University Press.

———. 1993. *The War Puzzle*. Cambridge: Cambridge University Press.

———. 1997. "The Realist Paradigm and Degenerative versus Progressive Research Programs: An Appraisal of Neotraditional Research on Waltz's Balancing Proposition." *American Political Science Review* 91:899–912.

Wagner, R. Harrison. 1986. "The Theory of Games and the Balance of Power." *World Politics* 38:546–76.

———. 1994. "Peace, War and the Balance of Power." *American Political Science Review* 88:593–607.

———. 2000. "Bargaining and War." *American Journal of Political Science* 44:469–84.

Wallerstein, Immanuel. 1979. *The Capitalist World Economy*. Cambridge: Cambridge University Press.

Walt, Stephen M. 1987. *The Origins of Alliances*. Ithaca: Cornell University Press.

———. 1989. "The Case for Finite Containment: Analysing U.S. Grand Strategy." *International Security* 14:5–49.

———. 1997. "The Progressive Power of Realism." *American Political Science Review* 91:931–35.

Waltz, Kenneth N. 1979. *Theory of International Politics*. Reading, MA: Addison-Wesley.

———. 1997. "Evaluating Theories." *American Political Science Review* 91:913–18.

Wang, T. Y. 1999. "U.S. Foreign Aid and UN Voting: An Analysis of Important Issues." *International Studies Quarterly* 43:199–210.

Warner, Michael, ed. 1994. *CIA Cold War Records: The CIA under Harry Truman*. Washington, DC: CIA History Staff, Center for the Study of Intelligence.

Wayman, Frank W., and Paul F. Diehl, eds. 1994. *Reconstructing Realpolitik*. Ann Arbor: University of Michigan Press.

Weede, Erich. 1984. "Democracy and War Involvement." *Journal of Peace Research* 28:649–64.

———. 1996. *Economic Development, Social Order, and World Politics*. Boulder, CO: Lynne Rienner.

Wheeler-Bennett, John W. 1963. *Brest-Litovsk: The Forgotten Peace*. London: Macmillan.

White, James D. 1994. *The Russian Revolution, 1917–1921: A Short History*. London: Edward Arnold.

Williams, Beryl. 1987. *The Russian Revolution, 1917–1921*. New York: Basil Blackwell.

Wittkopf, Eugene R. 1973. "Foreign Aid and United Nations Votes: A Comparative Study." *American Political Science Review* 67:868–88.

———. 1990. *Faces of Internationalism*. Durham: Duke University Press.

Wolfers, Arnold. 1962. *Discord and Collaboration*. Baltimore: Johns Hopkins University Press.

Wright, Quincy. 1942. *A Study of War*. 2nd ed. Chicago: University of Chicago Press.

Zahariadis, Nikolaos, Rick Travis, and Paul Diehl. 1990. "Military Substitution Effects from Foreign Economic Aid: Buying Guns with Foreign Butter." *Social Science Quarterly* 71:774–85.

Zimmerman, William. 1969. *Soviet Perspectives on International Relations*. Princeton: Princeton University Press.

Zinnes, Dina. 1976. *Mathematical Models in International Relations*. New York: Praeger.

Index

CPSIA information can be obtained at www.ICGtesting.com
Printed in the USA
LVOW10s0805061213

364166LV00001B/2/P